All My Loving

Every Parent's Guide to Bringing up a Child

Editors:

Low Poh Sim
Quak Seng Hock

OXFORD
UNIVERSITY PRESS

OXFORD
UNIVERSITY PRESS

Oxford University Press is a department of the University of Oxford.
It furthers the University's objective of excellence in research, scholarship,
and education by publishing worldwide in

Oxford New York

Athens Auckland Bangkok Bogotá Buenos Aires Calcutta
Cape Town Chennai Dar es Salaam Delhi Florence Hong Kong Istanbul
Karachi Kuala Lumpur Madrid Melbourne Mexico City Mumbai
Nairobi Paris São Paulo Singapore Taipei Tokyo Toronto Warsaw

with associated companies in Berlin Ibadan

Oxford is a registered trade mark of Oxford University Press
in the UK and in certain other countries

Published in Singapore
by Oxford University Press Pte Ltd

© Oxford University Press Pte Ltd 1999

First published 1999

Printed in Singapore

As parents, all of us have passed through the phase of both pleasure and pain, in bringing up our children. Pleasure in seeing them grow and develop, and how they reciprocate the love we give them. The occasional pain does occur when they fall sick, and rarely when their behaviour upsets societal norms.

Correct parenting, tdoes not come naturally in these days of sophisticated living and expectation of both developing and developed countries. Therefore, present-day parents need to know what ailments may affect their children; they need to know how they can produce healthy children and keep them healthy both physically and psychologically. In the olden days, our ancestors accept infant and childhood mortality from all sorts of diseases as part of human evolution. Epidemic visitations were considered as unavoidable tragedies which removed their beloved children from their midst due to wrongly perceived divine will. Not anymore now.

We now have effective and safe vaccines against many childhood infections so that we hardly see cases of diphtheria, tetanus, whooping cough, poliomyelitis, measles and childhood tuberculosis. Hepatitis B and hepatitis A are being controlled by vaccines, and many bacterial and even some viral infections can now be effectively treated by antimicrobial drugs. Gone were the days when parents refused to bring their children to Child Health Centres for vaccinations to protect their children from these diseases. And when parents refused to bring their children for vaccination, the staff of the Ministry of Health would visit their homes, hoping to vaccinate them, but the parents would hide their children to avoid such injections.

As we control infectious diseases, we can now pay more attention to the psychological development of the child, and here many factors affect the child even before the foetus is formed or before the baby is born. After birth, the baby has not stopped developing, and parents would have to know how to provide the developing child with the correct nutrition, especially breast-feeding. They also to provide the child with the correct stimulatory environment, so that intellectually and psychologically, their child will attain his genetic potential. Parents will have to know what part genes and the environment play in the optimal development of their child, and to provide and guide him, so that finally he will achieve their inheritance which is their due.

The above are only some of the facts that adults should acquaint themselves with before they embark on parenthood. It is with these in mind that the various writers who contribute to this book, have successfully addressed themselves to parents and would-be parents. These paediatricians have had wide experience in their various specialities, and have spent much time and effort, to assist parents to bring up their children in such a way that these children, as they grow into adulthood, will pass on such experiences in dealing with their own children when the time comes for them to assume the mantle of responsible parents. It is important to realize that a healthy child, both physically and psychologically, will lay the foundation for a healthy adult.

Emeritus Professor WONG Hock Boon
MBBS, FRCP(Edin), FRCP(Glas), FRCP(Lond)
FRACP, DCH(Lond), FRCP & CH (UK)
Professorial Fellow, Department of Paediatrics,
National University of Singapore
Consultant Paediatrician,
National University Hospital and
Thomson Medical Centre

This book has been written for parents and care givers as a guide to bringing up children. It will provide answers to some of the many questions raised by young and inexperienced parents who are in need of information on many common issues of parenting. The scope of this book covers the normal patterns of growth and development, the common childhood complaints, the common childhood illnesses in the first 5 years of a child's life. It gives advice that prepares the expectant parents for the arrival of their child. It provides comprehensive reading addressing many areas that can cause parental anxiety in the first month of the child. The book takes you through the many normal routines of child-rearing such as feeding your baby, bathing your baby, growth and development, immunizations, as well as toilet training.

The book also aims to keep you informed about common childhood illnesses and provides basic information on how to handle them. You can gain more understanding to these common childhood diseases and become more confident when you come face-to-face with them.

As you read on, it is our hope that you become better equipped as a parent and care giver to deal with the issues that may affect your child during these early years of life.

LOW Poh Sim
QUAK Seng Hock
Editors

Acknowledgements

We would like to show our appreciation to Professor S Arulkumaran, former *Head*, Department of Obstetrics and Gynaecology, National University of Singapore, for conceiving the idea of writing a parent's guide on child rearing. We also gratefully acknowledge the contributions made by Dr John Martin as reviewer, as his valuable advice has been instrumental in improving the quality of the presentation. (Dr Martin is *Consultant Paediatrician* and former *Medical Director*, Royal Liverpool Childrens NHS Trus – Alder Hey, United Kingdom.)

Dedication

To our own parents who have brought us up so well, and parents and parents-to-be.

JOSEPH Roy

MBBS, MMed (Paed)
Associate Professor of Paediatrics
National University of Singapore
Senior Consultant Neonatologist
Department of Neonatology
Children's Medical Centre
National University Hospital

KHOR Sek Hoon Elizabeth

MBBS, MMed (Paed)
Consultant Paediatrician
Department of Paediatrics
Children's Medical Centre
National University Hospital

LEE Bee Wah

MBBS, MMed (Paed), MD, FRCP(E), FAMS
Associate Professor of Paediatrics
National University of Singapore
Senior Consultant Paediatrician
Department of Paediatrics
Children's Medical Centre
National University Hospital

LEE Wei Ling
MBBS (Hons), MMed (Paed), FRCP, FAMS
Senior Consultant
Department of Neurology
Tan Tock Seng Hospital
Adjunct Associate Professor
Department of Paediatrics
National University of Singapore

LEE Woon Kwang
MBBS (NSW), FRACP(Paed), FAMS
Consultant Paediatrician
W.K. Lee Baby & Child Clinic
Gleneagles Medical Centre

LIM Sok Bee
MBBS, MMed (Paed)
Senior Consultant
Department of Neonatology
KK Women's and Children's Hospital

LOKE Kah Yin
MBBS, MMed (Paed), FRCP(E), FAMS
Associate Professor of Paediatrics
National University of Singapore
Consultant Paediatrician
Department of Paediatrics
Children's Medical Centre
National University Hospital

LOW Poh Sim
MBBS, MMed (Paed), MD, FRCP(E), FAMS
Professor & Head of Paediatrics
National University of Singapore
Senior Consultant Paediatrician & Chief
Department of Paediatrics
Children's Medical Centre
National University Hospital

MALATHI Ikshuvanam
MBBS, MMed (Paed)
Consultant
Department of Neonatology
KK Women's and Children's Hospital

MURUGASU Belinda
MBBS, MMed (Paed), FAMS
Associate Professor of Paediatrics
National University of Singapore
Senior Consultant Paediatrician
Department of Paediatrics
Children's Medical Centre
National University Hospital

QUAH Thuan Chong
MBBS, MMed (Paed)
Associate Professor of Paediatrics
National University of Singapore
Senior Consultant Paediatrician
Department of Paediatrics
Children's Medical Centre
National University Hospital

QUAK Seng Hock
MBBS, MMed (Paed), MD, FRCP(G), FRCPCH, FAMS
Associate Professor of Paediatrics
National University of Singapore
Senior Consultant Paediatrician
Department of Paediatrics
Children's Medical Centre
National University Hospital

QUEK Swee Chye
MBBS, MMed (Paed), DCH (Lon), FAMS
Assistant Professor of Paediatrics
National University of Singapore
Consultant Paediatrician
Department of Paediatrics
Children's Medical Centre
National University Hospital

SHEK Pei-Chi Lynette
MBBS (Hons), MRCP, MRCPCH
Assistant Professor of Paediatrics
National University of Singapore
Registrar
Department of Paediatrics
Children's Medical Centre
National University Hospital

TAN Cheng Lim
MBBS, FRACP, FRCP(E), FAMS
Senior Consultant Paediatrician & Head
Department of Paediatrics
KK Women's and Children's Hospital

TAN Yean Swee Angelin
MBBS, MMed (Paed), FAMS
Consultant Paediatrician
Angelin's Baby & Child Clinic

TAY Kiat Hong Stacey
MBBS (Hons), MMed (Paed), MRCP, MRCPCH
Assistant Professor of Paediatrics
National University of Singapore
Registrar
Department of Paediatrics
Children's Medical Centre
National University Hospital

VELLAYAPPAN K
MBBS (Sydney), MMed (Paed), FRACP, FAMS
Consultant Paediatrician
Singapore Baby & Child Clinic
Gleneagles Medical Centre

WONG May Ling
MBBS, MMed (Paed), FAMS
Assistant Professor of Paediatrics
National University of Singapore
Consultant Paediatrician
Department of Paediatrics
Children's Medical Centre
National University Hospital

YAP Hui Kim

MBBS, MMed (Paed), MD, FRCP(E), FAMS
Associate Professor of Paediatrics
National University of Singapore
Senior Consultant Paediatrician
Department of Paediatrics
Children's Medical Centre
National University Hospital

YEO Kah Loke Brian

MBBS, MMed (Psych), Dip Child Adol Psych (Lon)
Assistant Professor
Department of Psychological Medicine
National University of Singapore
Consultant Psychiatrist
Department of Psychological Medicine
National University Hospital

YEOH Eng Juh Allen

MBBS, MMed (Paed), FAMS
Senior Lecturer in Paediatrics
National University of Singapore
Senior Registrar
Department of Paediatrics
Children's Medical Centre
National University Hospital

YIP Chin Ling William
MBBS, MMed (Paed), MD, MRCP (UK), DCH (Lon), FRCP (E),
FAMS
Consultant Paediatrician
Singapore Baby & Child Clinic
Gleneagles Medical Centre
Adjunct Associate Professor
Department of Paediatrics
National University of Singapore

Contents

Preparing for Your Baby's Arrival

TAN Yean Swee Angelin

A new baby is coming! A joyful and a most anxious time especially if he is your first born. Adequate prior preparations will certainly help to alleviate the situation and minimize stress for all concerned. Often, expectant mothers have many issues to resolve. A number of issues such as breast-feeding, duration of leave and domestic assistance should be sorted out well before delivery. Often, consulting relatives or friends who have young children will help.

Preparations for you

With the expected date of delivery drawing close, it is important that mothers-to-be are physically and psychologically prepared for the tasks ahead. There are special areas with regard to personal hygiene following parturition, lactation and feeding of the baby, and dietary needs after delivery that need your attention.

What can I do to make the immediate postpartum period easier?

In Singapore, most of the deliveries are conducted in hospitals. Often, the immediate postpartum care takes place in the hospital. Different hospitals have different facilities and the care offered in each hospital is of high quality.

The aim of the postpartum period would be maximum rest for you especially if you have had an assisted delivery, for example, a caesarean section. Minimizing physical exertion and keeping all things within easy reach would certainly be beneficial to you. Too much physical exertion is not advisable as muscles are still lax postdelivery, hence muscle strains are more common. Items placed at standing height level would help to minimize bending. Stairs can sometimes be problematic especially after an assisted delivery. A remote call bell which can be easily purchased at many electrical retailers may be useful to minimize movements initially.

How do I maintain good personal hygiene?

An important aspect for your comfort and your well-being would be your personal hygiene.

Many traditional families believe that the new mother should not wet her head. However, you also have to balance personal hygiene especially if you plan to breast-feed. Perhaps, a good compromise would be dry shampoos which can be easily purchased at pharmacies and some supermarkets if you would like to minimize using wet shampoos. Singapore is hot and humid. Daily bath is necessary. Even in an air-conditioned room, regular bathing is mandatory. Hot water bath may be preferred by some individuals.

The postpartum bleeding also requires special maternity pads which are longer and thicker. Hence, it would be wise to buy sufficient maternity pads to last approximately 1–2 weeks.

Episiotomies and caesarean wounds require cleansing. A supply of sterile cotton balls and an antiseptic liquid cleanser like Chlorhexidine would help to minimize wound infections.

What is the best feeding method?

(See also *What is the best feed*? on page 7, Chapter 2: Your Baby's First Month and Chapter 3: Feeding and Weaning)

The decision to breast-feed your baby should be made before delivery. You should be fully aware of the benefits of breast-feeding. Similarly, you should also know the pros and cons of formula-feeding. The opinion of your spouse should be respected.

Breast-feeding is naturally the best for your baby. However, breast-feeding, especially in the initial few weeks, can be quite difficult and tiring for you. Some babies require very frequent feeds in the initial few weeks until a more reasonable routine is established. Hence, preparations are important to facilitate the feeding and minimize discomfort. Clothes and especially nightclothes with front openings, nursing brassieres and disposable or cloth breast pads would be helpful to make breast-feeding a less finicky and messy process.

One of the ways to overcome the tiredness during the initial period before your baby establishes a regular feeding pattern is to synchronize your sleeping hours. When your baby sleeps, you should also try to sleep. In this way, you would have adequate rest and this is an important factor for good milk flow.

A breast pump on standby to relieve engorgement would also be useful. First-time mothers whose ducts are not fully open would be more prone to generalized or localized engorgement which is certainly a most uncomfortable experience for the mother. Engorgement may also lead to breast infection or mastitis in the mother. Hence, preventive measures are important to reduce the risk of engorgement.

What are the other miscellaneous preparations?

Besides nutritious main meals, mothers and especially breast-feeding mothers would certainly appreciate healthy snacks and drinks within easy reach. Multivitamins should still be consumed postdelivery to restore any losses from postpartum bleeding and maintenance during breast-feeding. Calcium supplement is necessary especially during breast-feeding.

There should be a lot of short periods of rest as your baby sleeps a significant amount of time initially, so you can prepare leisure activities like reading and visual entertainment.

Preparations for your baby

The coming home for the newborn baby from the hospital is an exciting event. Much time has gone into the planning of your baby's room, the preparation your baby cot, the clothes, utensils for feeding and bathing. You would have received some practical tips on the care of your baby at the hospital's nursery. The time has come for you to be in charge of your baby at home.

What do I look out for general hygiene?

Spring cleaning your baby's room and bathroom should be done prior to the homecoming of the newborn baby. The aim is to have a clean and uncluttered room to greet your baby. Babies also tend to be more susceptible to insect bites. Hence, a good spray with an insecticide especially into corners a few hours just prior to your baby's homecoming would help to minimize the insects.

Meanwhile, the room should be comfortable, well ventilated with suitable lighting. When necessary, the curtains can be closed to keep the room dark while your baby is sleeping.

How can I make bathing a less scary and a more smoothly run activity?

A cheap infant bath tub which can be bought from the neighbourhood sundry shop or a more expensive version from the departmental or speciality store is necessary. One item each of the usual baby bath and baby shampoo should be bought prior to the delivery. There is no hurry to bulk buy as further supplies can be bought later if there is no skin reaction to the items. Preparation of baby bath items should also include cotton buds for cleaning the outside of the ears and nostrils. (Cord spirit and possibly antibiotic powder will often be provided upon discharge from the hospital.) Other items include hooded cotton towels and cotton face towels. Lastly, do not forget to watch the bathing demonstrations often available in the maternity ward before discharging from the hospital.

Hot water supply is needed for bathing your baby. Do make sure that your bathroom has a heater. The bathroom can be very slippery, especially when it is wet. The easiest way to avoid slipping is to keep the floor base dry while bathing your baby.

How can I make diaper changing a more efficient activity?

Diaper changing is done several times a day and hence logistics is important to minimize running around gathering items. Portability would also be important as you might move your baby from room to room very often. Hence, a plastic basket/fishing tackle box with the following items would be useful:

- cotton balls teased out into small balls out of a big roll of cotton in a container
- cotton buds in a container
- cloth/disposable diapers
- barrier cream/ointment for the diaper area
- clothes

A plastic diaper changing pad/small plastic mat to be placed on top of the mattress would help to minimize the spills or leakages. Some changing pads have inflatable sides to prevent your baby from rolling over and falling off.

Are there too many/too little clothes?

It is usually not necessary to buy many newborn clothes as many would probably be given as gifts. Clothes for the older infant can be selected at leisure later. You do not need to store bootees and mittens in large quantities as they are usually used in the short term only. Cotton napkins, especially hand-me-downs, are useful as they are not as warm and occlusive as disposable diapers. However, to minimize work, more disposable diapers can be used in the initial few weeks. The early stools (meconium) passed by your baby in the first few days of life is so sticky and mucilaginous that it is best to use disposable diapers. Many babies outgrow the small size diapers quickly, so it would be wise not to buy too many of this size. Swaddling blankets including cheaper flannel ones that can be sewn cheaply are a good idea in the initial few months especially in the first month as it keeps your baby warm.

What is the best feed?

Breast-feeding is certainly best for your baby. However, if you are unable to do so, formula-fed babies will also thrive well. Even partial breast-feeding is good for your baby so you do not need to feel guilty if you do not breast-feed your baby fully. Mental preparation for breast-feeding can be done at this stage.

Time-out to rest is also most important for the breast-feeding mother. Do remember that a well-rested mother will result in better milk production and a happy baby on hand. If necessary, other activities like changing diapers can easily be done by others so that you can concentrate on feeding your baby. Hospital nurseries generally practise a monthly milk rotation and hence your baby will be fed the milk of the month unless you have other requests.

Other useful items for formula-fed babies include the following:

- steam sterilizer with an automatic switch off mechanism
- four 120 ml bottles (not too many as your baby outgrows them quickly!)
- four 240 ml bottles (as they last longer)
- plastic bottle tongs and cleaning brush

What are the sleeping arrangements?

A height adjustable cot (as it can 'grow' with the child) would be a good buy. A firm mattress is also safer as otherwise, your baby may sink in too much into a softer mattress. Cotton cot sheets are preferable as it is much cooler for your baby. Cotton waterproof sheets which can be used below the cot sheets to prevent leakages are also useful. An optional baby alarm may be useful for those babies sleeping alone.

What are the types of wheels for the stroller?

A stroller which can be adjusted flat as babies often nap during outings would provide more flexibility for the parents. A Moses basket can be used temporarily if you prefer to get a stroller which is only partially reclinable as it lasts longer. An infant car seat which can be temporarily rented from the Automobile Association of Singapore (AAS) would be a safe mode of vehicular transport for the baby.

What are the kinds of toys to use?

Musical toys are useful as a newborn's hearing is initially better developed than his vision. Other toys can be bought later. Moreover, gifts for your baby are often toys, hence it would be good to minimize the duplication of toys. During the first few months, do avoid stuff toys or those made from fabric materials. They are difficult to keep clean and newborn babies do not really need them.

Preparations for your family

It is good that the parents-to-be spend time together and be relaxed and well rested prior to the birth, as the hard work will soon begin.

What are the preparations for the future care of my baby?

There are different child care alternatives depending on the varying family situations. If a maid is the choice of child care, she should be involved in all the different aspects of caring for the child, including the preparations prior to delivery. However, you should be absolutely certain that the maid is reliable and competent in taking care of the young baby. It is not advisable to leave your baby to a newly employed maid at home with no other responsible adult around.

When there are siblings

The impact of a new sibling upon your older child can be significant with effects seen even before your new baby is born. Your older child may rect in a variety of ways in anticipation of a new sibling who may be seen as a rival for your love. He may show regressive behaviour such as wetting or soiling. On the other hand, he may be happy to accept the baby. He needs to be psychologically prepared long before your baby is born. He needs to have reassurance from you that he is still being loved. He could be made to feel important as a 'big brother' or in having care-taking responsibilities of the new sibling that your family is expecting.

Siblings can be involved in many aspects of the preparation like decorating the room for the baby. They are also part of the excitement and joy of the new arrival. One way to include them in the expected excitement would be to prepare little gifts for them, so that when the newborn baby receives gifts, they will also be recipients of presents too!

Finally, do not worry as things will turn out better than expected.

2

Your Baby's First Month

Roy JOSEPH

Introduction

Your baby, prior to birth, existed in a parasitic stage, passively obtaining all his requirements from you, automatically and without human intervention. With birth and the cutting of the umbilical cord, your baby's secure state comes to an abrupt and potentially life-threatening halt. Of all mammalian offspring, none is so vulnerable at birth as the human newborn.

Although the transition to extra-uterine life is affected promptly, smoothly and successfully, your baby has a built-in system of a battery of reflex responses that serves to help him meet his physical and emotional needs. These reflex responses will steadily and gradually, over the next few months and years, be replaced by a series of voluntary and conditioned physical and emotional responses that enable your child to take his place as an independent individual in society. The actions are reflexively initiated by the basic feelings of cold, hunger, pain, and loneliness. Your baby will, over the ensuing weeks, gradually begin to associate the smell, sound, touch, and image of the person who meets the requirements and will develop a bond that strengthens by the day. This bonding process lasts about 2 years and it is with this bond that the foundation on which future mother-child interaction will be developed. Disruption of this bonding process by frequent and long separations, your aberrant behaviour, severe and prolonged physical illness in your child and the lack of a primary care giver are capable of producing psychological disturbances and if severe, secondary physical disturbances.

From the moment of birth, every second of life calls for the active participation and contribution from you and your child. This requires knowledge on your part and the ability of your baby to learn. You will realize the value of knowledge and the experience of others in helping you look after your newborn baby. This knowledge and experience would have been obtained previously from listening to one's own parents and/or watching other close relatives as they were looking after their own children. Living conditions and attitudes created many opportunities for this natural learning to take place. Alas with education and affluence came small nuclear families, a desire for privacy and parents who have not had the opportunity to closely observe and learn the art of child rearing.

If you are in this state, this chapter will provide you with a foundation on which you can develop your child rearing expertise. As for those who have already had some experience, the contents are useful in enriching your experience. Child rearing is more of an art than a science because each parent-child pair is a unique unit. The information in the following pages will become useful when you uniquely apply it to look after your baby.

In this chapter, a description of the form and function of the newborn baby and the significant changes that occur in the 1st month will be highlighted first. These changes, in a way, are measurable indicators of health and outcomes of good care. The areas in which care has to be provided will be then covered and this will be followed by a discussion on the management of variations and the detection of ill health. Attainment of these health indicators should reassure you that your baby is well, boost your confidence and encourage your subsequent efforts.

Your newborn baby: Appearance and functional characteristics

A newborn baby is in many ways different from adults. The physical appearance, the facial expression, the behaviour and even the way the baby breathes can bring much excitement and at times anxiety to first-time parents. The following are some normal features observed in newborn babies.

Posture

The posture of your baby is the most obvious finding when observing him. In the prone position (lying with the face down), your baby adopts a predominantly folded posture. His arms are bent to one side, his pelvis high and his knees drawn up underneath his abdomen. In the supine position (lying with the face up), he lies on his back with his elbows partially bent and with his arms held close to his chest. His legs are also half bent at his knees and held with a slight spread at his hips. With his head in the mid-line, his limbs on either side will have a symmetrical posture.

Size

(See also **Growth in the first month** on page 17 and Chapter 4: Normal Growth Development — **What is physical growth?**)

Birth weight and length vary greatly among healthy newborn infants. The range of birth weight is from 2.5–4 kg. About 5 per cent will be lighter and an equal number heavier. Extremes of birth weight are associated with a higher risk of difficulties in the newborn period. Babies with a birth weight under 2.5 kg or above 4.0 kg are labelled as Low Birth Weight and Large respectively. Body length will range from 45–55 cm. Major factors that determine birth weight and length are duration of development inside the mother, the mother's health in pregnancy, the ability of the placenta to deliver nutrition, heredity, race, and birth order. Girls are smaller and so are twins and first-born babies.

Reflexes

Reflexes are automatic and fixed reactions to particular stimuli or changes in the surroundings that are present in the newborn baby. These primitive reflexes are thought to be a legacy from man's earliest ancestors, when such actions were vital for an infant's survival. The presence of these reflexes is an indication of the normality of your baby's general condition and the central nervous system. Most of these reflex responses would have disappeared by about 3 months of age, being replaced by voluntary action. This happens when your baby learns to associate a particular action with the fulfilment of a certain need.

Some of the more readily recognizable reflexes are the rooting, grasp and Moro reflexes. If one side of your baby's cheeks is gently touched, he will turn his head in the direction of the touch. This is the rooting reflex. It ensures that he will seek out your nipple when his cheek is brushed by your breast. The grasp reflex makes your baby clench his fist automatically if an object is placed in his palm. If a finger is slipped into each palm, your baby will grasp them so tightly that he can support his own weight. The Moro reflex is seen when your baby is startled. His arms and legs will be outstretched and then drawn inwards with his fingers curled as if ready to clutch at something.

Vision and hearing

Your baby is asleep most of the time except for a brief period before and after a feed or when disturbed. His eyes will shut when suddenly dazzled by a bright light. His pupils respond to light. When held erect, his eyes will open and will follow the human face that is brought close to him. The hearing mechanism is fully formed at birth but the amniotic fluid in the ear canal can cause a few hours of deafness. Your newborn baby also reacts to harsh sharp sounds. By 10 days, he will respond to a loudly ticking watch or voice and soon responds to sounds of different pitches and loudness. Sudden sound will cause blinking. Your baby will be visibly startled by a loud noise. He can cry energetically but stops in the presence of steady soft sounds. His eyes but not his head may turn towards the source of a soft steady sound.

Breathing pattern

Your baby's breathing is gentle at a rate of about 60 per
minute soon after birth, rapidly settling to about 30 per
minute within 6 hours. The breathing pattern is not
very regular and close observation will reveal a
variation in the frequency with regular short periods
when there is no breathing. These periods can easily
last about 10 seconds and should not be associated with
a bluish change in colour. Healthy babies tend to have
a generalized light pink colour after birth and a light
golden colour due to jaundice after a few days.

The umbilical cord which is initially thick, jelly-like
and whitish in colour, will rapidly begin to dry, shrink
in size, and darken. This may be associated with a
normal foul odour and mild redness around the base.
After about a week, the dried up cord will detach and
drop off, leaving behind a stump that is moist and
lightly discharging for about another day or two.
Distinct redness and/or swelling of the umbilicus or
persistent discharge are suggestive of an infection and
medical opinion should be sought.

Physical features arising from the birth process

Some aspects of your newborn baby's appearance may
surprise or even alarm you. All are quite normal and
will usually disappear within a day or so. These include
a misshapened or swollen head, swollen puffy eyes,
tiny yellowish white spots covering his face, throbbing
fontanel, distended abdomen, swollen genitals, bright
pink, purple or even blue skin colour, a greasy white
substance called **vernix** on some parts of his body, fine
downy hair called **lanugo** on some areas of his body,

especially his back, and maternal blood smeared on his body due to tearing or cutting of vaginal tissues.

Less commonly, a baby may display the following characteristics which are not harmful. They include instrument marks on his head after a forceps delivery. A cephalhaematoma is a soft swelling seen on the side of the head and is caused by bruising during birth. The swelling will spontaneously subside in about 2 months. Before that, it may initially enlarge and later harden. On the way through the birth canal during labour, a baby's head becomes compressed. Because his bones of the skull are loosely connected, the pressure can cause his bones to overlap, creating a ridge that can be easily felt and often seen. The overlapping bone will return to its normal place within a few weeks. Red spots in the white of his eyes are small areas of bleeding caused by pressure on his neck during delivery, snuffy breathing and frequent sneezing caused by a shallow nasal bridge are other features. A baby, if premature, will be smaller and light with a large head, brighter pink colour, eyes widely spaced and closed, nails short and skin thin with little fat.

Growth in the first month

Significant development occurs over the ensuing weeks and by 1 month, there are significant changes in appearance and behaviour in your baby. His weight will decline in the first few days as a result of the loss of body water and the utilization of body stores. There can be about a 10 per cent drop from the birth weight, reaching a low by about the 7th day; then it begins to increase and the birth weight is usually regained by

10–14 days. Subsequent weight gain increases at the rate of about 30 g a day for the next 3 months. His head circumference will increase by about 0.5 cm a week and his length by about 0.75 cm a week.

There are three broad trends in muscle development and body control — outward, head to foot, and big to small. Central body muscle control is attained before those at the extremities. Head control comes before hauling the body with the hands. Early movements are wild jerks of the whole body trunk or entire limb. Only very much later does controlled movements occur around the smaller joints. Your baby lies on his back with his head to one side and his limbs straightened and stretched. At rest, his hands are shut and his thumbs turned in, his head flops when his body is lifted but will within a few seconds, activate his neck muscles to keep his head in line with his body. His eyes will now clearly turn towards a source of light. He may stare at a window or a bright wall. His eyes will follow a moving, nearby light of a flash lamp and will alertly watch your face when being fed by you. Sudden noise may cause stiffening, blinking, quivering, stretching, and crying. His eyes and head may turn towards any sound heard. A soothing voice may stop whimpering. He will cry if in hunger or in discomfort and will gurgle when contended. Crying will cease if he is picked up and talked to. Most of his time is spent sleeping.

Your baby, at 1 month, cannot yet hold up his head. Yet, his body has made tremendous progress. Millions of new connections have been made in his brain producing much improved muscle tone, breathing, swallowing, and temperature control. He would have gained about 600 g, increased his length by about 3 cm, and his head circumference by about 2 cm. Day by day, during this 1st month, you watch him grow in size and develop in complexity of responses to his environment. The first milestones of your baby's life are moments to be cherished and remembered.

Care of your baby

Following the delivery of your baby, there will be many procedures done to assist him in coping with living outside the womb. Steps are taken to ensure that he has a clear airway to breathe, that his body temperature is maintained and that he is protected from infection.

Procedures after birth

To aid breathing, air passages are cleared with a mucus extractor as your baby's head emerges. He may be held upside down to prevent inhalation of mucus. Oxygen may be given through a mask or, if necessary, through a tube passed into the trachea (windpipe). The umbilical cord may be severed as soon as your baby's air passages are clear and regular breathing is established. One clamp is placed on the cord about 15 cm from your baby and a second 7.5 cm nearer you. The cord is then cut between these two points. Blood is collected from the cut of your baby's end of the cord and examined to detect two conditions, G6PD deficiency and congenital hypothyroidism, both of which are capable of producing mental retardation.

Immediately after birth, your baby's condition is briefly checked to ascertain the adequacy with which the transition to life outside the womb is being accomplished. He is then weighed. His body length and head circumference are then measured and recorded. As your newborn baby's temperature can drop dramatically after birth, it is essential that he be wrapped in a warm dry blanket and placed in a warm crib. If you have decided to breast-feed and the condition of your baby is satisfactory, he may be handed to you for feeding. This is desirable as your baby's suckling stimulates milk production in the breast and also helps the uterus to contract. Within 24 hours of delivery, your baby will be given a full medical examination. This includes a check for life threatening and morbidity producing abnormalities.

Maintenance of body temperature

It is possible for your baby from birth, to regulate his body temperature in responses to changes in temperature around him. But the body mechanisms that allow him to do this are still inefficient. Cold is generally more of a problem than heat. A baby who is inadequately dressed in a cold environment needs a lot of energy to keep himself warm. A baby who has been chilled, normally responds by using energy to create additional body heat — but he is unable to store his heat and is thus forced to continue his efforts until he is relieved by outside warmth. Serious problems can occur if the air temperature drops suddenly and markedly when a baby is asleep. It seems that a baby's temperature control mechanisms start to function only when he is almost awake. A controlled bedroom temperature and swaddling are strongly recommended.

If a baby has become chilled, it is important to warm him up before adding extra clothing — otherwise, the extra clothing (which is at room temperature) will merely keep in the cold. If the chilled baby is lethargic with reduced respiration and pulse rates, medical attention should be sought at once. High environmental temperatures are less likely to cause serious problems than low ones. A baby will soon cry if he is too warm and the problem is easily identifiable and corrected.

Care of the umbilicus

The umbilical stump and the umbilicus (after it falls off) are common sites through which germs can enter and invade the body. Till not so long ago, it was common for a variety of animal and plant products to be applied on the umbilical stump to prevent bleeding and infection. Such practices, though well meaning, have caused high mortality through the development of tetanus and other bacterial infections. Regular and frequent (6 hourly) application of cord spirit onto the umbilical stump will suffice to keep bacterial growth under control. There is also no need to protect the umbilicus by wrapping and covering it.

Prevention of infection

In the absence of congenital abnormalities, infection is a major source of morbidity and mortality even in mature infants. Your newborn baby is particularly pre-disposed to infections because his physical barriers, like the skin, are easily breached. In addition, the resistance is low and finally, your baby which is born with a sterile skin can easily be contaminated and subsequently be colonized by virulent disease producing germs that are transmitted by health care workers.

Prevention is attained by firstly taking steps to maintain the integrity of the physical barriers, namely the skin and the membranes that line the body orifices. This involves regular general cleansing of the skin through a bath that is given at least once in 24 hours. A bath is part of a baby's daily routine and is usually given either just before the mid-morning or the early evening feed. It is usually possible to give a new baby a tub bath, but an all-over wash or sponge bath may be recommended for the first few weeks. Whatever bathing method is used, all necessary equipment must be on hand. This includes the items used during the bath itself, and in addition, towels, a clean diaper, and fresh clothing. Handling a baby during the bath may seem a daunting prospect to the new parent. In practice, however, most people soon master all the procedures they will need to know.

When lifting your baby or carrying a young baby, it is important to support his neck to prevent it from jerking back; supporting the neck with your hand or arm is all that is needed to prevent an alarming startling reaction. Secondly, remember to provide support to his trunk at the level of his hips and finally, bring your baby close to your body so that his limbs can establish contact and not be allowed to float in the air. Your baby is likely to be startled if he is picked up suddenly. Talking as you approach him will remove the element of surprise. Bathe him in a warm room 35–38°C, using water comfortable to your elbow. Use mild soap or baby cleaning lotion. When a tub is used, he may be soaped before or after placing in the tub.

For a sponge bath, take off your baby's clothes above the waist. Apply soap to his neck, chest arms and hands. Pay special attention to the folds and creases. Carefully rinse his body with clean warm water. Pat dry with a soft towel. Unpin the diaper but do not remove it. Turn your baby over, supporting his neck with one hand. Apply soap to his back, and also lower the diaper to his buttocks. As before, pay attention to all folds and creases. Rinse his body carefully with clean warm water. Pat dry and turn him to his back. Collect everything you will need and wash your hands. Sit down with your baby on a big towel on your lap. Clean his eyes and nose. Clean his face gently with a wash cloth or cotton dipped in warm water.

In the tub bath, remove your baby's clothes, leaving his diaper until the last. He is now ready to be soaped. This may be done either before or after he is placed in the tub. If he is to be soaped in the tub, this should be done quickly to prevent lather drying on his skin. Using hands or a cloth, apply soap to his body and limbs. Use front to back movements in the genital area. Lower him into the tub — supporting his head and back, and grasping his ankles with your forefinger in between them. Continue to support his head and back with one hand while soaping or rinsing with the other. To prevent any chafing, always make sure that he is patted completely dry, particularly around the navel and wherever the skin is folded, for example, neck, armpits, and groin. Baby powder, lotion or cream may then be applied as required. Your baby is now ready for a fresh diaper. Babies should never be fed just before a bath, but a feed would always be welcome once the bath is finished.

In between baths, the perineum (the area between the genitalia and the anus) will need to be cleaned after each urination or defecation by your baby. If his skin remains in contact with urine and faeces for an extended time, it will become irritated, macerated, and then infected. The infected site then become a portal for the entry of pathogens (disease producing germs) into the blood and then to other parts of the body. Other areas of the skin that can easily become macerated are the intertriginous areas (e.g. axilla, neck, groin). Maceration is prevented by minimizing the duration of contact with irritants to the skin and keeping the area cool and dry. Another way in which infections can be prevented is by preventing colonization of your baby by virulent pathogens. This is best achieved by early exposure of your baby to the generally harmless bacteria that is found on you. Consumption of breast milk will result in the transfer of antibodies and harmless bacteria found in breast milk to your baby. As the hands of the care giver can easily become a source of infection, strict hand washing before and after handling a baby is required on the part of health workers and the mother. If formula milk is being offered, one has to ensure that it is prepared without being contaminated.

Promotion of bonding

A reliable and continuous loving relationship experienced from birth, provides a baby with a firm basis for future development. Research suggests that close physical contact and not food, is the most important factor in the formation of a baby's first emotional attachment — with parents or parent substitutes. The tasks of the newborn baby are to adjust physiologically to extra-uterine life, to develop appropriate psychological response and to assimilate experientially with increasing capacity to postpone and accept substitutes. The tasks of the mother are to sustain the baby and herself physically and pleasurably, to give and get emotional gratification from nurturing, and to foster and integrate the baby's development.

Maternal-infant bonding

Babies like to be held in close body contact — being particularly happy in positions that stimulate clinging and a reassuring cuddle will often work wonders when feeling upset. Aids such as baby carriers and baby carriages may be a blessing to mothers, but if used excessively, can deprive a baby of valuable physical contact. Baby slings or backpacks worn by parents are a useful alternative. Not every mother falls in love with her baby immediately. This is more common if the mother and baby were separated after the birth, or if the birth was traumatic for the mother. Try not to feel guilty — just take each day as it comes, caring for your baby as well as you can. In time, your love for your baby will develop. Until such time, talking with other mothers will reassure you that your feelings are not unusual nor permanent.

The presence of the following psychological disturbances should alert you that the bonding is not taking place in a smooth and predicted manner. Evidence in your baby of minimal psychological disturbance include feeding and digestive problems, sleep irregularities, excessive sucking activity, excessive movements, crying and irritability, and difficulty in comforting. Evidence of extreme disturbance consist of lethargy, failure to thrive, inability to be comforted, unresponsiveness, infantile autism, and developmental arrest.

Management of normal variations in behaviour and appearance

Variations in behaviour and appearance of your newborn baby may worry you and your spouse. Not uncommonly, you and your spouse seek professional advice on normality or otherwise of certain features like your baby's cry, the appearance of his skin, the presence of spots or rashes, his general behaviour, and shape of his head.

Anxiety in parents

Your newborn baby brings many changes to you and your spouse. Feelings of anxiety in the early days are quite normal. Many mothers suffer from a short period of depression after giving birth — 'postpartum blues' are probably caused by hormonal changes in the mother's body. If depression lasts for more than a few days, the mother should consult her doctor. Anxiety about coping with the baby's needs is very common — particularly for new mothers whose lives were busy even before the new arrival came. It is in such cases that understanding and experienced relatives and friends, babysitters, play groups for older children and groups where mothers can discuss their problems can be so useful.

A major problem is that, initially, the parents do not know their baby's typical behaviour pattern. In time, they will learn what to expect but meanwhile, their baby will make his needs known by crying. Specific aspects of care such as feeding, cleaning, bathing, and changing may seem problematic to new parents but will soon become second nature. Some fathers feel neglected after the arrival of a new and demanding baby. Understanding is needed on both sides in the partnership of parenthood, and a mother should encourage her husband to take an active interest in the care of their child. Parents should avoid neglecting their own needs. Self-imposed imprisonment can lead to harmful resentment.

Babies do not ask for or require total sacrifice — only love, food, and warmth. Evidence of mild psychological disturbance in the mother is indifference to the baby, mixed or changing feelings towards him and his needs, self doubt and anxiety, intolerance of his characteristics, over- or under-response to him, premature or inappropriate expectations and dis-satisfaction with the role of motherhood. Alienation from the baby, severe depression, excessive guilt, complete inability to function in maternal role, denial or trying to control the baby's needs, severe clashes with the baby and venting of dissatisfaction on the baby are signs of severe psychopathology, and professional assistance should be urgently sought.

Jaundice

A yellowish discoloration of the skin and lining membranes of the eyes and gums, jaundice is a common observation in about a third of all healthy newborn babies. The yellowish colour is due to the deposition in the tissues of the yellow pigment called **bilirubin**. Bilirubin is formed by the normal breakdown of haemoglobin when the red blood cell dies. In the liver, the bilirubin is converted to a water soluble compound that can be excreted in the bile and through the gut. When bilirubin is present in very large amounts, there develops a possibility of it exerting a toxic effect on certain parts of the brain to produce a disease called **kernicterus**. Kernicterus, when severe, results in death; otherwise, it produces permanent brain damage and impaired hearing. The level of bilirubin is a factor that determines whether a child will become kernicteric. In mature term babies, values above 450 mmol/L or 25 mg/dl (17 mmol/L = 1 mg/dl) are believed to significantly raise the likelihood of kernicterus. (The other factors are the amount of free bilirubin [bilirubin that is not bound to albumin and which can freely diffuse into the brain], the binding capacity of the blood, and the state of health of the brain cells.) Pre-term babies, particularly if they are sick, are more susceptible to the damage from bilirubin than the term baby.

Physiological jaundice

In the 1st week of life, physiological jaundice develops in the healthy baby because the rate at which bilirubin is formed is greater than the rate at which it is metabolized and excreted by his body. In physiological jaundice, there is only a limited rise in bilirubin levels such that jaundice is not apparent till the 3rd day, reaching a peak by about the 4th–5th day. It subsides subsequently and becomes barely recognizable by about the 10th day of life. Maximum values are usually below 256 mmol/L or 15 mg/dl and do not endanger the baby's health.

G6PD deficiency

Individuals with this lifelong genetic disease which usually affects only males and is inherited from the mother, have decreased levels of the enzyme G6PD (Glucose 6 Phosphate Dehydrogenase) in their red blood cells. As a result, the red cells may be easily haemolysed (broken down) when exposed to triggers like naphthalene in moth balls, fava beans, some of the sulphur drugs, certain drugs used in treating malaria and infections. When many red cells are haemolysed, bilirubin will be produced in large amounts and severe jaundice can develop quickly, raising the likelihood of kernicterus. The disease is common in some races — about 4 per cent of Chinese males in contrast to less than 1 per cent of Indian and Caucasian males. In Malay males, the incidence is about 2 per cent.

Severe jaundice

In a small but significant number (approximately 25 per cent of prematures, 25 per cent of babies with G6PD deficiency, 20 per cent of Chinese babies and less than 10 per cent of Malay and Indian babies), bilirubin levels rise to beyond 256 mmol/L within a few days of life. In such instances, physiological jaundice might not be the only reason for the bilirubin to reach such values and the baby will need to be investigated.

Phototherapy

In phototherapy, the unclothed baby is exposed (with his eyes covered by an eye pad) to light emitted from a bank of ordinary fluorescent bulbs for about 48 hours. During phototherapy, light energy in the blue spectrum acts on the bilirubin in the skin, converting it to a non toxic and water soluble substance. In the majority of babies, the bilirubin levels do not rise much once phototherapy is started. Hence, the bilirubin levels can be very effectively kept at safe levels and kernicterus prevented.

The current strategy to prevent kernicterus is for phototherapy to commence when bilirubin values exceed 256 mmol/L in mature babies. Particularly in western countries, there is now a shift to a more conservative approach and phototherapy is only started when the values in healthy term babies go beyond 300–340 mmol/L. This is because there is growing evidence that values between 256 and 340 mmol/L are indeed safe for a mature and healthy baby and the philosophy of offering intervention only when there is clear evidence of benefit.

The bilirubin level can be estimated with some degree of accuracy by observing the intensity of jaundice. However, it is not consistent and is subject to the experience of the observer and the natural skin colour of the patient. Thus, estimation of the bilirubin value by testing the blood is often necessary. Your role as a parent is to learn to detect jaundice and present your jaundiced baby to a health worker for a decision on the need for a blood test to be made. As a rough rule, if jaundice is easily recognizable only over the face, the serum bilirubin is probably below 220 mmol/L or 12 mg/dl. On the other hand, if the jaundice is easily recognizable in the extremities, the possibility of the bilirubin level being over 256 mmol/L is high.

Crying

Crying is the only way a young baby can communicate with his parents; if he cries, it may be an indication that something is wrong. Babies have characteristic ways of crying depending on what is troubling them and most parents soon learn to distinguish between cries for different reasons. Normally, the causes are straightforward and once they have been dealt with, the crying stops. Frequent causes include hunger, distension caused by swallowed air, general discomfort, and loneliness. Crying may also be caused by disturbing a child during cleaning or dressing. A baby crying for no apparent reason is probably only asking to be cuddled. Some reasons are, however, more difficult to remedy.

Notable among these is colic which is a severe abdominal pain that recurs daily (and often at a fixed time of the day) in some babies from about the age of

2 weeks and which cause great distress to the parents because of their inability to relieve the crying. Another difficult problem is that of dealing with what are sometimes called 'hypertonic' babies. These babies are particularly tense and may start crying at even the slightest noise or handling. Many suffer from colic and are prone to long periods of inconsolable crying. In time, these babies also settle down, but for the first few months, it is best to disturb him as little as possible; mild sedatives may at times become necessary. If crying is in any way unusual, particularly persistent or if your baby appears in any way unwell, medical advice should be sought without delay.

Diaper rash

Patches of redness and spots in the diaper area can be a cause of great discomfort. It can result from sensitivity to soap, bleaches or fabric rinses used on the diapers, powders or lotions that are applied directly to the skin, or from irritation caused by wet or dirty diapers. Treatment involves boiling diapers and rinsing with an antiseptic rinse, use of one-way liners or disposable diapers, frequent change of diapers, avoidance of waterproof pants, use of a barrier cream, and keeping the area exposed to air as much as possible.

The traditional method of cleaning diapers is by washing. The stools are first scraped from the diaper and then the diaper is rinsed and washed in very hot soapy water. Diapers should also be boiled for a few minutes to sanitize them. The task of cleaning diapers has been made easier with the development of special sanitizing products. In this method, the diaper that has been scraped clean is rinsed and then immersed in a sanitizing solution in a plastic pail for about two or more hours and then rinsed several times in clean water. Diapers are ideally dried in the sun or in an automatic drier. Both methods destroy many bacteria and thus have a disinfectant function.

If it is not convenient to appropriately clean, sanitize and disinfect diapers, the use of disposable diapers would be required. To make laundering easier, many people favour using a muslin or a disposable liner along with cotton outer diapers. Plastic pants are usually worn over the diapers, but should be avoided if the baby is suffering from diaper rash. Disposable diapers either have a plastic outer lining or are worn under specially designed plastic pants. Although comparatively expensive, disposable diapers are often preferred by people who are short of time or away from home. Constant use of disposables can, however, cause chafing or diaper rash in some babies.

Regurgitation and vomiting

Following a feed, your baby needs to be burped. Burping removes the wind that has been swallowed during feeding. Babies will often bring out small quantities of stomach contents. This process usually takes place without apparent effort on the baby's part and is called **regurgitation** or spitting up or posseting. Formula-fed babies posset materials that look like cottage cheese while breast-fed babies posset a thin, milky liquid. Regurgitation is common and normal and is not likely to be associated with poor feeding, lethargy, temperature disturbances, or continued decrease in weight. The tendency to regurgitate resolves spontaneously as the baby grows, and is fairly uncommon once he has turned over. It occurs due to physical reasons like a small stomach that is easily over-filled with milk or swallowed air, a short oesophagus (food pipe), ineffective or uncoordinated contractions of the oesophagus, and a weak muscular valve at the junction between the end of the oesophagus and the stomach. Rarely, it may be due to milk intolerance.

Though the majority of regurgitating babies need no intervention, they sometimes demonstrate discomfort and poor sleep. This may create much anxiety in their parents and the babies are often subject to unnecessary change in their feeding; many are loosely and incorrectly diagnosed as having lactose intolerance or cow milk allergy and started on soy-based formula (lactose free and cow protein free). Among those who have intense symptoms, the pressure to do something is great. Remember that only a small proportion may benefit from the administration of medications, particularly those that regulate the activity of the muscles of the digestive tract. If the stomach contents are expelled forcefully and in significant amounts, vomiting is the appropriate term. The same reasons for regurgitation can also cause your baby to vomit. Moreover, vomiting can be due to actual diseases like milk intolerance, infection, and intestinal obstruction. Healthy babies may also vomit, but only once or twice a day and not every day. If the vomitus is expelled a good distance away from the child, projectile vomiting is the appropriate term used.

Medical opinion should be sought when regurgitation or vomiting is associated with weight loss or poor skin turgor, lethargy or extreme irritability, fever, bile, blood or faeculent material in the vomitus, diarrhoea or constipation, and abdominal distension.

Variations in stool colour and consistency

The stools (bowel movements) of babies vary in appearance according to age and the method of feeding. During the first few days of life, the baby passes meconium stools which are sticky and green-black in colour. These stools consist of the waste products that are accumulated in the intestines during the last weeks before delivery. As the baby adapts to milk feeding, the stools become green brown and are known as **changing stools**. When milk feeding is established, the stools become mustard yellow. The transition from changing stools can take a few days or as long as 4 weeks.

The frequency of passing stools can vary enormously. Some breast-fed babies produce stools after each feed during the first few months. Others may produce stools as many as 15 times a day. Bottle-fed babies tend to produce fewer stools — between one and four times a day. In general, the stools of a breast-fed baby are softer and less well formed than those of a formula-fed baby. Constipation (passage with difficulty of hard stools) is more common with formula-fed babies. Adding some brown sugar or maltose to the formula is likely to be of help. Laxatives should not be given except on the basis of medical advice (rarely given in the 1st month). Blood in the stools of newborn babies usually originates from maternal blood that was swallowed during delivery. Streaks can be due to fissures in the anus.

Cradle cap

Cradle cap is a common condition found in newborn babies in which greasy white or brownish scales stick tightly to the scalp. The same scales may be seen on the eyebrows, forehead, and behind the ears. The scales do not produce pain or itchiness but may create a picture of concern. They spontaneously disappear by about 6 months of age. There are a variety of scalp shampoos or just plain oil that may be applied to reduce its presence.

Breast lump

Female hormones which stimulate the mother's breasts to enlarge and produce milk are transferred from the mother to the baby during pregnancy. Thus, many babies — both males and females — are born with lumps of breast tissue under their nipples. In some babies, this lump is large and very visible and when gently squeezed, may extrude a drop or two of a whitish and watery liquid often referred to as **witches milk**. The lump will spontaneously regress and should be left alone unless it becomes red and painful or if it discharges pus or blood.

Vaginal bleeding

The vaginas of newborn girls will produce intermittently, a clear or milky white mucus over the first few weeks. This discharge is the result of the stimulatory effects of the maternal hormones — the same hormones that cause breast swelling. With birth, the level of these hormones will fall rapidly and this precipitates bleeding in the baby — like menstruation. The amount is little and will neither harm the baby nor is it a sign of precocity. If bleeding continues, there may be an underlying clotting abnormality or a structural abnormality in the genital tract, both of which will require evaluation.

Hiccups

Most babies hiccup often. This is usually because swallowed air in the stomach pushes up against the adjacent diaphragm. Hiccups stop on their own.

Pink coloured urine

During the 1st or 2nd week, some babies excrete a chemical in their urine which stains nappies a soft pink on one or two occasions. This is not blood. If it persists or the red colour intensifies, bring in the stained napkin to a doctor.

Bowed legs and curved feet

Babies have to fold up substantially in order to fit into a uterus. Their legs are thus crossed over each other and over the abdomen. In the process, an inward bend to the legs and feet develop. Most of the bending disappears within about 2 months.

Detection of ill health

As the baby is a simple creature, its response to illness is very straightforward. The following symptoms would raise the possibility of ill health — persistent refusal to suck, excessive vomiting, diarrhoea, abdominal distension, failure to evacuate faeces, pale stools, blood stained mucked stools, lethargy, weak cry, decrease in the tone of the muscles, stiffening of the limbs and/or the trunk, bluish discoloration of the lips or extremities, and rapid or laboured breathing. Illnesses evolve and complications develop rapidly in babies. Thus, the recognition of any of these signs should prompt an immediate visit to the doctor.

Breast-feeding

Social evolution, characterized by mothers choosing or having to work outside the home, families desiring more free time, and the proliferation of nuclear families has caused radical changes in the manner in which newborn babies are being fed. In Singapore, less than 50 per cent of mothers make an attempt to breast-feed their babies, the remainder citing a variety of excuses. By about 6 weeks, only less than 15 per cent are still breast-feeding. In contrast, in the United Kingdom, about two-thirds initiate breast-feeding and a third is still breast-feeding 6 weeks later.

Colostrum

For the first few days, until the milk 'comes in', your baby feeds on the colostrum that is present in the breasts. Colostrum is of great value to your baby as it is particularly rich in antibodies that will increase his resistance especially to intestinal infections. The colostrum or first milk is adequate for all of your baby's nutritional needs as it is also rich in nutrients. Gradually, the creamy yellow colostrum will change into the mature milk which has a thin or watery appearance.

Mechanism of breast milk production

The production of milk depends on adequate stimulation of the breasts. There is no better way to increase milk supply than by the frequent sucking of a hungry baby. When your baby sucks at your breast, nerve impulses are carried to his brain, causing the release of hormones. One of the hormones, **prolactin**, is responsible for the manufacture of milk by the milk producing glands in the breast, while the other hormone called **oxytocin** causes the 'let down' or ejection of the milk. A tingling in the breasts may be felt, or milk dripping or spraying from one breast as the baby feeds from the other. Uterine cramps may also be experienced in the early days, ranging from very mild to severe especially if the baby is not your first one. These are signs that the 'let down' reflex is at work. Sometimes, the 'let down' feeling will occur without you being aware. It can be prevented by pain, tension, and fatigue. Being comfortable and relaxed is helpful.

Latching to the breast

A normal infant is put to the breast for a few minutes at each side either immediately or a few hours after birth. This results in a small amount of colostrum and more importantly, the stimulation to produce milk. You could feed your baby seated on a chair with your feet supported on a low stool or cushion. A cushion on your lap may help to support your baby. You could also lie comfortably with pillows behind you and under your knees. Your clothes and brassiere should be opened wide enough to allow your baby to have close and direct contact with your breast. Cuddle your child for a

moment before bringing him to your breast. If you
sense that you are not relaxed, try slow deep breathing
or the relaxation techniques that are taught during the
antenatal classes. Think positively and have happy
thoughts. Gaze, smile and talk to your baby as you
cuddle him.

Gently touch your baby's mouth with the nipple. There
will be an instinctive opening of his mouth and you can
then guide your nipple and some of the areola
(pigmented area surrounding the nipple) just into his
mouth. Next, draw him close to you. Your nipple may
slip out, in which case, just repeat the whole process.
The sensation of your nipple against his palate
stimulates your baby to suck. Some babies may need a
drop of colostrum squeezed out to get them begin
sucking. Placing your baby in the correct position
encourages successful feeding and avoids damage to
your nipple. His chin must drive into your breast to
enable your nipple to reach his palate, so he needs to put
his head back and up. If his head becomes too flexed,
your nipple will touch his lower jaw and tongue and his
nose will be too close to your breast. Helping his chin to
thrust forward and his head to tilt backward is hindered
by the pressure on the back of your baby's head but is
improved by supporting your baby's back to the shoulder
level, with your baby facing you, chest to chest.

If it hurts when you are feeding him, the positioning at
your breast is incorrect. Break the suction by inserting
a finger in the corner of his mouth and reposition him.
Do not also compress your breast or distort its shape as
the milk ducts may get kinked. Some babies will be
reluctant to take your nipple initially. Be reassured
that this is common. Keep bringing your baby to your

breast and after a few attempts, he will accept your nipple. If he is sleepy, coax him gently to your breast, but do not force him. It is better to offer the feed a little later when he is more aroused. Many mothers feel insecure and inadequate at first and are only too glad to change to bottle-feeding whenever the slightest difficulty arises. Your lactation consultant will resist such a request and use sympathy, understanding and skill to encourage you to gain confidence in handling your own baby.

Rooming in

During the early days, your breast will need frequent stimulation and your baby too will want to come to your breast often. This is facilitated by rooming in. He thus spends all the time with you in your room and only briefly spends time in the nursery. This enables you to feed him whenever he demands. If he must be in the nursery, request that he be brought whenever he fusses or at least every 3 hourly. Frequent feedings are ideal, but hospital routines may sometimes make this difficult. If it happens, do not fear that breast-feeding will fail. From the beginning, it is most likely that your baby will wake and require feeding at night. For the first night or two, you may be tempted to allow him to be fed by bottle while you sleep. Unless you are really exhausted or if a medical condition warrants, it is better to give your baby the night feed. The stimulation is valuable for milk production and once milk production is well established, the emptying of the breast is useful in preventing engorgement.

Particularly during the 1st week, most of the feed is obtained within 5 minutes. Thus, the length of time that your baby is on the breast bears little relation to the amount of milk received. Babies commonly feed every 2 or 3 hours. After a few weeks, the frequency will reduce to about 3 hourly. Complementary (top up) feeds are rarely necessary even in the 1st week and should be avoided and used only when absolutely necessary. The feel, taste, and smell of the rubber teat and the taste of formula milk is quite different from that of your breasts, and refusal to suck arising from nipple confusion might arise. If complementing becomes necessary, plain boiled water or expressed breast milk administered by a dropper or spoon is preferable to formula milk via a nipple. By the end of the 1st week, your milk supply will be plentiful and your baby will take eight or more feeds a day easily. Intestinal hurry is common at this stage and frequent loose stools are common and not to be taken as a sign of illness.

Cracked nipples arise usually as a result of malplacement of your baby on your nipple such that the whole of the areola is not in your baby's mouth. Pulling him off abruptly is another cause. If your nipple cracks, he could be kept off your breast for a day or two, and a bland ointment like lanolin applied to the nipple frequently, like every 3 hourly. (See Chapter 3: Feeding and Weaning — Sore nipples.)

Engorgement usually occurs when feeding is not on demand and your breasts become very full and tight and you feel uncomfortable. The engorgement is caused not only by the milk, but also by the vascular swelling which accompanies the early stages of milk production. Massaging and expressing your breasts before and after a feed, application of a cold compress or expression of the milk under a shower or with a manual pump will, in most instances, suffice to reduce the swelling and discomfort. If engorgement fully sets in, the assistance of an experienced midwife should be sought (see Chapter 3: Feeding and Weaning — <u>Breast engorgement</u>).

During the first feed of the morning or when the breast is very full, the milk may spurt out and a ravenous baby may in association swallow excessive air which may be regurgitated later with milk. This is often accompanied by a distressful crying. This may be reduced by manual expression of the first 30 ml of milk and which can be given to your baby later (see Chapter 3: Feeding and Weaning — <u>Expressing milk</u>).

Lag in milk supply

At about 2 weeks of age and about a month later, you will notice that your baby appears to need more milk than usual. Usually, the increasing appetite will be met by increasing milk supply to meet needs for your baby's growth. The appropriate response is to follow your baby's need and allow him to suck more often for a time. He will soon settle down. Sufficiency of milk supply can be monitored by observing the urine output. The presence of at least six to eight pale wet nappies in each 24-hour period indicates that the milk supply is adequate. In addition, a 120–180 g weekly increase in body weight supports the notion of adequate milk supply.

Contraindications to breast-feeding

Radioactive medications (a form of treatment of thyrotoxicosis), cytotoxic drugs (treatment of cancer), or lithium (certain types of psychiatric disturbances) are transmitted in significant concentrations in the breast milk and are capable of endangering a baby's health. You should thus not breast-feed if you are receiving any of these medications. If you are on carbimazole (a drug used in treating thyrotoxicosis), you may continue to breast-feed but your baby's thyroid function must be monitored. Antibiotics that you may be on will be secreted in minute amounts in the breast milk and will not harm your baby. The likelihood of being sensitized may be there. Most drugs, therefore, may be safely taken by the mother without fear of harm to the baby. Nevertheless, do not take a drug unless there are definite indications.

Breast-feeding may prolong jaudice in your newborn baby but this is not a reason for you to stop breast-feeding. There is established evidence that the human immunodeficiency virus (HIV) type 1 can be transmitted through breast-feeding. When there are safe alternatives to breast-feeding, it is advised that HIV infected mothers do not breast-feed their babies in order to reduce the risk of transmitting this deadly virus to their babies.

Formula-feeding
(See Chapter 3: Feeding and Weaning —
How do I choose a formula?)

In the rare situations when you are unable to breast-feed, your baby needs to be fed with a formula milk. All the infant formulae that are present in the market have been significantly modified to bring them close to that of breast milk, both physically and chemically. They are thus safe and no one brand is really superior to another. There will be minor differences between them which the manufacturer will make a big issue of. However, your baby will not mind the differences. It is possible that a baby may have difficulties with a particular brand. The observation, however, is quite rare and is not a reflection of the inferiority of the brand but more a manifestation of the individuality of your child.

The size of the hole in the teat should be such that individual drops of milk form quickly when the bottle is inverted. Weekly check of the nipple size is required. A hole that allows a steady stream is too large and one through which drops form albeit slowly is too small.

Feeds may be given on demand or by the clock at 3 or 4 hourly intervals. Most babies will be happy with either; a few may distinctly show a preference for one schedule. Like so many areas in child rearing, you will have to find out what suits your child best. The feeding requirements of a baby gradually increase from about 30 ml/kg day on Day 1 rising by about 20 ml/kg each day until a maximum of about 150 ml/kg day by about 7 days. For a 3-kg-baby who is receiving eight feeds in 24 hours, this works out to about 15 ml per feed rising daily by about 5–10 ml per feed and reaching a maximum of about 60 ml per feed by the end of the 1st week. Many babies will take much more but really do not need to. A few appear to be satisfied with slightly less.

The appropriate indicator of the adequacy of the milk intake is the rate of weight gain. A good number of bottle-fed babies may grow much more and a small number of breast-fed babies may put on less weight. In the absence of an illness, babies who put on less than 20 g a day averaged over a 2-week period need to be medically reviewed. Frequent passage of small amounts of greenish mucked stools is commonly seen when there is under-feeding. Supplemental water is not needed unless the baby is exposed to a high environmental temperature. The weather in Singapore is fairly mild and does not produce marked elevations in indoor temperatures. Further, most babies rarely go outdoors. Thus, additional water intake is rarely necessary.

The 1st month of a baby's life is an important period in his life. Both the baby and mother have much to learn from each other. This learning process may appear to be daunting. It is not as thousands of successful mother-baby pairs have shown. A mother, with confidence in her own abilities, a social support system, a certain amount of knowledge and plenty of love for her baby, will be rewarded with a lifetime of joy as she and her family prepare the baby for his ultimate independent existence and watch him attain it.

Each baby is unique. The information which you have just read is a general description that would fit most babies in the 1st month of life. Your baby may be seen to be different in some areas. That does not make him abnormal. It is just a reflection of his uniqueness. You will find that each time you refer to this chapter, you will see your baby in a different perspective; your insight of your baby will thus deepen. This will help you understand and nurture your baby. Read ahead into the subsequent chapters; this will help you anticipate and prepare for the changes that are ahead.

3
Feeding and Weaning

QUAK Seng Hock & WONG May Ling

Introduction

Infant-feeding has experienced a great deal of changes during the last few decades. This is due to the better understanding of neonatal physiology and advances in technology. A number of modifications to infant foods have been made. As a result, infant food markets are flooded with many brands of infant formulae and infant foods. Meanwhile, there is a remarkable resurgence of interest in breast-feeding, particularly in Western Europe and the United States. Better educated mothers have shown an increasing tendency to breast-feed because they understand that breast milk is the best infant food for their babies.

Babies are not miniature adults. There are a number of physiological differences between children and adults, particularly in growth and food intake. During the first few years of life, there are many changes that take place. Infancy is a period of most rapid growth and development of the entire postnatal human life. This has tremendous implications on infant-feeding.

How do I feed my baby?

Breast milk is most suitable for human babies and is

an almost complete source of all required nutrients. It is nutritionally adequate for normal babies up to 6 months of life, provided that the mother is healthy and well nourished.

Compared to cow's milk, breast milk is relatively low in protein. The high protein content of unmodified cow's milk is not suitable for infant-feeding. A number of complications had been documented in the past, mainly because the human baby is unable to handle the high protein load. Some of the complications can lead to permanent damage and cause death. Besides, human milk protein differs qualitatively from cow's milk protein. The latter is almost entirely casein whereas the former consists of equal amounts of casein and whey proteins which are readily digested and absorbed by the gastrointestinal tract of the baby.

The mineral content in human milk is low compared to that in cow's milk. These include sodium, potassium, calcium, phosphorus, and many others. The kidneys of newborn babies are not able to handle this mineral load which is present in cow's milk. Excessive urinary water loss, dehydration, and renal failure might occur if newborn babies are fed with unmodified cow's milk. Hence, breast milk, which has low mineral content, is eminently suitable for newborn babies.

Human milk is rich in certain nutrients compared to cow's milk. It contains about 40 mg/l of vitamin C compared to about 20 mg/l in cow's milk. It has the highest content of lactose among all mammalian milk and is also the sweetest mammalian milk.

Besides nutrition, breast-feeding offers many other advantages. Breast milk contains various immunoglobulins, macrophages, leucocytes which are not found in formula milk. These substances are capable of protecting the babies from bacterial infection or invasion at the surface of the gastrointestinal tract. The macrophages are capable of producing antibodies and are programmed by the maternal immunologic protection system, thus offering the baby protection from a variety of infections.

The modern era of artificial feeding dates back to the beginning of this century. In recent years, there is an increasing availability of infant formulae and variety of infant foods. Artificial feeding during infancy has been marred by various erroneous ideas and mishaps which have resulted in permanent handicaps and in some cases, deaths.

With advances in technology and better understanding of neonatal metabolism and physiology, formula-feeding is currently safe and can substitute breast-feeding in the majority of cases. However, infant-feeding is not simply a biological response to the metabolic demand of a baby. It is a complicated process and complex web of behaviours involving actions and reactions of other people around the baby. Much joy can be derived from successful infant-feeding.

What is breast-feeding?

Breast-feeding implies a baby's sucking directly from the breast and ingesting the milk. Strictly speaking, total breast-feeding excludes the feeding of expressed breast milk because the process of expressing, bottling and storing may expose the baby to the same risk of contamination as a bottle-fed infant. The interactional aspects of breast-feeding and immunological properties of breast milk may be lost. However, when the mother is away at work or when the baby is hospitalized, expressed breast milk feeding may be necessary and is an important method of maintaining milk supply.

Breast-feeding your baby

Breast-feeding will be successful when the baby is healthy and suckles frequently, and when the mother wants to breast-feed and is confident in her ability to do so. The vast majority of women can breast-feed their babies. Only a small percentage (less than 5 per cent) may be unable to do so temporarily or not at all. In a rural society, breast-feeding causes little trouble or concern for the new mother. Often, she has learnt from her mother and watched what relatives and friends have done. It is natural for her to put her baby to the breast after birth and to let the baby suck on demand. However, in an urban society such as Singapore, breast-feeding has become quite uncommon. Many young mothers have not observed breast-feeding or breast-fed before. As such, breast-feeding must be encouraged in and supported by all expectant mothers.

How can I succeed in breast-feeding?

Breast-feeding is a natural and physiological process and nearly all mothers can do it. However, it does not mean that they do so 'instinctively'. Normal feeding requires a technique that has to be learnt, especially for the first baby. Suckling of the young is a learnt process rather than an instinctive behaviour. If a young and inexperienced mother has a problem with breast-feeding, she has no informed knowledge of what to do. However natural the process may be, she must still be taught of what to do if her baby refuses to suck, if her nipples hurt, or if her milk supply seems inadequate. In an urban society, where breast-feeding is less common compared to rural communities, it can be difficult for a mother to find support and advice. Fortunately, 'Breast-feeding Mothers' Support Groups' are available in many big cities such as Singapore. Expecting mothers should attempt to get into contact with such support groups as early as possible. In Singapore, 'The Breast-feeding Mothers' Support Group' is a voluntary organization run by a group of mothers who have breast-fed their children and who offer encouragement and advice to other women wishing to do the same.

The decision to breast-feed your baby should be made well before labour. All expecting mothers must have the genuine freedom of choice whether to breast-feed their babies or not. However, they should be fully informed about the pros and cons of breast-feeding before making the choice. Breast-feeding is always an emotional subject. It is linked to the basic events of life, and is part of motherhood and total sexual experience.

The main prerequisite for successful breast-feeding is the confidence that one can do it. The confidence of experienced women may be unshakable; inexperienced women have to develop it. In an urban society, alternatives to breast-feeding are readily available and support for breast-feeding is often inadequate and haphazard. Instead, young mothers are surrounded by influences which actively undermine any confidence they have.

How do I prepare my nipples for breast-feeding?

Nipple examination is part of routine antenatal examination. Some women have inverted, flat, short, or non-protractile nipples. These problems should be detected early and appropriate steps can be taken to overcome them. Most nipples stick out a bit from the surrounding areola. Occasionally, they appear flat or even appear to 'turn in', partly or completely. These are called 'inverted' nipples. Fortunately, severely 'inverted' nipples are not common. Expecting mothers can examine their own nipples. Try to gently pull out (protract) each nipple. It may seem to slip away under your fingers. If it is truly inverted, you simply cannot pull it out at all. If you can pull out or protract the nipple for a short distance, this is just a short nipple. Flat-looking nipple can protract very well and should cause no problem during breast-feeding.

A truly inverted nipple can be problematic. This must be overcome if breast-feeding is to be successful. The first step is to put on nipple shields before wearing the brassiere. Such nipple shields are commercially available at most pharmacies. Women with inverted nipples should use them daily from about 6th–7th month of pregnancy. At the same time, they should regularly do the 'pulling' exercise which consists of gently pulling into the protracted position. It may be done while taking a bath, upon waking up, or before going to sleep.

From the second trimester of pregnancy, colostrum is present in the milk glands and can be expressed. It is not necessary to milk out the colostrum regularly. However, it may be beneficial in preparing your nipples mechanically and yourself, psychologically for breast-feeding.

What must I eat during lactation?

There are a few important factors which are essential for good milk production. Lactating mothers must have adequate rest, be physically relaxed and the baby hungry and sucking vigorously. Besides these factors, lactating mothers must have a good nutrition with adequate water intake. A breast-feeding mother needs 300–500 extra calories daily to successfully feed her baby. Another 300 calories needed by her baby are supplied by the fat she had laid down in pregnancy. A breast-feeding mother should maintain a well-balanced diet and eat according to her appetite. Excessive dieting is not advisable during lactation and will adversely affect milk supply.

A lactating mother is the most efficient baby-food factory and she can make use of a wide variety of raw materials and make them into a highly specialized and complex liquid food with a wastage of less than 10 per cent. A breast-feeding mother may secrete large quantity of high-quality protein daily in her breast milk. Extra protein intake is required. The addition of 20 g of protein to a normal diet is generally recommended. In every culture, certain foods are offered to the nursing mother in the belief that they help to produce milk. Often, such food do not have any role in the promotion of lactation. It is more important to concentrate on a well-balanced diet. Avoid the complicated arithmetic of calculating calories and percentage. As a general rule, a lactating mother should take about one quarter more than she used to take before pregnancy. A pregnant or lactating woman should eat as well as a man.

Besides protein, daily water intake must be adequate. While breast-feeding, drinks should be available by the side. You should drink to quench thirst and to maintain a good urine flow. Generally, water, milk, clear soup, soy bean milk, fruit juices, and other beverages such as *Milo* and *Ovaltine* are suitable. Soft drinks and alcoholic drinks are to be avoided. There is no truth that drinking more cow's milk will produce more breast milk and you should not feel compelled to drink cow's milk if you are intolerant to it.

What are common problems associated with breast-feeding?

Breast-feeding is an enjoyable experience. When the flow of milk is well established, the mother is happy and the baby is satisfied. However, there are a number of problems associated with breast-feeding.

Breast-feeding jaundice

Neonatal jaundice is extremely common and most newborn babies would have some degree of jaundice during the first two weeks of life. Most of these babies are well and the level of jaundice is well within the 'safety' range. Sometimes, breast-feeding can prolong the jaundice for a few more weeks. However, this usually does not have any untoward effect and there is no reason to stop breast-feeding. Breast-feeding mothers should avoid taking unnecessary drugs or 'herbal medications' as many of these substances can aggravate the jaundice of the young baby. You should discuss with your paediatrician to find out about the cause of the jaundice in your baby as early as possible so that the appropriate steps can be taken.

Premature baby

Prematurity is a fairly common problem and such babies usually need special care. Some of them may need mechanical assistance for their respiration. Depending on the degree of prematurity and other associated abnormalities, a premature baby may not be able to suck and swallow in a coordinated manner. Artificial-feeding via the venous route may be necessary. However, as soon as the baby is able to make use of his intestine, breast milk would be the best choice. It is, therefore, very important that you establish good flow of breast milk, express and store the milk in anticipation of feeding your baby as soon as he is ready for it. During the early stage, feeding through a tube may be necessary. Your neonatologist would discuss with you the choice of the route of feeding, the amount to feed, and the necessary precautions. You should visit your baby regularly if he is in the nursery or intensive care unit.

Obviously, when the premature baby is unable to suck, you need to express your milk and feed him through a feeding stomach tube. The precaution required is to maintain cleanliness and prevent contamination of your expressed milk. Sometimes, the milk needs to be stored overnight. Most neonatal units are able to store breast milk by refrigeration. However, there are strict limits for the length of time expressed breast milk can be stored without getting spoilt:

- A maximum of 24 hours if kept at 4°C, i.e. in domestic refrigerator. Do keep it on the top shelf and right at the back of the refrigerator.
- A maximum of 2 weeks if kept in the freezer compartment of a refrigerator.
- A maximum of 3 months if kept at −20°C (or colder) in a deep freezer.

As each bottle of expressed milk looks similar to another, you should date every container clearly in order to avoid confusion.

Twin pregnancy

All mothers have milk in both breasts and many mothers have milk for more than one child. Healthy twins, born on time, have no difficulty with breast-feeding. A mother who feeds two babies produces a very large amount of milk. She should eat and drink adequately herself. The two babies can be fed separately or simultaneously. If you choose to feed the twins simultaneously, you will have to find a comfortable position for the three of you. Often, it is good to have some cushions around and have one baby under each arm, with their feet towards your back, or one in front and one under the arm.

Baby with cleft lip or palate

A baby with cleft lip or palate will have some problems with feeding. If only the soft palate is cleft, breast-feeding is usually not a problem. All that is necessary is for your baby to be fed in a relatively upright position to prevent the milk from going into his nose. If only the upper lip is cleft, you can often place your finger over the opening. This will block off the cleft. Sucking will be difficult if both the lip and the hard palate are totally cleaved. Your paediatrician and plastic surgeon will often help to feed your baby by using special feeding bottle and teat. Sometimes, an occlusion device can be inserted into his mouth. Surgery is the way to treat it and should be planned at the most appropriate time so that your baby is well and free from infection before the operation. As such, nutrition is important to your baby both before and after surgery.

Expressing milk

There are different methods of expressing breast milk. Hand expression is convenient and effective. Before expressing, it is of utmost importance that you wash your hands thoroughly. Do tie back your hair as it is likely to get in your way. Make yourself comfortable and ensure privacy.

The milk ducts are channels radiating from the nipples. They are felt to be like lumps under the skin and can be easily palpated at about 1–2 inches from the areola. This is where milk is collected and where you should be exerting pressure to eject the milk. Press your fingers gently and release repeatedly. Rotate your fingers around your breast until all the ducts are milked. You need to express your breast alternatively every few minutes to give time for the other breast to fill up again. Do not be disappointed if only a few drops are expressed initially. With practice, your milk flow will improve. The whole process of hand expression is about 20–30 minutes. Generally, 50–60 ml can be expressed from a full breast. There are a number of things you can do to encourage milk flow:

- Feel relax and comfortable.
- Stay in the privacy of your room.
- Do a little gentle nipple rolling or pulling.
- Stroke your breast gently towards the nipple.
- Think of your baby.
- Do some deep breathing with your eyes closed.

Using a breast pump

There are a number of breast pumps available commercially. They are effective but many mothers experienced some pain during use. You should not use them if your nipples are cracked or sore. The same principle of cleanliness applies. All parts of the pump must be sterilized. When using a breast pump, try to relax in order to encourage better milk flow. Use the pump gently and avoid using excessive suction which causes pain. Switch to hand expression at the first sign of sore nipples or severe engorgement.

Breast problems

There are a number of problems associated with breast-feeding which are more commonly encountered during the early period of breast-feeding. They include sucking difficulties, too little milk, breast engorgement, sore nipple, block ducts, and infection. Most of these can be overcome and should not be a reason to stop breast-feeding.

Sucking difficulties have been discussed earlier. Problems with flat or retracted nipples should be solved before the baby is born. Most healthy babies suck easily and naturally. However, some babies need to learn to suck. In such cases, great patience is required in feeding them. You should not give up trying and at the same time, you should not exhaust yourself by incessantly trying to succeed. A period of rest is mandatory between feeding — both for you and your baby. The presence of an experienced person who is familiar to you will be of great help.

Sucking is a reflex action for any normal newborn baby. The presence of the nipple in the mouth would trigger off this reflex and the baby will start sucking and swallowing. Sometimes, the nipple is too short and may not be able to get right inside the baby's mouth to trigger off the reflex. This is why flat nipples may cause problems in the early days of breast-feeding.

Flat nipples can be managed or improved by the following method. Firstly, manipulate your nipple a little to make it more erect and easy to grasp. Secondly, it is often helpful to remove some of the milk so that your breast is softer and thirdly, gently and patiently put your baby to your breast for another try. Your nipple and areola must be put into his mouth. Sometimes, you may have to press him quite closely to your breast. If you think that your breast is blocking the nostrils of your baby, use your finger to hold your breast clear of his nose. Do not pull his head away.

In some cases, the nipples are too big and the baby seems to gag and choke when the nipple is put into the mouth. It is because the long and big nipple touches on the soft palate of the baby and this makes the baby gag. This can be corrected by holding the baby a little away from the breast.

One common problem frequently raised by mothers is 'too little milk'. This can be particularly worrying before breast-feeding is fully established. You should not be discouraged as this is not an uncommon experience. Generally, low supply is caused by rigid feeding schedule, fatigue, poor positioning of the baby and hormonal imbalance caused by various factors such as oral contraception and menstrual problems. As discussed earlier, good nutrition, adequate rest and motivation are essential for successful breast-feeding. Night suckling is a strong stimulus to increase milk production. Frequent sucking and complete emptying of the breast is another important stimulus. Poor milk production can be due to the baby being unable to suck vigorously. Such examples include premature babies, sick babies, or neurologically abnormal babies. In such cases, the problem can be overcome by manual expression or using a breast pump to empty the breast at regular intervals.

After successfully establishing breast-feeding, most mothers will not feel the sense of fullness or engorgement. This is often interpreted by some mothers as a decrease in milk production. This is not the case. In fact, milk production is as good, if not more than the period when the breasts are engorged. You should not be worrying that your baby is not getting enough milk because you do not feel the engorgement. There are a number of simple rules to help you decide whether your baby is receiving enough milk. If the baby is gaining weight adequately, whatever the amount you have produced is adequate. Generally, most babies put on about 20–30 g daily during the first 3–4 months of life. During the first 7–10 days, weight gain is negligible. Adequately fed babies are alert, happy, contented, and sleep well. Their skin is firm and smooth, their eyes bright. Generally, a good urine flow is one of the features of adequate feeding and most babies wet their nappies after every feed.

Breast engorgement

During the early stage of establishing breast-feeding, the breasts may feel full, uncomfortable, and even painful. Some mothers may have no discomfort at all. Hence, there is great variation in terms of breast engorgement which is partly due to increased blood flow to the breast and partly due to excessive milk in the breasts. The increase in blood supply would spontaneously decrease after a few days. Milk production would automatically decrease to match the demand of the baby after a few days. However, if you are extremely uncomfortable, breast engorgement can be managed by expressing the excess milk. This provides rapid relief of pain and other symptoms. Some mothers are afraid to express the excess milk because they fear that they may continue to produce more milk than necessary. This is not true as milk production almost always decreases to match the requirement of the baby.

Sore nipples

(See Chapter 2: Your Baby's First Month — *Rooming in* (the paragraph on cracked nipples on page 42)

Sore nipples may occur at any time during lactation. It is more common during the early weeks of breast-feeding. Often, it is due to sudden exposure to unaccustomed action of sucking, excessive cleaning of the nipples with soap, faulty sucking techniques, and bad position during feeding. The nipples are well supplied with pain nerve fibres and are extremely sensitive. Small lesions can be extremely painful. Sore nipples do not have gross wounds and they only appear a 'little red'. The pain is worst when the baby first begins to suck as it is the stretching of the skin when pain is felt. It gets less as nursing proceeds, especially after the ejection reflex is working and the milk is flowing. You may be glad to know that sore nipples seldom lasts more than a week. However, it may seem a long time when the nipples are painful and prevention is easier than cure. This is why the nipples must be examined antenatally and short or flat nipples corrected as early as possible.

In spite of all the precautions, sore nipples may still develop. Although it may sound cruel, frequent and short nursing promote speedy healing. The painful wound heals in spite of frequent nursing. It is unwise to stop suckling for many hours because the crust would crack open as soon as the baby sucks. Let the baby suckle on the unaffected side first if only one nipple is affected. The initial sucking is strongest and most painful. When the 'let down' or ejection reflex has started, change the baby over to the painful side. Nursing the baby at a different position may help. Protect the nipple with a thin coat of any edible oil in between feedings. Lanolin or *Vaseline* are good and harmless agents. Avoid using strong soap at the nipples and areola regions. There are times when the nipples are extremely painful and it may be necessary to discontinue breast-feeding for a little while. It is essential to express the milk regularly to prevent infection and maintain milk production.

Persistent sore nipples

(See Chapter 2: Your Baby's First Month — *Rooming in* (the paragraph on cracked nipples on page 42 and <u>Sore nipples</u> on page 62)

Occasionally, sore nipples can persist for longer duration and the doctor should be consulted when sore nipples persist longer than expected. It may be due to fissures or crack, thrush, or other infections of the nipples. However, wrong posturing is a common cause of persistent sore nipples. Make sure that your baby's mouth is in the correct position. The gums should be 'biting' over the areola area during sucking. A fissure may be slow to heal especially when it is complicated by thrush infection.

It is not uncommon for a baby to have oral thrush and the infection spread to the nipples, resulting in persistent sore nipples. The baby's mouth should always be checked. Thrush infection appears as a white coat over the tongue or on the inside of the cheeks. They appear like milk curds. If you are not sure if they are milk curds or thrush, try to wipe them away. If the white coat can be removed easily, it is milk curd. If not, it is probably thrush and can be treated with some oral medications. It is best to consult the paediatrician to confirm the diagnosis and for treatment.

Persistent crack nipples may necessitate stopping of suckling for a few days. It is reasonable to apply an antiseptic cream as soon as a fissure is suspected. The use of a nipple shield temporarily may help.

What is artificial-feeding?

Artificial- or formula-feeding is common in most industrialized countries. In spite of the hazards and problems associated with bottle-feeding, many children thrive well on formula milk without any problem. When it is not possible to provide breast milk to your baby, another source of milk should be found and formula milk is a convenient alternative. Throughout the world, millions of babies have been bottle-fed since birth for many years. These babies have grown up to be healthy adults. They do not suffer from any nutritional deficiency and are also healthy mentally. It is safe to bottle-fed when carried out properly although formula-feeding in developing countries often leads to an increase in incidence of diarrhoea and its complications.

How do I choose a formula?

There is a wide range of milk formulae available. They are usually imported from Europe, North America,

Australia, or New Zealand. They have different packaging and are very different in prices. Many factors influence a mother's choice of formula milk. Sometimes, it is the cost. However, the cheapest brand is not always the choice because the more expensive one might have a better status symbol. The choice might depend on the attractiveness of the container, the best sales promotion, or availability.

Bottle-feeding

Unmodified full cream cow's milk is not suitable for human babies. The saying that 'cow's milk is meant for cows only' is quite true. However, infant formulae are highly modified and are formulated according to certain standard or requirements set by the professional bodies or World Health Organization. There are minor variations among the various commercial brands. Varying amounts of vitamins are used to fortify the formulae. You should choose a brand which has a content most similar to that of breast milk. The mineral or salt content should be as close as possible to that in breast milk. The protein, fat and/or sugar contents are already adjusted to make them more like those in breast milk. Some brands replace some of the casein protein with more soluble whey protein. In some, the fat has been replaced with vegetable oils which have a pattern of fatty acids more similar to those in human milk. The final decision is yours and you should try to use the same formula all the time. It is seldom necessary to change from one brand to another.

How do I sterilize bottles and teats?

Before delivery, you should get ready all the feeding bottles and utensils for sterilization. Feeding bottles are usually made of clear plastic or glass. They should be of the upright version and wide mouthed to make it easy to clean the interior of the bottles. Beware that the markings or calibrations may be in millilitres (ml) or in fluid ounces (oz). Make sure that you are familiar with the markings and always follow the same unit to avoid making mistakes. It is always wise to have a number of bottles and teats so that you only need to sterilize them once or twice a day. The teats should be of good quality to withstand boiling. The hole in the teat should allow a steady flow of drops when the bottle is held upside down. You may control the flow by either tightening or loosening the cap of the bottle. Nowadays, there are a number of teats available commercially with anticolic mechanisms. They may not allow milk to drop freely as the flow of milk only commence when the baby sucks.

Besides bottles and teats, you should get a bottle brush for cleaning the interior of the bottle, a pair of tongs, and a big pot with lid. Wash all the utensils immediately after use with soap or detergent, using a bottle brush for the bottles. Scrub the teats with salt to remove milk curds. The safe and effective way of sterilizing is by boiling. Place all the bottles, teats and caps in the pot with about half to one-third full of boiling water and cover the lid. Boil for 5–10 minutes and leave the pot covered until the utensils are to be used. If you are using a pair of tongs, they should be sterilized too. Keep the handles of the tongs above water. With practice, it is possible to fix each teat to the bottle with the use of a pair of tongs using 'non-touch technique'. This means that you can use one clean hand to hold the bottle without touching the area around the opening and use the sterilized tongs to fix the teat and cap the bottle. It is not practical to boil after each feed. Having four or five bottles will cut down the number of boiling to twice a day. Each bottle and teat must be boiled before feeding.

Sterilizing agents are available commercially nowadays. They are convenient to use. However, it is essential that you follow the instructions on the pack/box carefully.

How do I prepare formula milk?

It is absolutely essential to read the manufacturer's instructions and measure both the powder and water carefully. Most of the formulae are reconstituted with one level scoop of powder to 30 ml of water. Some brands are supplied with a bigger scoop meant for one scoop of powder to 60 ml of water. It is essential that the formulae are prepared in strict accordance with the manufacturer's instructions. Never use the scoop supplied by one brand to prepare the formula of another brand.

It is during the preparation of formula that most of the mistakes occur. Firstly, you must clean your hands thoroughly with water and soap. Contamination of milk occurs during this stage of milk reconstitution. Measure out the amount of powder into a pre-sterilized bottle. Cap the can of milk powder properly to prevent contamination. Add about half the required boiled hot

Important steps in reconstituting formula milk

water. Cap the bottle and shake it to dissolve the powder. It is not advisable to use a spoon or other instrument to stir the milk as this increases the chance of infection and contamination. Most brands of infant formulae are 'instant milk' which means that the powder has been homogenized and can dissolve in hot water without difficulty. After dissolving the powder in hot water, reconstitute the milk to the correct volume with boiled cool water. This will bring the milk to a lower temperature. You can still check whether the milk is too hot by dropping a few drops on the back of your hand. If it is hot to you, it is definitely not suitable for your baby. You may cool the milk by running tap water over the bottle. During the process, avoid opening the cap or touching the teat. After the feed, it is mandatory that the leftover milk in the bottle be discarded.

'Ready to feed' preparations are available for many brands. These are liquid formulae. Such preparations are already constituted and can be fed directly without any dilution. They are convenient to use. However, the shelf-life of such preparations is shorter than the powder forms and cannot be stored for prolonged period. Always check the expiry date.

How much do I feed my baby?

The amount of milk to feed varies from baby to baby. Generally, the daily total volume of milk taken by babies is about 150 ml/kg body weight (ranges from 100–200 ml per kg body weight). In the first few days, most babies take less than this amount. The total amount of milk is then divided equally into seven or eight feeds and this is the amount of milk you should feed your baby each time. For example, if your baby is 3.2 kg in body weight, the total daily milk intake will be about 480ml (150ml X 3.2 = 480ml). This volume is divided into eight equal feeds at 3 hourly intervals and thus your baby should take about 60 ml each feed. Obviously, some babies feed on more and some feed on less than this amount. You can either increase or decrease the volume according to the demand of your baby.

It should be noted that babies respond to anything that is put into the mouth by sucking. Hence, not all 'cries' are 'hunger cries'. You should always find out why your baby cries as it is very easy to over-feed your baby by offering him a bottle each time he cries. Common causes of crying besides hunger include wet nappies, dirty nappies, and other physical causes of discomfort.

How do I feed my baby?

You should always make yourself and your baby comfortable during feeding. Use an armchair with good back support. You may need one or two pillows to support your arm that is holding your baby. Make sure that the bottle is held at an angle so that the whole teat is filled with milk. If the bottle is held too horizontally, your baby may suck in too much air instead. Most babies will be able to complete a feed in some 10–20 minutes. If your baby finishes a feed in less than 5 minutes, you are feeding him too rapidly. In such cases, it is due to the rapid flow of milk and you can regulate the flow by tightening the cap of the bottle or using a teat with a smaller opening. Rapid flow of milk increases the risk of choking and aspiration of milk into the airways. It should be avoided.

On the other hand, feeding too slowly is also unnecessary. You should always check the flow of milk if your baby is sucking vigorously and yet he does not seem to be able to finish the milk. Too slow a flow of milk increases the amount of air swallowed by your baby and thus causes colic. Meanwhile, you should be aware that 'sick babies' are unable to feed well. Sometimes, babies with congenital heart disease can manifest as 'slow feeding'. You should consult your paediatrician if your baby is persistently difficult to feed without any obvious reason. Do not change the formula without finding out the real cause.

There are times when a baby is unable to complete a feed at one sitting. Do not keep the reconstituted milk for more than half an hour at room temperature and re-feed the baby. Milk is a good culture medium for bacteria. Each feed should be freshly prepared and discarded if not used within half an hour.

After the first couple of months, you may be able to decrease the number of feeds to six times a day and omit the midnight or early morning feed when your baby is sleeping. However, some babies still demand these feeds after a few months of age. You can increase the amount of milk during the late evening feed so that your baby will sleep for a longer period before waking up to demand for another feed. On the other hand, if you are breast-feeding, you should not avoid night feeding as night suckling increases milk production. Furthermore, breast-feeding at night can be easily carried out. All you need is to bring your baby to your breast and your baby will do the rest of the work. You may even continue to suckle your baby as you sleep.

How do I burp my baby?

As babies suck and swallow milk, a small amount of air is also swallowed at the same time. The swallowed air can cause abdominal distension and discomfort. The problem is more severe when the feeding technique is faulty.

You can help your baby to bring out the swallowed air by 'burping' him halfway through a feed and at the end of it. This can be achieved by different techniques. You can either support your baby in a sitting position with one hand and use the free hand to gently rub or pet his back or hold up your baby so that his head rest over your shoulder and then gently tap or rub his back. Sometimes, some mothers find it easier to burp their babies lying in a prone position. It takes only a few minutes for a baby to bring out the air. Often, a small amount of milk is brought out at the same time and this is perfectly normal.

When do I change the milk for my baby?

Like breast milk, infant formula milk is sufficient for the baby without any complementary foods for up to about 4–6 months of age. It is because by this age, babies develop the ability to 'chew' and are ready to be weaned to semi-solid foods. Nutritionally speaking, the demand for energy and nutrients for babies at this age cannot be met by liquid milk alone. Solid foods are needed. However, if your baby is born prematurely or has other medical conditions, you should consult your paediatrician about the choice of weaning food and the timing of weaning as the requirement of a premature baby is quite different from that of a normal newborn baby. For normal babies, the appropriate time to change to a 'follow on' formula is at about 6 months of age.

When do I give vitamins and iron to my baby?

Breast milk is adequate for newborn babies and requires supplementation with only vitamin D and iron. Although the small amount of iron contained in breast milk is well absorbed, breast-fed babies require iron supplementation from about 6 weeks of age. Vitamin D deficiency is uncommon in tropical countries. With adequate exposure to sunlight, there is no dietary requirement of vitamin D. Breast-fed babies may develop rickets when vitamin D is not given, presumably because of the absence of adequate exposure to sunlight. A dietary supplement of 400 IU of vitamin D is recommended for breast-fed babies.

The fluoride content of breast milk is low. It is recommended that 0.25 mg daily supplement of fluoride be given for fully breast-fed babies after the first 6 months of life. You should discuss with your paediatrician before starting your baby on vitamin D.

If your baby is formula-fed, you should be aware that all infant formulae are fortified with vitamins nowadays. Except for iron, there is no real need to give your baby extra vitamins. Excessive intake of vitamins is not only unnecessary, but also harmful, particularly the fat soluble ones. These are vitamins A, D, E and K. Excess fat soluble vitamins are not excreted by the body and can cause disease.

What is weaning?

For a normal term baby, the appropriate time to introduce some semi-solid meals is after the 4th month of age. Weaning should be carried out gradually over a period of time. Cereal, traditionally the first solid food offered to babies, is well tolerated. Rice-based cereal is preferred by most mothers locally as rice is the main staple food in this country. However, other cereals such as wheat, corn or oat cereals are perfectly acceptable. Mashed potatoes can also be used. It should be noted that plain cereals and potatoes are all starches or carbohydrates, and the amount of protein present is very small. Many commercial brands have added sugar, milk powder, and other edible substances. Remember to read the labels carefully.

Weaning

Home-cooked rice cereal (polished or unpolished brown rice) or commercially prepared plain cereals, can be made into a semi-solid paste or gruel and fed by spoon to your baby. Usually, you may like to time a meal at mid-day and another one during the evening so that they coincide with the lunch and dinner hour of the family. During these meals, offer the cereal by spoon. At the beginning, your baby may have difficulty or even reject the cereal offered. Be patient. It only takes a few days for your baby to get used to it and will accept a few spoonfuls of cereal each time. You may offer him milk after the cereal if you think that your baby has not taken enough of the meal.

When your baby has taken and tolerated one type of cereal well, you can then introduce other variety of cereals gradually. Never introduce several food items at one time. After he has tolerated a few days of cereal, vegetables can be introduced. Leafy vegetables such as spinach or 'kang kong' are rather soft after steaming. They can be easily mashed and offered to your baby together with the cereal. Carrots are preferred by some mothers because they are sweet and have high vitamin A content. Other leafy vegetables available locally include *chye sim*, *kai lan* and *bayam*. Sweet potatoes and pumpkins are suitable alternatives to cereals as they can be smashed into a gruel after cooking.

Protein is the other food item which should be introduced to your baby after he has tolerated cereal and vegetables. Locally, *tofu* (soy bean curd) is widely available and can be easily minced with the cereal for the baby. The advantage of *tofu* is that it is a very good source of protein and contains high quantities of essential amino acids. The calcium content of *tofu* is high and is eminently suitable for young babies.

The other source of protein is fish. You can easily obtain a wide variety of fish locally. Make sure that all the bones are removed. Fish can be mashed up and minced with cereal for feeding babies. One common mistake is to give only the gravy of cooked protein to babies. The 'meaty' part must be given. Hard-boiled egg yolk is another good protein. Proteins from pork, beef, and mutton are tough and cannot be easily made into a semi-solid state for infant-feeding. As such, they are usually introduced at a later age.

The choice of proteins for your baby is influenced by the eating habit and history of allergy in your family. Obviously, if you want your baby to be a vegetarian, the choice of proteins is more limited. In such cases, beans and nuts are good alternatives and they should be well cooked and minced before offering them to your baby. Depending on your family, you may like to avoid certain protein if one of the immediate family members is allergic to it. It is a good practice to delay introducing protein until 6 months of age if there is a strong family history of allergy. Always consult your paediatrician in such cases.

Other than making sure that your baby is well nourished, you should also cultivate good eating habits at this age. The eating habit at this age will influence the eating behaviour in later life. Your baby should enjoy eating and have a well-balanced diet. Within a short period of time, most babies can be successfully weaned to two semi-solid meals a day. In proportion, the amount of milk consumed daily will decrease to about three to four times.

Fruit should be introduced during weaning. There are many choices of tropical fruit locally. Common fruit such as papayas, bananas and chikus are suitable for babies at weaning. These fruit are soft, tasty and can be easily be mashed into a 'paste' or semi-solid state for feeding. Occasionally, some parents prefer to give apples to their babies. Apples are well tolerated by young babies. However, they are harder than papayas or bananas and must be carefully scrapped or cooked before they are offered to your baby. Other fruit include grapes, dates, raisins, and prunes.

Fruit juices can be given to young babies from about 1 month of age. Initially, they may take only a small amount in diluted form. Common choices are orange or apple juice. There are times when parents believe that oranges will induce increased amount of phlegm in the child. Cough and phlegm are more commonly due to viral infection of the respiratory tract, and the association of these respiratory symptoms with the consumption of orange juice may be coincidental. Prune juice is useful particularly when your baby is a little constipated. The feeding of fruit juice from a feeding bottle should be discouraged. Try using a spoon. This is to prevent the practice of putting the baby to bed with a bottle containing cariogenic liquid. 'Nursing bottle' caries is a common problem in babies when this is practised after your baby's teeth have erupted.

Once your baby has started on solids, it is a good idea to bring him to the dining table during meals. He is part of the family and should be included during meal times as part of the family social activity. Seeing everyone else eat is a good encouragement to your baby. However, do not offer him your food from the table unless they are soft and can be swallowed by him. Solids such as peanuts should be avoided at this age because the nuts are hard and can easily be aspirated into the lungs.

Why do I change the formula milk?

As mentioned earlier, breast milk and infant formulae are adequate nutritionally for infants till about 6 months of age. By this age, you should have successfully weaned your baby to at least two meals of semi-solid diet a day. Meanwhile, if you choose to continue to breast-feed your baby, which is the best thing to do, it is not necessary to introduce other formula milk at this moment. Your baby is able to derive all the necessary nutrients from the weaning diet and breast milk. The number of food items your baby is able to take after successful weaning increases tremendously. There is no doubt that solid meals are much more important to your baby nutritionally and you should concentrate on solid meals rather than introducing formula milk.

However, a number of milk manufacturers have marketed 'follow on' formulae for babies 6 months and older. They are meant to replace the regular infant formula used from birth to 6 months of age. Before considering changing to 'follow on' formula, you should wean your baby to weaning diet first. It is after successful weaning that you may consider changing the infant formula to 'follow on' milk. These formulae are slightly different from regular infant formulae in terms of their composition, particularly the higher protein content. Never introduce full cream milk or fresh milk at this age as they are not suitable for babies and should be avoided until after infancy.

What are the other dietary supplements?

After weaning, many other food items can be introduced to your baby. At the age of 4–6 months, most babies have started teething and many of them like to bite things which they can get hold of. Their gums irritate them and they drool. You can provide him with a 'teething biscuit' or a slice of apple for him to chew on. They enjoy biting on something hard and 'play' with food in their mouths. Make sure that you are watching your baby all the time as he may choke. Avoid food items which have added sugar or artificial sweeteners. Sweet foods tend to satisfy your baby quickly, resulting in poor appetite during meal times. Furthermore, your baby might reject other foods which are not as sweet. Avoid refined and processed food too. They might contain unnecessary ingredients. Before you purchase any food for your baby, always read the labels carefully.

Avoid adding table salt to your baby's food during his 1st year of life. Once on a weaning diet, the amount of salt intake increases tremendously. Adding table salt or soy sauce will further increase the intake and this is not recommended. Your baby's kidneys are not able to handle this sudden increase in salt which has to be excreted.

Can I give my child sweets and candies?

Often, parents offer their children sweets, candies, chocolates and other food items as rewards. You should be aware that it is best to avoid cultivating the habit of taking 'sweet' food. Healthy eating habit should be cultivated and nurtured from young. A hug or a kiss will show your love for your baby equally well.

Furthermore, young children may accidentally choke on the sweet and this can be troublesome.

Can I give my child hawker food?

In Singapore, hawker centres are everywhere and they provide a wide range of local foods. In some centres, Western and Japanese foods are also available. Eating at these centres is very convenient and reasonably cheap.

When choosing food at these places, hygiene should be your first concern. Although safety checks and strict regulations are enforced by the authority, unhygienic practices are still encountered.

The same principles about healthy and balanced diet should apply. If you are not cooking at home, you should not allow your child to take a certain dish for a prolonged period of time. Vary as widely as possible in order to have various nutrients from different sources. Avoid those with excessive food flavouring. Take those which are not too oily and have more fibre. Provided your child is able to tolerate spicy food, early exposure of young children to such food is permissible and is often influenced by ethnic culture.

Can I give my child fast food?

This applies to older children who are able to take meals like the adults. They are at least a few years old. With advertisements and peer pressure, many young children prefer fast food than the conventional dishes. It is very convenient and fashionable to have a meal at these fast food restaurants.

In terms of nutrition, fast foods do not give a balanced diet. They are either too high in protein and fat or too low in vegetable contents. Occasional meals of such food are acceptable for children. However, its frequent and regular consumption should be discouraged.

Conclusion

Whether you are breast-feeding or bottle-feeding, you will soon realize that infant-feeding is a very enjoyable process. Unfortunately, many mothers are unable to do so themselves because of other commitments such as work and social functions. The task of feeding their babies has been given to their domestic maids. As far as possible, try to feed your baby yourself at least once or twice a day. Your baby needs your presence and company.

Always remember that infant-feeding is the period of time when you can actually nurture the health and cultivate eating habits of your baby. With correct approach and effort, your baby should grow up healthy and become a healthy adult who enjoys eating and knows what to eat.

References

Breast-feeding mothers' support group (1998) Practical hints on breast-feeding. Singapore.

Cameron, G. & Hofvander, Y. (1983) Manual on feeding infants and young children. Third edition. Oxford University Press, United Kingdom.

Helsing, E. & King. F.S. (1983) Breast-feeding in practice, a manual for health workers. Oxford University Press, United Kingdom.

4
Normal Growth and Development

LOW Poh Sim

Introduction

A normally developing child is expected to be continually active physically, to have an enquiring mind that is intensely curious about the people and things in his environment while developing a personality that seeks good relationships with others around him.

Physical growth and development encompass change in the size and function of the child. Intellectual growth and development in later infancy and childhood can be measured by communicative skills and the ability of the child to handle abstract and symbolic materials. Emotional growth and development is seen as the child's ability to establish supportive bond of feeling, the capacity for love and affection, the ability to handle anxieties arising out of frustration, and the ability to control aggressive impulses.

Normally, growth and development of the body, intellect and personality progress harmoniously and with relative predictability in rate and outcome. In the abnormal situation, there is dissociation of growth with intellectual and behavioural developmental progresses. Growth and development besides being programmed genetically are also subject to an intricate relationship with nutritional, social and cultural influences which can result in individual variability of the final growth and behaviour patterns.

What is physical growth?

Growth is an increase in body size and can be measured with some degree of reliability by height, weight, and head circumference. It is important for parents to note that the rate of growth is greater in the first 4–6 months of life and the rate slows down thereafter during the later half of the 1st year. Birth weight doubles by 4–6 months and trebles by about 1 year of age. The average birth weight is 3–3.5 kg and so most 1 year olds would weigh about 9–10 kg. The average length of term newborn babies is 50 cm and this increases during the 1st year by 25–30 cm. Height does not double until between 3 and 4 years of age. Head growth, especially during the first 6 months of life, needs careful monitoring. Large and small head sizes are both warning signs of developmental problems. The anterior fontanelle (the soft spot on top of the head which may be felt to pulsate) of the baby may become effectively closed from 9–18 months.

Teething in infancy also follows a time-table which again varies from child to child. The deciduous teeth (milk teeth) appear in most babies between 5 and 9 months. The first teeth to erupt are the lower central incisors, followed by the upper central, and then the upper lateral incisors. The lower lateral incisors follow, the first deciduous molars, the cuspids and second deciduous molars appearing in that order. By the age of 1, most children have six to eight teeth. However, teething varies from child to child and in some normal children, there may be as few as two teeth at 1 year of age. The average physical growth parameters during the first 2 years of the child's life are summarized in Table 4.1.

Table 4.1 Average physical growth parameters:
First 2 years of life

Age	Occipito-frontal circumference	Height	Weight	Dentition
At birth	35.0 cm +2 cm/mth (0–3 mths) +1 cm/mth (3–6 mths) +0.5 cm/mth (6–12 mths)	50.0 cm	3.0–3.5 kg (Doubles by 4–6 mths) (Trebles by 1 year)	Central incisors – 6 mths Lateral incisors – 8 mths
1 year old	47 cm	75 cm	10.0 kg	First molars – 14 mths Canines – 19 mths
2 years old	49 cm	88 cm	12.0–12.5 kg (4 times birth weight)	Second molars – 24 mths

What is meant by development?

Development is an increase in complexity in functional abilities. The purpose of development in a child is for the helpless babe to gradually develop abilities that would allow him to achieve 'independence'. There are four areas to be achieved towards independent living in a social environment. The child has to achieve upright body posture free of his hands and be able to move from one place to another. He would also have to develop hand skills that would allow his fingers to manipulate and with seeing and looking, he would be able to direct his hand movements for precise purposeful activities. He has to acquire spoken language to communicate with others and in order to live harmoniously with people around him, he has to evolve a set of socially and culturally acceptable behaviour.

Some rules in infant development

Some important rules that govern the pattern of infant and child development are as follows:

■ Infant development occurs in an orderly and predictable manner. The sequence of development is the same for every child. Inherently, the sequence of control of muscles starts from the head and neck before the child gains truncal control and finally develops control of the lower limbs. He progresses from hand-mouth to foot-mouth play. In the same way, the child will first learn to control big movements involving the upper portions of the limbs (arms and thighs) before being able to control his fingers and toes. Attainment of a particular skill builds on the acquisition of earlier skills. It is a known fact that a child is not expected to walk before he has learnt to sit and is not be able to run before he can walk.

■ Although the sequence of developmental patterns is fixed by nature, the pace of the development varies between individuals. For each developmental milestone, there is an acceptable norm to the timing of its attainment by the child, and each child's developmental path is unique to himself. For instance, for walking without aid, one child may walk earlier (at 11 months) while another does not walk until 16 months. Still, both children have achieved the milestone within the limits of normality.

■ Development is primarily a function of the brain's maturation. Developmental progress can, however, be enhanced and augmented by learning and training to achieve the full potential. The pace of development can be modulated by external contributions from the family, the style of care giving, and the financial, social and cultural backgrounds which put the child in an advantageous position for learning. However, the final achievement cannot go beyond that which the particular brain is capable of supporting.

Nurturing a child's development

Nature and nurture influence and determine a child's developmental capabilities. Heredity determines the potential abilities of the child while the environment determines the extent to which the child can fulfil his potential capability. Parents and care givers have the important duty of providing their child with guidance and care to ensure their healthy physical growth and mental development. The opportunity to learn is important for any growing child. In the natural environment of the home and in the company of playthings, the child receives early training and stimulation to develop normally.

There are two views with regard to the child's need in the process of development. One view held by Arnold Gesell is that a child is a robust, healthy, biologically organized developer who, with a little support from his parents, will probably develop into a normal healthy adult. In a healthy environment, children as individuals can develop along their own developmental trajectories. In another view, John Watson portrays the omniscience of parental influence in making the child into whatever they want him to be. Present day practice advocates a middle-line system that would balance the interests of all family members in creating a conducive environment towards child development.

A child needs constant family-member input in order to develop into a normal, competent person. It is clear that in the first few years of life, children need a great deal of individual attention from adults with whom they have a loving relationship. Fathers are as important parents as mothers. They also play a special role in their children's development.

Getting a child to behave

A child's behaviour is important for social interaction. It is believed that the child's behaviour can be modified and shaped by discipline in childhood. Positive reinforcement of behaviour can be effected through pleasant rewarding actions and negative reinforcement achieved through some form of punishment. Positive reinforcement is a more effective way than punishment in bringing out desirable behaviour from children. There is a need to set limits to the behaviour of children from time to time through restraints or measures amounting to punishment.

What is child development?

There are four different areas of a child's development,

which in a normal child, proceed in an integrated manner. These areas are as follows:

• Gross motor development
• Vision and fine motor development
• Hearing and speech
• Social behaviour and play

Gross motor development

Gross motor development begins from the child achieving head control, rolling, to sitting and then through standing and ambulating. The ability to move smoothly through these developmental steps depends, among other things, the normal muscle tone, strength, and coordination. The toddler usually walks on a broad base, slightly crouched and with arms stretched out and forward for better balance. The walking is also hesitant and interrupted. As the child attains better balance, the movements are carried out much more smoothly, with the base narrowing and arm swing evolving, leading to the adult pattern of walking by 3 years of age. The expected norms of gross motor development are outlined in Table 4.2.

Vision and fine motor development

A baby, at the age of 1 month, is already able to gaze at brightness of the window and at brightly coloured objects. He can turn his head and eyes towards light and is able to watch his mother's face while she feeds or talks to him. By 3 months of age, he is visually very alert to moving objects and can follow movements of adults within his field of vision. He begins to show pleasure when the feeding bottle gets into sight.

Progression in gross motor development: (a) Sitting, (b) Crawling, and (c) Standing

Table 4.2 Motor development in the first 5 years of age

Age	Gross motor skills	Fine motor skills
1 month old	Lying on stomach, head up	Hands tightly fisted
3 months old	Good head control Lying on stomach, head up and rests on forearms	Hands unfisted
6 months old	Rolls over Sits with support, propping up with own hands Bears weight in legs when supported to stand and bounces	Reaches for an object, puts the object to mouth, may be able to transfer the object from hand to hand
9 months old	Does commando crawls Sits without support, gets into sitting position Pulls to stand Creeps on hands and knees	Grasps a cube with palm, racks objects with fingers into palm Uses immature pincer grasp
12 months old	Crawls Stands alone Walks with one hand held/cruises/independent steps	Pokes/points with index finger Claps hands Waves Releases an object

Table 4.2 (cont'd)

Age	Gross motor skills	Fine motor skills
18 months old	Walks well alone Climbs onto furniture Walks backwards Throws a ball while standing	Releases a pellet into a small container Builds tower of up to four cubes Scribbles spontaneously Draws a single stroke crudely Beginning to show hand preference
24 months old	Walks upstairs with hand held or holding to rail Jumps in place Kicks ball Walks downstairs with rail Throws ball over hand	Builds tower of six cubes Imitates vertical strokes Turns pages singly, enjoys picture books
2 years old	Runs well Jumps with two feet together from low steps	Imitates drawing a horizontal line and a circle
3 years old	Walks alone upstairs with alternating feet Walks downstairs two feet to a step Rides tricycle Stands momentarily on one foot	Copies a circle, imitates drawing a cross Draws a man with head and one or two other parts Matches two or three primary colours Cuts with scissors
4 years old	Walks or runs up and downstairs, one foot to step Throws, catches, bounces and kicks a ball	Holds and uses pencil with good control (like adult) Draws a man with head, legs, trunk, arm and fingers Matches and names primary colours correctly
5 years old	Skips, hops Climbs, slides and swings skilfully	Copies a square and a triangle Writes a few letters spontaneously Draws a house with a door, window, roof Colours pictures neatly within outlines

Fine motor development begins with the child engaging in finger play and watching his own hand movements at about 3–4 months of age. Reaching for an object, bringing an object to mouth, transfer of the object from hand to hand, development of the pincer grasp occurs in sequence as shown in Table 4.2. Putting the fist to the mouth and mouthing an object for oral exploration is a normal phase in infant development. This behaviour should, however, not persist beyond 18 months of age. It is important to realize that fine manipulative precision is dependent not only on the development of hand skills, but also on normal vision. As part of social interaction, a 1-year-old child uses his newly acquired fine motor skills of pointing, clapping hands, and waving. During the 2nd year, the fine motor

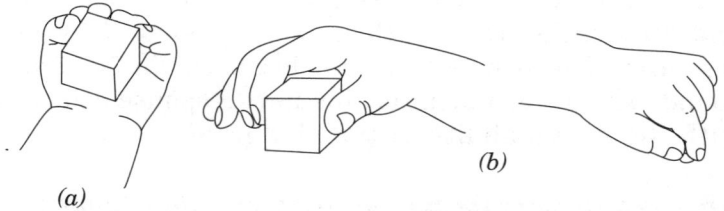

Progression in fine manipulative skills: (a) Palmar grasp and (b) Princer grasp

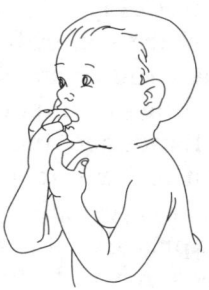

Putting objects and their parts into mouth

skills develop to allow the child to use objects as tools. He uses the pencil to draw and the blocks to build. Manual dexterity improves working hand in hand, with cognitive development enhancing the child's ability to solve problems. He learns that by fine manipulation of the key, the toy car starts to move or the music is turned on by pushing a button. The expected norms of fine motor development is outlined in Table 4.2.

Hearing and speech

In the newborn baby, responses to sound are entirely reflex — the so-called startle response. These are elicited by loud sounds. The first response to a quiet sound is for the baby to keep still for a few seconds. This can be seen as early as 3 weeks of life. Between 8 and 10 months, the startle reflex is replaced by new response. The baby turns and localizes the source of sound. The development of this new response coincides with the baby's ability to turn his head.

What is necessary for normal language development?

The development of speech is closely associated with the ability to hear. Delays in language development are more common than delays in other domains of development. Parents are generally less familiar with language milestones and may not be aware that vocalization and babbling are important fore-runners of speech acquisition. Language includes the ability to receive and understand what is heard (receptive language) and that of expressing what the child wants to communicate (expressive language). Expressive language may be spoken words (verbal) or communicated through actions and gestures (non-verbal).

Judging a child's language development by what he speaks can be erroneous as well as an incomplete assessment. A child may be able to hear but not comprehend what he has heard and can yet echo what is heard without meaning what he says. A child who has no spoken language yet may be receptive as well as expressive with appropriate actions and gestures and yet communicate non-verbally with others effectively. Cognitive deficit is the most common reason for language delay. All children who have delayed language development should, however, undergo hearing testing to rule out hearing loss. A hearing-impaired child usually has normal babbling at 6 months but will lose this ability as well as verbal expression over time. A 1-year-old child who is deaf may seem to be able to hear as he is able to follow a command with a gesture relying solely on visual cues. Table 4.3 shows a check list of language milestones for the first 5 years of life.

What are the serious problems that can cause language delay?

In an otherwise normal child, speech delay is much more likely to be due to 'late maturation'. However, serious problems such as mental retardation and autism must be recognized early as these conditions need aggressive intervention.

In a non-verbal child, it is important to note how the child communicates what he wants and how much you think he understands what is being said to him. The child's behaviour around others is an important observation to make. A child who is hyperactive but not purposeful in what he does has broader functional

Table 4.3 Development of language skills during the first 5 years of age

Age	Receptive	Expressive	Warning signs
1 month old	Is alert to sound	Cries	No response to sound — Deaf?
2 months old	Looks at speaker	Smile Coos Vocalizes	
3 months old		Chuckles Echoes Cries discriminately (hunger, pain)	
4 months old		Laughs Says "ah-goo" Listens to speaker and vocalizes in response	
6 months old	Localizes (laterally) source of sound	Babbles "baba, gaga"	Absent babbling indicates possible hearing deficit
8 months old	Plays peek-a-boo	Mimics sounds	
10 months old	Comprehends "no" Answers to name when called	Says "Dada/Mama" appropriately Waves bye-bye	Inability to localize sounds, may indicate hearing loss
12 months old	Looks at familiar family member when named Follows commands like "give me"	Says first word Imitates simple sounds Uses immature jargoning	
14 months old	Looks appropriately when asked "Where is (familiar object)?" Follows commands without gesture	Says two or three words	

Table 4.3 (cont'd)

Age	Receptive	Expressive	Warning signs
18 months old	Points to three body parts Points to self Carries out simple instructions	Knows 10–25 words including "thank you", "Let's go", "I want" Names one picture on command	
24 months old	Points to four to six pictures Carries out 2-step commands Understands "me/you"	Knows 50+ words Uses 2- or 3-word sentences (noun-verb) Refers to self by name Uses "I", "you", "me"	Non-communicative speech (echoing, repeating by rote memory) may indicate autism
2 years old		Knows full name Knows 200 or more recognizable words	Stuttering common
3 years old	Listens to stories, knows nursery rhymes	Gives full name, sex and maybe age Carries out simple conversations Asks many questions Counts up to 10 (by rote)	
4 years old	Enjoys jokes Listens to stories	Sings nursery rhymes Tells long fantasy and imaginative stories Counts up to 20 (by rote)	
5 years old	Enjoys riddles	Speaks fluently	

disturbance of his brain of which a lack of language development is just a feature. A child who appears to be in a world of his own with an inability to relate to others and who also avoids eye contact may be autistic. Such a child does not feel a need to communicate with others, and language development is deemed to be superfluous.

The typical 3-year-old speaks in well-formed, simple sentences of three or four words. A 3-year-old can count three items and the 4-year-old four items. A 5-year-old can be expected to use complete sentences of about five words and would be able to count ten or more objects.

When do I have to worry about common speech disorders?

A common concern of parents in their child's speech is poor articulation which is very common in children younger than 3 years of age. Strangers can usually only understand 25–50 per cent of what a 2-year-old child says and up to 75 per cent of what a 3-year-old child says. By the age of 4, the child's speech is 100 per cent intelligible to strangers. Some common errors are made in producing sounds such as 'r', 's', 'l', 'sh' and 'th' and may continue till 7 years of age.

Lack of fluency (stuttering) in children between 2 and 4 years of age is often transient. Persistence or worsening of stuttering beyond 4 years of age warrants medical attention. As a group, girls are more advanced than boys in language acquisition. Reading is not expected before 6 years of age. Knowledge of letters, words and symbols is acquired before reading begins.

Social behaviour and play

During the preschool years, children are rapidly developing patterns of social behaviour. In this chapter, only the development of social skills with regard to early social responses to people, and the development of independence in eating, dressing, and toileting are discussed. Issues pertaining to psychosocial and emotional developments are being addressed in Chapter 7. Table 4.4 summarizes the early social behaviour of a child.

What is the role of play in child development?

Play is not as frivolous as it looks. It does somehow contribute to the development of the child. Children actually learn through play. Children acquire new skills through manipulation of a toy and then practise it over and over again until they master it entirely before going on to something else. Play is a place for exercising newly discovered skills and mastering it — as in working jigsaw puzzles or figuring how things work by fixing or even pressing a button. Children talk more during play and their language is more complex and more sophisticated. There is a reciprocal relationship between play and learning. Learning leads to more sophisticated play and play provides a kind of mastery that leads to more learning. A child engaged in pretend play stretches his imagination to create a world of his own. Children spend so much time in play and the major learning experience is through play. Play contributes to the child's physical, intellectual, emotional and social development. In games between two children or a child and an adult, there is mutual interaction and turn-taking.

Table 4.4 Development of social behaviour and play in the first 5 years of age

Age	Behaviour
5-6 weeks old	Smiles Stops crying when picked up or spoken to Shows responsive vocalization
3 months old	Gazes on mother's face during feeding Smiles, coos, shows excited movements to familiar situations like feeding or bathing
6 months old	Grasps small toys Puts everything to mouth Puts hands to bottle, pats it during feeding Shakes rattle for sound May begin to show anxiety with strangers
9 months old	Distinguishes strangers from familiar faces Claps Plays "peek-a-boo"
12 months old	Holds and drinks from cup Puts toys to mouth less often Helps with dressing Stops drooling Gives toys to adults on request Plays "pat-a-cake" Waves bye bye
18 months old	Holds cup between both hands, drinks with little spilling Takes off shoes, socks Does not put toys to mouth Still wets, may have bowel control Imitates simple daily activities such as feeding dolls
2 years old	Spoonfeeds self with messing Indicates toilet needs Is usually dry through day Is very curious, demanding for attention and easily frustrated Is rebellious, temper tantrums Is little aware of dangers

Table 4.4 (cont'd)

Age	Behaviour
3 years old	Feeds self without spilling much Washes and dries hands and face Is dry by day and night Puts on pants, shoes and socks but cannot button Understands sharing Is active in make-belief play
4 years old	Towels dry after a bath Brushes teeth Dresses completely, distinguishes front from back Is independent and strong willed Understands turn-taking
5 years old	Bathes or showers without assistance Understands rules for games Understands meaning of clock-time

Play contributes towards a child's physical development. The active child exercises his limbs and muscles, improving the acquisition of motor skills, balance, and coordination. Grasping objects, catching a ball or kicking a ball improves the child's motor coordination and judgement of distance. Matching different shapes through their appropriate slots helps the child in appreciating shapes and manipulating of the object through the right slot. Fitting a square block into a round hole soon becomes an error of the past. Building tower blocks improves the child's perceptual motor skills.

Play also helps cognitive development. Through play, children come to test the validity of their beliefs, to grapple with what they do not understand. The ability to manipulate reality and to think metaphorically, is developed further through pretend play. Pretend play allows the child to try out new concepts and new ways of thinking, to come to grips with them, to master them, and then to go on to some new challenge.

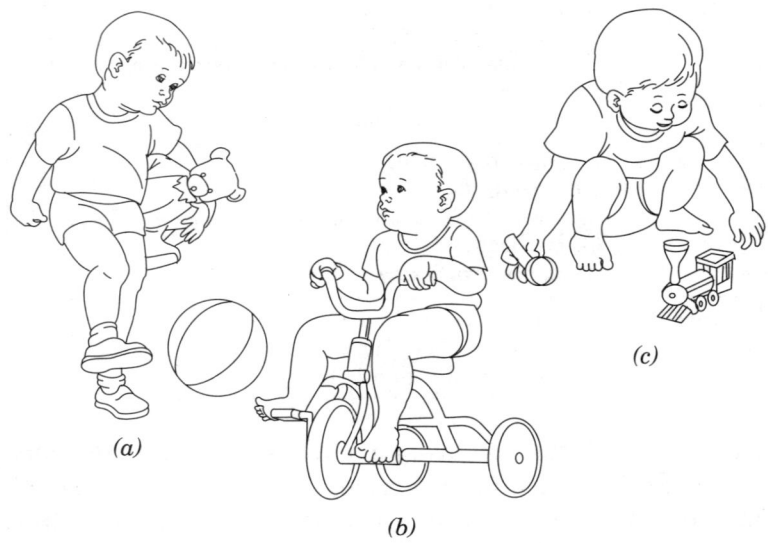

Improving motor skills through play

Play also contributes to emotional health. Children who enjoy playing and those who play more seem to be happier. Those who are good at play or who are fun to play with, seem to get other emotional benefits besides the joy of play itself. Those children who play well also gain the good effects of having friends.

Eye contact is an extremely important social skill and is the most basic way of making contact with another person. Children's games nearly always involve interactions with other people, so they are especially important to social development. The child learns the concept of turn-taking and sharing. He learns to obey rules (as in the game) and about team spirit. The concept of competition is also taught in play. The child learns to experience the joy of winning and the misery of losing.

Socialization can be achieved through model plays. Children as young as a few months old tend to imitate the behaviour of those around them. As they grow, they can draw lessons from the consequences of their own behaviour. Children learn values and imbibe real life experiences through mass media like the television. It is important that the system of values proposed to children and other significant persons be congruent with the actual behaviour of these same individuals.

What is cognitive development?

In the defined areas of development discussed above, there is not a domain for cognitive development. Intellectual development depends on learning that contains three components — attention, information processing, and memory. Intellectual development is reflected in increasing abilities to comprehend, reason and make judgement and decisions, and to solve problems. The ability to apply previous experience and lessons learnt to current situations is also a measure of intellectual capability. It has been found that language skill is the single best indicator of intellectual potential. Problem-solving skills are the next best measure. Cognitive function can be objectively measured using an intelligence quotient (IQ) test. However, IQ assessment in children younger than 3 years old may be unreliable as cooperation from the child is necessary during testing.

What is the significance of global and isolated developmental delay?

In a normal child, the different areas of development proceed in an integrated manner. The level of attainment in the developmental milestones is reflective of the state of maturity of the brain. Global developmental delay would strongly suggest brain damage or mental retardation.

When there is an isolated area of delay in development, it is less likely to be due primarily to problems in the brain. A child with an isolated delay in gross motor development may have a problem with the muscles, ligaments, joints or bone instead of a problem of poor brain control of limb movements or coordination. An isolated problem of poor fine motor skills may be the result of impaired vision or hand and finger malformations. Hearing impairment can result in speech delay without brain dysfunction. A child may be poor in social interaction from lack of social exposure.

What are the early warning signs of developmental problems?

Not all children do things at exactly the same time and the same way. Variations can occur naturally and can also occur according to the experiences and opportunities of the child. It is not easy to be certain about a week's delay (25 per cent delay) in a child's development when he is only 1 month old. However, a baby whose development continues to be behind, this rate of 25 per cent delay would be more easily detected given time when the gap in the development compared to children of the same age is obvious. By 6 months, the baby would only be able to do what a $4\frac{1}{2}$-month-old child would do and by 1 year old, the child only has the abilities of a 9-month-old.

The mother is usually the first to suspect any abnormal developmental patterns in her child. Her suspicion that her child is not seeing, hearing, moving his limbs or taking notice like other children of his age, is an important warning sign. Delayed motor development, lack of normal visual alertness, inattentiveness to sounds, delayed development of vocalization or speech, lack of interest in people or playthings, and abnormal social behaviour need medical attention.

For gross motor development, a child rolling over before 3 months of age may have stiff limbs. Poor head control by 5 months is a matter for concern. Persistent toe walking needs medical attention.

For development of hand skills, particular attention should be given to hands which are persistently fisted at 3 months of age as this is an early indication of hand dysfunction. Hand dominance (fixed preference for the use of one hand) before the age of 18 months may indicate weakness of the unpreferred hand. As right-handedness is the expected norm, parents may realize late the child's inability to use the left hand in the early months of life. On the other hand, if the baby does not uses his right hand to reach for an object, parents are more likely to notice that something is wrong with the right hand and less likely to assume that the child is left-handed. Mouthing of objects should not persist beyond 18 months of age.

Failure to alert to environment stimuli like sound or sight in the 1st month may indicate problems in the baby's hearing or vision. The inability of the baby to fixate on and the inability to follow moving objects are important warning signs of poor vision. Gaze avoidance is significant of probable abnormality. Absence of babbling at 6 months may indicate hearing deficit. Lack of spoken words by 18 months needs assessment and close monitoring. Persistence of echolalia at $2-2^1/_2$ years old is abnormal.

Parents should, therefore, seek help when their child is noticeably slower than children of his age especially when he is not walking or talking when other children are doing so. Parents should also seek help if their child's action and behaviour seem different from other children or if parents find difficulty in understanding and relating to their child.

5
Immunizations

LEE Bee Wah & SHEK Pei Chi Lynette

Introduction

Vaccination or immunization is a very important aspect of your child's medical health care. These vaccines protect your child against certain serious infections. Before the vaccine era, many of these diseases were major causes of death and sickness, particularly amongst children. Diphtheria, measles and poliomyelitis used to kill thousands of children a year, and left many more with severe crippling diseases. Even today, these diseases can lead to lung infections, brain damage and liver or heart failure in children who are not protected. With the introduction of vaccination in the mid-20th century, we have, over this short span of time, achieved global eradication of small pox and elimination of tetanus, polio and diphtheria in many populations including Singapore.

How do vaccines work?

When disease-causing organisms (virus or bacteria) enter the body, the body fights the infections by producing antibodies and other specific immune defences. Unfortunately, before these defences can be built up to protect the body, the infection causes disease, which can lead to serious complications and even death. Vaccines can confer protection without causing a disease. Vaccines consist of oral or injected preparations of dead or weakened disease organisms (virus or bacteria) which can stimulate the immune system, but they do not cause the symptoms of disease themselves. When administered, the body develops protective immunity to that particular disease. Some vaccines induce prolonged or even lifelong immunity, and can be given just once. But others may only induce a temporary immunity and require repeated injections (called boosters) in order to maintain immunity against such diseases.

What are the vaccines available?

Unfortunately, we do not have a vaccine for every known infectious disease. The characteristics of some infectious organisms, especially those with many different sub-types, make vaccine development a problem. However, a lot of research is currently ongoing and large sums of money are being spent to discover new and better vaccines.

What are the types of childhood vaccines?

Vaccination has been shown to be so effective that the World Health Organization (WHO) recommends that a number of well-established vaccines be given to all children born in every population. This programme is called the Expanded Programme of Immunization. The vaccines include BCG (tuberculosis), diphtheria, tetanus (lockjaw), pertussis (whooping cough), poliomyelitis, hepatitis B, and measles. Since the rubella (German measles), and mumps vaccines have been combined with measles, it is common that all three are given at the same time in many countries, including Singapore. In addition, these vaccines are heavily subsidized by government bodies and are often given free in almost all communities. They are also made compulsory either by legislation or by requirement for school entry. The reason being that vaccination not only protects the individual who is vaccinated, it also protects those in contact with him, as many of these diseases are highly contagious. Only when vaccine coverage is high (more than 90 per cent) in a population can the entire population benefit from the elimination of these diseases from the community.

It is also very important to maintain careful surveillance of vaccine coverage as a drop in the coverage often results in disease epidemics. An example is the recent outbreak of diphtheria in Russia when political and social circumstances reduced vaccination coverage in the population. The childhood vaccination schedule of Singapore is shown in Table 5.1. Currently, there are eight injections in the first 18 months of life to complete this immunization schedule.

BCG vaccine

BCG is the most commonly given vaccine in the Expanded Programme of Immunization. It protects against tuberculosis which kills more people worldwide than any other infectious diseases. This disease is experiencing a resurgence with the advent of AIDS (acquired immunodeficiency syndrome). BCG vaccination is 50–80 per cent effective in protecting against the most severe forms of childhood tuberculosis — meningitis and miliary disease — even though its protection against adult tuberculosis is doubtful.

DTP vaccine

DTP vaccinates against diphtheria, tetanus, and pertussis. These are serious illnesses that cause death or severe damage to the health of children. The side-effects include swelling and redness at the injection site, or fever for a day or two. Sometimes, your child may be a little more fussy. Recently, a combined diphtheria, tetanus and acellular pertussis vaccine, DTPa, has been introduced. DT, consisting of tetanus and diphtheria toxoids, is a booster given to older children and adults.

HBV vaccine

Hepatitis B vaccine protects against the commonest cause of chronic liver disease in our population. It is given to Singapore children at birth. It is a safe vaccine with almost no serious side-effects reported.

MMR vaccine

Measles, mumps and rubella (MMR) vaccine protects against diseases that were once very common among children. They cause diseases ranging from mild symptoms to severe complications like infection of the brain, lungs, or the unborn baby. Rubella during early pregnancy frequently results in foetal infection and may produce a spectrum of congenital malformations known as the congenital rubella syndrome. The MMR vaccine has an excellent safety record with fever and rash as the more common side-effects.

Polio vaccine

Live oral polio vaccine, OPV, helps to prevent poliomyelitis. This used to be a common cause of paralysis and death. Another type of polio vaccine, inactivated poliovirus vaccine is given as an injection rather than by mouth. With the elimination of polio in the United States, immunization using the injection form for the first two doses has been introduced as there is an extremely rare complication of mild polio after the oral vaccine (estimated at one in 1 million doses), even though the oral vaccine generally confers better immunity. OPV is given to Singapore children as part of the immunization programme. There have been no reports of paralytics polio in Singapore that is caused by the vaccine.

What are the new vaccines?

There are also some 'optional' vaccines available for children. They have not been put into the immunization programme because most of these vaccines are relatively new, currently too costly to subsidize, and in some cases, the disease may be relatively less common in some communities. *Haemophilus* type b (which causes meningitis) and chicken pox are the 'optional' vaccines that you may consider for your children.

Hib vaccine

Serious *Haemophilus* type b infections were an important cause of disease in many Western populations. The most dreaded of these infections is meningitis (infections of the brain covering) as this can lead to permanent mental and neurological disability. In Singapore, as in Hong Kong, this infection is not as common although it does occur. Hence, parents may choose to protect their children against this infection by vaccination.

Chicken pox vaccine

Chicken pox vaccine is relatively new. It was introduced into the childhood immunization programme in the United States in early 1995. Chicken pox is generally considered a mild illness in young children. It can, however, be very serious and even life threatening in newborn babies, adults, and patients with depressed immunity. It is also a social burden. For example, it is not uncommon for chicken pox to 'strike' during school examinations. Chicken pox vaccination is optional in Singapore. If a child has not had chicken pox by the time he reaches 10–12 years old, vaccination should be considered as the infection tends to be more severe in adolescents and adults. Moreover, the vaccination schedule for those above the age of 13 is two separate injections, whereas for those before their 13th birthday, a single injection is effective.

What are the types of travel vaccines?

Before going on holiday or migration, protection against certain infectious diseases in the form of vaccination should be considered. Some vaccines are compulsory when travelling to certain countries. See Table 9.1 for more details on the vaccinations necessary or recommended when travelling overseas.

Table 5.1 Vaccination contraindications, precautions and common misconceptions

Vaccine	Valid contraindications	Invalid contraindications (Vaccines may be given)
General for all vaccines	Previous anaphylactic reaction to a vaccine is an absolute contraindication to subsequent doses of that vaccine Anaphylactic reaction to a vaccine constituent is a contraindication to the use of vaccines with that substance Current moderate or severe illness Precautions[1] • Pregnancy	Mild to moderate local reaction such as soreness, redness or swelling Low-grade or moderate fever following vaccination Mild current acute illness with or without fever Current antimicrobial therapy Convalescent phase of illness Prematurity (the schedule for immunization is the same as that for full-term babies) Recent exposure to an infectious disease
DTP/DTPa	Encephalopathy within 7 days of administration of the vaccine Precautions[1] • Fever of higher than 40.5°C within 48 hours of vaccine administration • Collapse or shock-like state (hypotonic-hyporesponsive episode) within 48 hours of vaccine administration • Seizures within 3 days of vaccine administration[2] • Persistent inconsolable crying lasting more than 3 hours within 3 days of vaccine administration • Guillain-Barre syndrome within 6 weeks of vaccine administration • Progressive neurological disorder or if the diagnosis of the neurological impairment is still unclear	Family history of convulsions Family history of adverse reaction to DTP/DTPa Personal history of febrile convulsions[2] Children with a personal history of afebrile seizures, which are well controlled and unlikely to recur, may be vaccinated. The American Academy of Pediatrics recommends using DTPa[2]
OPV	Immunodeficiency state, whether primary or secondary, including HIV infection Immunodeficient household contact	Current antimicrobial therapy Mild diarrhoea Breast-feeding household contact

Table 5.1 (cont'd)

Vaccine	Valid contraindications	Invalid contraindications (Vaccines may be given)
IPV	Anaphylactic reaction to neomycin or streptomycin	
MMR	Anaphylactic reaction to neomycin Anaphylactic reaction to eggs Immunodeficiency state Precautions[1] • Thrombocytopenia or a history of thrombocytopenic purpura[4] • Recent (within 3 months) immune globulin administration	• Nonanaphylactic reactions to eggs or neomycin • Immunodeficient household contact • Pregnant household contact • HIV infection if there are no overt clinical manifestations • Tuberculin skin testing[3]
Hib	None apart from general contraindications	
Hepatitis B	None apart from general contraindications	
Varicella	Anaphylactic reaction to neomycin or gelatin Immunodeficiency states, including HIV infection Precautions[1] • Family history of immunodeficiency • Recent (within 3 months) immune globulin administration	

[1] The benefits and risks of administrating a specific vaccine to an individual under the given circumstances should be considered. If the risks are believed to outweigh the benefits, the immunization should be withheld; if the benefits are believed to outweigh the risks (e.g. during an outbreak or foreign travel), the immunization should be given. On theoretical grounds, it is prudent not to vaccinate pregnant women unless the benefits outweigh the risks.

[2] Paracetamol should be given prior to administration of DTP or DTPa and for 24 hours after in children with a personal or family history of seizures.

[3] Measles vaccination may temporarily (4–6 weeks) suppress tuberculin reactivity. MMR vaccine may be given after or on the same day as tuberculin testing.

[4] In most instances, the benefits of vaccination with MMR will be greater than the risks, particularly in view of the even greater risk of thrombocytopenia following measles or rubella.

Adapted from American Academy of Pediatrics. Appendix II. In G. Peter (ed.), *1997 Red Book: Report of the Committee on Infectious Diseases.* 24th edn. Elk Grove Village, IL: American Academy of Pediatrics; 1997: 676–680.

What are the other vaccines available?

Other vaccines not commonly used in children include influenza vaccine which protects against flu caused by the influenza virus. This vaccine is particularly popular during the winter season in temperate regions as epidemics tend to occur at this time. The vaccine has to be given annually as the virus strains change every year. During epidemics, children with muscle diseases or severe lung diseases may benefit from this vaccine.

Are vaccines safe?

Generally, the vaccines in current use are safe and very effective. In the great majority of children, the side-effects are mild and can go away after a few days. Serious reactions are very rare. The benefits to the individual and the community as a whole far outweigh any risks. Hence, it is important to note that the disease causes much more problems than the vaccine.

Typical side-effects of vaccines are sometimes fever, and in even fewer vaccines, rashes. Fever can be quite high after the triple antigen vaccine (tetanus, diphtheria and pertussis) which is given in infancy. Medication such as paracetamol is usually prescribed, and can be administered soon after vaccination as a precautionary measure or when fever occurs. The pertussis (whooping cough) component is generally the cause of the fever. It can also cause some redness and swelling at the injection site, and irritability and crying can occur 24–72 hours after vaccination. Fortunately, most of these adverse reactions are not serious and are self-limiting. However, in view of the possibility of high fever and therefore convulsions in those susceptible, there is a tendency not to immunize children who have had convulsions previously. If there are breast-feeding mothers or pregnant women in the home, your child can still be vaccinated according to the schedule.

In an effort to reduce the side-effects of pertussis vaccination, a newer preparation called the acellular pertussis vaccine, has been tested and made available recently. This vaccine is modified to contain parts of the pertussis organism as opposed to the original preparation which contains killed whole organism. The newer vaccine is not widely available as the cost of this newer preparation is considerably high and up to 20 times the price of the original formulation.

It is fortunate that vaccination coverage for childhood vaccinations in Singapore is very good, and an important reason for this is the excellent acceptance of vaccination by the public. The coverage of these vaccines is more than 90 per cent of the target population. In other countries, there are anti-vaccine groups which lobby against vaccination. Amongst the medical community, it is felt that misinformation, a lack of understanding of the vaccination process, and even distrust of the government which legislates immunization requirements are the main reasons for the support that these groups manage to garner from unsuspecting parents.

In some populations, these groups appear to have very strong influence and prey on the innocence of many parents who are swayed to believe that vaccination will harm their children. These groups work through the media and even the Internet where websites are created by these groups. There is a danger that these anti-vaccines group may lobby sufficient support to reduce immunization coverage of the population to a critical point that puts the community at danger of disease epidemics.

What happens if the vaccination schedule cannot be met?

It is a good idea to keep a good record of your child's immunizations. Your baby's health booklet, which is given to all babies born in Singapore, is a useful book to keep the records. These records will be checked when your child enters primary school.

Occasionally, the immunizations may have to be postponed and the most common reason is flu or some other febrile illness. In such situations, the scheduled immunization will be postponed 1–2 weeks later when the child has recovered. However, if the illness is more serious, there may be a need to delay even longer. It is generally permissible to carry on with the immunization schedule no matter how long ago the last injection was given. For example, if the DTP vaccination has been delayed or interrupted for 2 months because of illness, vaccination can resume from that point as if there had been no interruption. However, it is not advisable to shorten the interval between injections as this may affect the immune response. In other words, we should not contemplate hurrying through the immunization schedule, for example, rushing to complete the immunization(s) because of travel.

What is the future of vaccines?

A great deal of work is being done to develop vaccines for the other common infectious diseases. There is prospect that a vaccine for rotavirus (a common cause of diarrhoeal illness in children) may be available for use very soon. Other vaccines being worked on are those for respiratory viruses and dengue fever.

The other area of vaccine development lies in combined vaccines. In other words, multiple vaccines are being mixed together so that a single injection will provide immunity to many diseases. However, combining vaccines is not as simple as putting them together in the same syringe. It has to be ascertained that the risk of side-effects is not increased and the immune response is just as good. Currently, we are already using combined vaccines, for example, the triple antigen and the measles, mumps and rubella (MMR) vaccine. Vaccines, which contain up to five different components, are already available. These combined vaccines will help to reduce the number of injections required and therefore would ultimately reduce the cost and improve the convenience of administering vaccines.

In conclusion, immunization is an important part of maintaining the well-being of our children and population. It should be taken seriously and the immunization schedules maintained. It is with such a concerted effort that we may be able to achieve the global eradication of certain dreaded infectious disease, like the success we had with small pox (Table 5.2).

Table 5.2 Immunization programme for preschool children

Protect against	Birth	1 month	3 months	4 months	5 months	6 months	12 months	15 months	18 months
Tuberculosis	BCG								
Diphtheria Tetanus Pertussis (whooping cough)*			DTP* 1st dose	DTP* 2nd dose	DTP* 3rd dose				DTP* 1st booster
Poliomyelitis			OPV 1st dose	OPV 2nd dose	OPV 3rd dose				OPV 1st booster
Measles Mumps Rubella (MMR)								MMR	
Hepatitis B (optional)	HBV 1st dose	HBV 2nd dose				HBV 3rd dose			
Hib vaccine** (optional)			Hib 1st dose		Hib 2nd dose			Hib Booster	
Chicken pox								#Varicella vaccine	

* Acellular pertussis vaccine is also available.

** You can ask your paediatrician about this vaccine. Schedule may be modified depending on the vaccine used.

\# Chickenpox vaccine can be given at anytime from 12 months onwards.

6
Common Childhood Complaints

TAN Cheng Lim & TAY Kiat Hong Stacey

Infants

Babies are adorable and are bundles of joy to parents most of the time. However, there are times when their poorly understood behaviour becomes a distress to their parents. This is especially so when parents could not figure out what their baby is upset about. Parents often request help when their babies have poor sleep patterns or excessive crying, or are fussy for no obvious reasons.

Crying

Crying is part of normal behaviour in babies. The baby sends his distress call through crying. Appropriate feeding or changing the wet nappies may be all that is necessary to sooth the crying baby. Excessive crying in babies is distressing to parents and care givers. Organic causes for crying must not be overlooked.

It is always distressing for parents to hear their baby cry. It disrupts the peace at home, annoys the neighbours and may even cause arguments between parents or with their grandparents as to the cause of and the best solution to crying.

What are the causes of incessant crying and how do I deal with a crying baby?

If you have to rule out a medical cause for prolonged crying, the most common reason why your baby cries is because he is hungry or uncomfortable from being wet or feeling too warm or too cold. However, you should seek medical advice if the crying is incessant or associated with fever, vomiting, diarrhoea or other worrying symptoms. Under such circumstances, the cry could be just one clue to a whole list of possible causes which could be serious.

A relatively common and often distressing cause of prolonged crying is infantile colic which usually happens in the first 3 months of life. Colic itself has multiple causes and the resultant pain experienced will make a baby cry.

Hunger as a cause of crying is relevant as it is the only way a baby expresses himself and draws the attention of his mother to his hunger. Most mothers are able to distinguish from the nature of the crying — whether her child is crying from hunger or for other reasons. If the crying ceases after feeding, either with breast milk or formula feed, hunger is the most likely cause. Other causes of crying related to feeding include over-feeding, intolerance of the baby to lactose or allergy to milk.

A baby who is over-active, a poor feeder, a screamer or a bad sleeper can be very taxing, especially to inexperienced mothers. It can result in anxiety, mental and physical exhaustion, depression, and ill health of the mothers. In such extreme situations, medical help is necessary to assess the psychosocial factors involving the baby and each individual family member. For example, psychological factors such as an unwanted pregnancy, failure at breast-feeding, or poor self-esteem on the mother's part may be the underlying factor. It would then be important to obtain the father's understanding in helping the inexperienced mother gain confidence in finding her own feet to successful motherhood.

Colic

When an otherwise healthy baby cries for prolonged periods of time, even belting out piercing screams, drawing up both legs and getting rid of some wind, the diagnosis is usually infantile colic. These attacks usually occur in the evenings and tend to affect babies only during the first 3 months of life, hence the terms 'evening colic' or '3 months' colic'.

What must I do if my baby has 'colics'?

The pain is probably due to wind locked in a loop of bowel and your baby can sometimes be relieved by burping or getting rid of some flatus or by lying him prone (lying with face downwards) for a short period of time. When such attacks are prolonged and distressing, medical advice should be sought. The doctor may prescribe a mild sedative once he has ruled out anything serious. Fortunately, as previously stated, the condition rarely persists after the age of 3 months.

Colic is very common in an otherwise healthy baby. While the exact cause of infantile colic is not fully known, the best advice that can be given is to prevent your baby from swallowing excessive air during feeding if he is not breast-fed. The feeding technique must be correct with the milk bottle properly tilted so that the milk covers the teat completely, and the hole in the teat must not be too large or too small. Your baby must always be burped after his feed.

You should consult a doctor if colic is severe or is associated with fever, vomiting, diarrhoea, blood in the stools, or abdominal distension. The cause could be due to disturbances of the gastrointestinal or urinary tract from causes such as lactose or milk intolerance, urinary tract infection, or conditions as serious as appendicitis or intestinal obstruction.

Sleep problems

It is important for young parents to expect interrupted sleep once or twice a night for the first 3–6 months of their newborn baby's life. After all, young babies need frequent feeds.

What is the normal pattern sleep in babies?

By 6 months, about 70 per cent of babies sleep for a 6–8 hour stretch. However, at 6 months of age, about 25 per cent of babies will continue to wake up regularly at night throughout infancy for one reason or another.

Sweet slumber

What are the causes of sleep problems?

Sleep problems occur in up to 10 per cent of children. In many cases, the problem arises during bedtime and may be a result of parental anxiety. Older children may be fearful of lightning and thunder or of getting nightmares. Other reasons include fear of parental separation when there is marital discord or fear arising from a recent death in the family.

How do I deal with sleep problems?

In tackling the problem of sleep disorders in a baby, the use of a security pillow, a favourite toy, a night light or reassurance by leaving your child's bedroom door open could help. It is not advisable to allow your fearful baby to sleep with you as it may prove difficult to stop such a habit. If necessary, your baby could temporarily be allowed to sleep with another sibling.

Sympathetic support, reassurance and encouragement are essential for alleviating sleep problems. Punishment or angry threats should never be used. Bedtime should be set at a regular time and the period before it should be a relaxed and restful time with no frightening television programme to watch. Other measures which might help would include a hot drink or a short bedtime story. In really difficult cases, your doctor would prescribe a mild sedative.

Teething

Teething is a normal process of eruption of a baby's primary teeth starting around 6 months of age and completing at 18 months of age. However, this process is variable and can occur any time between 3 months and 3 years of age.

What are the common problems associated with teething?

The symptoms of teething include drooling of saliva, an increased need to bite on something or to thumb suck, and an increased irritability together with reduced milk intake.

During such periods, encourage the use of teething rings for your baby to bite. If necessary, cold foods such as yoghurt, ice-cream or jelly may be tried. Teething rusks or biscuits would also be appropriate once the teeth start to erupt.

The common belief that teething is associated with low-grade fever or occasional loose stools is hard to disprove. However, it can be stated categorically that teething does not give rise to high fever, febrile convulsions, or frank gastroenteritis.

Toddlers and preschoolers

Raising a child who is in the process of developing an independent mind and character can often be trying for the parent. The 'terrible twos' is a notorious period of testing for the parents as the child learns to assert himself. Later on, the issues of separation and other anxieties assail the preschooler. The parent's response to the child's behaviour can influence the child's personality and outlook in future. Knowing what constitutes normal and abnormal behaviour in a child is essential for parents to make the right decisions for the child's welfare, and prevents over-reacting to a child who is 'playing up' and avoids ignoring a child who is really unwell. Crying and sleep problems will be discussed in the following section to help parents recognize symptoms and signs that may need medical attention.

Crying

A crying child can be as distressing as that of a newborn baby to his parents, and is often a source of embarrassment as well. Crying may merely be a cry of distress or discomfort, but may also be a forerunner of a mammoth tussle of wills between parent and child.

Why does my child throw tantrums?

Children from 18 months to 3 years of age may be particularly prone to throwing tantrums as the expressive language is not fully developed yet, and crying is often a cry for help or a sign of frustration. Tantrums on their own are seldom a symptom of a serious underlying problem and can usually be channelled into more rational forms of communication. The older child and toddler may respond to constructtive distractions or re-directing techniques. Most children learn to handle stress without resorting to temper tantrums, so you need to stay calm during an episode, and talk to your child about better ways of expressing anger or discomfort. Often, you may need to consciously avoid confrontation with your child and spanking or hitting him during the episode. He may be just as frightened by his emotions, and needs to be shown that there are more peaceful ways of dealing with the area of frustration. Most of all, your child needs encouragement from a parent who listens.

Taming the tantrums: The ten commandments

- Do listen to your child, but tell him that the behaviour is unacceptable.
- Do take your child away from a public place.
- Do stay around your child to make sure that he is safe.
- Do show your child how to verbalize his frustration.
- Do stay calm and reassure your child that he is still loved.

- Don't give in to your child's demands.
- Don't hit or hurt your child.
- Don't force your child to snap out of the tantrum immediately.
- Don't allow your child to hurt himself or the people around.
- Don't deny or ignore the frustration and the emotions that your child may be feeling.

Tantrums should disappear with time, but persistent temper tantrums beyond the age of 6 should not be taken lightly, and a doctor should be consulted to exclude any serious behaviour problem.

What are breath-holding attacks?

Breath-holding attacks are some of the most frightening experiences that you can be put through. The typical scenario is that of a child playing happily, then because of an upsetting incident, such as a push by a sibling or a fall, the child starts crying and stops breathing until he turns blue. While distressing to observe, these episodes are actually benign and self-limiting, and the child is unlikely to suffer unless he is hurt in a fall.

Breath-holding attacks occur in children from 1–5 years of age, and may often be manifested when the child is frustrated or angry. They may occur in up to 5 per cent of children, and is not a reflection of any serious underlying disorder or any disciplinary problem.

There are two types of breath-holding spells — the **cyanotic** type and the **pallid** type. The cyanotic type is more common. The child will often give a cry, exhale, and stop breathing. There may be limpness and loss of consciousness, with the child turning blue (cyanotic). When the brain senses the lack of oxygen, breathing will restart spontaneously again, and the child will emerge from the attack. Each spell usually lasts for less than 1 minute. There may be difficulty in distinguishing seizures from breath-holding attacks as the child may actually have some jerking and stiff posturing of the body especially if the spells last longer. These are not seizures, but are what is known as 'brain stem release' phenomena, which is a reaction of the brain to low oxygen levels. A physician should be consulted if the parents notice these episodes for the first time, so as to help to exclude seizures that may be more dangerous to the child.

Pallid attacks are also dramatic and frightening events provoked by a painful and unexpected stimulus such as a fall or a bump. The child turns pale, rarely cries, and becomes limp and unconscious. After the initial limpness, the child may go on to have stiffening and jerking of the limbs, which are also not a seizure activity but merely 'brain stem release' phenomena. The child will wake up from the spell spontaneously.

These breath-holding spells are all benign, and children do not die during the attacks, although the appearance of the child may be frightening enough for his parents to want to commence CPR (cardio-pulmonary resuscitation). They grow out of these episodes, and there is no likelihood of the child developing epilepsy subsequently.

Your greatest task does not lie in the handling of the breath-holding attack, but in the management of your child between attacks. Often, parents are so frightened of the bizarre manifestations that they avoid confrontation with the child as often as they can, which usually means giving in to the child's every whim and fancy. You still need to enforce rules and discipline. The best approach is simply to behave as though nothing has happened. Occasionally, distracting your child with music or other interesting activities may avert the spells. If your child has frequent breath-holding with crying and temper tantrums, then ignoring him for 5–10 minutes after he has regained consciousness is likely to send the message that such behaviour is unproductive. There is no necessity to massage your child as it does not shorten the episodes in any way.

Mouth-to-mouth resuscitation is also not necessary as the spell will automatically abort once your child becomes cyanosed. Rarely, if the loss of consciousness lasts for a significant period of time, your child may have some jerking similar to a seizure, and you can put him on the side on a level surface to avoid airway obstruction and aspiration of any secretions into the lungs. Praise or cuddling for good behaviour should be practised on a normal basis, and temper tantrums and breath-holding spells should be ignored so that your child learns that breath-holding is unproductive. The episodes should gradually decrease with time.

How do I manage wolf crying during separation situations?

Many children are sent to day care or nursery when they are only a few years old. During this time, there may be a great deal of anxiety that may be expressed by the child crying frequently, especially when going to school. When your child starts going to school, he may also start showing separation anxiety in wanting to sleep with you or your spouse or by starting to complain of various symptoms such as headaches or stomachaches. Separation anxiety may be seen early, dating from the toddler stage, and your child may show distress if you or your spouse is not in sight or has just left the room. For toddlers, you may need to keep reinforcing that you are close by and will come quickly if your child is in distress. Making frequent voice contact is also useful if you or your spouse cannot be in the same room as your child all the time.

You need to recognize that there may be a lot of fear for your school-going child in staying in an unfamiliar environment with unfamiliar people. Your child is also naturally more attached to you or his care giver(s) at this stage. His fear should not be taken lightly and he should not be mocked, teased, or even threatened over separation distress. You need to show your child that the new environment such as the school can be a fun, interesting and safe place and not a hostile or dangerous place. Introducing your child early to his teacher so that he learns to regard his teacher as a close friend will help. Familiarizing your child with the interesting aspects of the school grounds some weeks before going to school is also likely to make him more willing to explore and discover his new environment when the time comes.

You should resist the temptation to bribe your child for controlling the symptoms of the distress. Stopping him from crying is a short-term measure that may save you from distress, but he may also end up developing repressed fear and emotions. As your child becomes more comfortable with the new environment, the crying and the tantrums are likely to decrease as well. Occasionally, although your child is becoming more independent, he may still cling to you on and off to get reassurance. Nonetheless, your child who shows separation anxiety is likely to just be a normal healthy child who feels secure with you and a familiar home environment.

Recognizing that your child is merely 'crying wolf' is not always easy for you. Sometimes, the timing of the symptoms may give a clue, for example, stomachaches whenever he has to go to school or has a test or an unpleasant task later in the day. Some somatic symptoms may also become more intense especially around the examination period. Often, your child may not be able to verbalize his fear and may not even be able to recognize that the behaviour has its roots in fear and anxiety.

Quiet and withdrawn behaviour or hyperactive and disruptive behaviour, may be associated with the onset of the symptoms. Sometimes, knowing that your child is 'crying wolf' may even be discovered retrospectively when his symptoms disappear miraculously after being kept home from school. If he is experiencing real discomfort, the intensity of the symptoms may be a clue that all is not well. If the symptoms are associated with other manifestations, for example, vomiting or diarrhoea with abdominal pain, or fever and change in conscious state with headache, medical consultation is necessary. A medical practitioner will be able to exclude significant medical conditions.

When would I know that the crying is real?

Your child who cries is often easily comforted, but if there is persistent crying or irritability, there may be a possibility of something more significant that may be the root cause of the crying. In the toddler age group and in early childhood, your child may not be able to express the sense of discomfort except by crying. Fortunately, however, if your child is unwell, there are some important markers that may indicate what the problem may be. You should not ignore symptoms such as fever, pain, vomiting, or change in behaviour such as drowsiness and confusion.

When should I cry for help?

You should call your child's physician if he:
- appears to be in pain
- has inconsolable crying for several hours
- has had recent trauma, fall or has been shaken (shaking a baby can result in bleeding in the brain)
- appears drowsy or disorientated
- refuses to feed or is vomiting

You should call for help if you become excessively frustrated by your child's crying and are in danger of hurting him. Relatives or close friends may be able to give you the break that you need.

Sleep problems

Sleep in a child can be a battle ground for some families, or a real source of worry in others. Getting a toddler to sleep can be a mammoth task for some parents. Where to sleep and how to get the child to bed can be a problem that lasts into the late hours of the night.

"Mummy, where are you?"

How do I make my child go to bed alone?

Some of you have a 'family bed' which is shared with your child or even children, but this may not be advisable as he gets much older. A toddler or child can be coaxed into sleeping in a separate room at night, but this process may be expected to take time. Reassurance may be all that your child needs to feel safe at night. Often, he may make frequent visits back to your bed at night, especially if he has had a nightmare or has any worries — perhaps, even of monsters under the bed. A night light or your presence before he falls asleep is likely to help in the transition stages. Patience and continued assurance of your proximity will definitely help.

How do I make my child sleep well?

Putting your child to sleep can sometimes be difficult. Some children may be more interested in playing than sleeping, and others may even throw tantrums at bedtime and refuse to lie down or stay in bed. The key to successful rest at night is a pleasant and predictable bedtime routine. This may take the form of a bedtime hug and kiss or a bedtime story. You and your spouse should be involved in this routine, and exciting activities such as strenuous physical activity or scary television programmes should be avoided just before sleeping. If your child protests or cries each time at the designated bedtime, you should be firm and the protests should be ignored in favour of the bedtime rule.

Your child's comfort at night is also important. In hot and humid Singapore, a fan or the air-conditioning is likely to be a necessity. Over-heating with long sleeved pyjamas or heavy blankets should be avoided. A light covering, depending on the temperature, is likely to be all that is necessary.

At night, you may also notice your child twitching or having jerking movements of the limbs. These movements are innocuous, and are known as 'sleep myoclonus' and often happen in the early phases of sleep. Some grunting noises and heavy breathing sound should not be fussed about either as these may be due to the lax tissues surrounding your child's relatively smaller airways in sleep.

Every child varies in the amount of time spent sleeping at night. Some may be fairly dependent on one or several naps throughout the day. The best gauge of adequacy of sleep is the child's activities during the day. If your child is not lethargic or sleepy during the day, he is probably getting enough sleep at night.

What are the fears of sleeping?

Nightmares are part and parcel of a child's nightlife, but can be exceptionally distressing at times. They are unpleasant or frightening dreams that the child is often able to recall when he wakes up. They occur in REM (rapid eye movement) sleep — a stage of sleep where the subconscious is the most active. If your child wakes up crying from a nightmare, comforting and a cuddle is all he needs. A hug, a night light or a teddy bear will help. Letting your child know that you are in close proximity, or leaving the bedroom door open is likely to give reassurance as well. Talking to your child the next day about the bad dream and helping him to imagine a nice ending to the dream can take away a lot of fear arising from the nightmare. Smaller children may find it difficult to distinguish fantasy and reality, and frightening or exciting events or television programmes should be avoided just before bedtime.

Night terrors can be far more distressing than nightmares, but fortunately, it does not occur often. They often occur in children from 4–7 years of age, occurring in the deeper stages of sleep. Your child may wake up terrified and screaming, thrashing around in bed and not responsive to your comforting. What often frightens parents most is that the child does not appear to be aware of his surroundings, although he seems to be awake. These episodes are actually not harmful or painful to him, although very disturbing to watch. He is not aware at the time of the night terror and has no recollection of it ever happening the following day.

Daytime stresses or even traumatic life events may bring on night terrors. The timing of the night terror may coincide with the relevant event. Decreasing daytime stresses may help to decrease the incidence of such episodes. To avoid night terrors, you can determine roughly when these events occur, and wake your child up about 15 minutes before the expected time, then allowing him to fall asleep again about 5 minutes later. These night terrors should decrease, and the nightly wakening can be discontinued a week after the episodes stop.

Most children do have night terrors, but some may have them more than once in a while. Night terrors will do your child no harm, but they do need to be handled by calm and experienced adults.

Sleep walking tends to occur in the older child of 6–15 years of age. It tends to run in families and occurs more in boys than in girls. When a child sleepwalks, he is in an altered state of consciousness and can only be awakened with great difficulty. He appears to be awake, but is actually asleep and is at danger for hurting himself. If a child is found to be sleepwalking, he should be led first to the bathroom as he may be looking for a place to relieve himself. He should then be led back to the bedroom and put to sleep again. He should be protected from injury as far as possible, especially if he is found to be in a dangerous situation or if he has wandered to an unfamiliar place.

Locking doors and making sure that your child does not sleep on the upper level of a double-decker bed is important. Avoiding lack of sleep and tiredness is also important in decreasing your child's tendency to sleepwalk. Some also advocate early awakening, similar to that described in night terrors, to decrease the frequency of sleepwalking. You should not keep trying to wake your child up during an episode as you may find this extremely difficult to achieve, and he may also be bewildered if woken up forcibly.

7
Normal Child Psychology and Behaviour

YEO Kah Loke Brian

Bonding

The long-awaited moment when a mother is able to hold her newborn baby is the physical beginning of the mother-child attachment. The nuzzling of the newborn baby on the mother's breast for comfort and sustenance is genetically imprinted and sustained in the many hours that the mother and child share in these special moments. The cooing words of the mother, the smell of her breast and milk, the enlargement of the pupils when the mother's eyes meets with the child's, all serve to reinforce the beginnings of this attachment. It is further strengthened when the child feeds at the mother's breast, the sustenance the child derives from the milk gives the mother pleasure and strength in the knowledge that not only did she bring this being into the world, but is also able to feed and provide for his continual well-being.

This special bond is important in the child's future emotional growth and personality development. The image of a constant, caring figure that is found in infancy and early childhood is deeply ingrained into the child's psyche. Developmental psychologists would term this the formation of an internal working model that the child has of himself, of others, and of the world. A secure bond between the child and a consistent and caring attachment figure enables the child to feel confident and secure that he is loved and worthy of being loved. He can then confidently explore his surroundings and develop his intellect. Conversely, a child who has had numerous changes of care givers or have been brought up in an impersonal institution would feel insecure, unsure of his self-worth, thus creating problems for his emotional development. This has been linked to a rise in conduct disorders and delinquency later in life. This focus on a consistent care giver cannot be over-emphasized.

In the past, it was felt that it would only influence later attachment security and intimacy. It is now held that the quality of this attachment bond influences a child's future sociability, language development and level of explorative play besides his ability to form friendships and intimacy. The current emphasis on emotional intelligence focuses on the child's abilities of sociability; of being able to recognize and deal with emotions in others and in himself. A child with a strong secure attachment bond, is one who has high self-esteem, who will then be able to have the confidence to socialize. He is able to cope with disappointments and defeat as he is firm in his belief that he is an innately capable person, worthy of consideration and love.

The issue regarding the attachment bond is that one consistent care giver is needed. It need not necessarily be the mother. It could be the father or a grandparent. While it is noted that children do have attachments to multiple care givers, it is recognized that even amongst this finite number of care givers, there is a consistent hierarchy. When the child needs comforting, invariably one unique attachment figure is always chosen.

The implications of this research are manifold. The first few years of life are crucial in a child's developmental psyche. It is important that a consistent nurturing care giver be there for the child. Ideally, this should be the mother, but if not, the father or a member of the extended family can be a suitable substitute. A domestic maid, however, who is there for the first few years, but would have to leave at the end of a contract, is not a good substitute. Being there at all times for the child requires time and patience. Although pre-planning for this time and maximal interaction during this period is ensured, the concept of 'quality time' is ideal as there is no substitute for 'just being there' time for the child. With the formation of an attachment bond to a care giver, the child would develop proximity-seeking behaviour and a need to interact with this care giver. In the face of danger or in times of insecurity, the child would always go towards the care giver. This behaviour is seen at around 18 months of age and sometimes referred to as 'stranger anxiety'. With time, a secure child is able to cope with this anxiety and interact in a new environment. This usually happens at around 3 years of age when he is ready to leave the confines of his mother and mix more with his peers — the time when play school usually starts.

Stimulation and choice of toys/activities

The amount of stimulation that is optimal for each child depends on his temperament and age. Some children are slow to settle and begin on new tasks whereas others cannot focus too long on certain activities and require more stimulation to stay engaged.

For the young baby, he has been programmed to recognize and engage with human faces and facial features. He will automatically select to engage with a face rather than with an inanimate object. If the face is able to move, make cooing high-pitched noises and laugh, the child would focus and respond even more to it. Making or drawing faces with thick black ink on white paper would be a very suitable stimulation. At this point, the child's colour perception is not fully developed and his ability to focus would be enhanced if there are pictures or objects in highly contrasting colours or background. Commercial products in the form of black and white drawings in books, cot protectors, posters and hanging mobiles are now widely available. Care givers need to ascertain when a child requires settling and when he is ready for stimulation. Talking to a child in short sentences or in varying pitches serve to engage the child better. Eye contact is crucial. It is biologically programmed that the focal length of vision for a baby is the distance between the mother's breast and her face, ensuring him to be able to engage with the mother optimally even when breast-feeding.

At the preschool age, the child begins to explore the external environment. He uses all his five senses, his colour perception and visuo-motor skills are now more developed. Objects that are easy to grasp, noisy when moved, colourful to the eye and non-toxic when mouthed, would be ideal. Hence, to stimulate motor skills, crawling, and eye-hand coordination, colourful building blocks, rolling balls and cylinders can be utilized. At the same time, the preschool child learns and imitates from his environment. Creative toys that simulate the home, school or play environment allow the child and his playmates to enhance the development from solitary play to interactive play. Hence, toy household utensils, work tools, blackboards, policeman's hats, doctor's stethoscopes and barber's shavers would allow children to re-enact their daily experiences.

It is normal for a child to have a comfort object, be it a doll or a blanket, that he turns to for solace. Parents sometimes reinforce this behaviour by encouraging their child to have his favourite object to sleep with to reduce tantrums. Most children will outgrow these tendencies with the warmth and support from their care givers.

To achieve learning stimulation, it is recommended that instead of rote learning from posters depicting the alphabet, parents can enhance their child's participation by utilizing more of the child's senses in education. Newer toys try to cater more to a child's sense of touch and movement. Letters of the alphabet that are formed in colourful sand, allow the child to trace the figure besides just looking at it. Addition and subtraction can be taught with weighing scales and coloured sticks, allowing the child to play besides learning mathematical concepts. Computer programmes and abacus classes now abound, where not just visual but tactile stimulation are brought into play at a young age in a fun atmosphere to enhance learning.

At the primary school level, the child interacts and is influenced much more by his friends. His choice of toys is thus dictated by what his friends desire, what is in 'fashion', advertised by the media or endorsed by their role models. Computer games are more elaborate and many are becoming more noisy, colourful, violent or frightening in order to stand out in this busy market. At this stage, parents are more involved in deciding the types of toys and games that the child wants to have as he is now more active in the selection of the toys in the first place. It is felt that we have to encourage the child to participate more in sports, music or drama to counterbalance the obsession with remote controlled toys, videos, video compact disks (VCDs), computer programmes, and fantasy games.

Parents need to be personally involved with the child. Sending a child for computer class, ballet class or swimming lessons is not enough. When parents actually join their child in these activities, talk to him and encourage his interests, it becomes not just another chore or routine to the child, but rather real quality time to be savoured. Whether the child participates in one or many activities depends on his inherent interests. There is a risk that some parents send their child to such enriching activities because they did not have the chance to do so when they were young and hence their enthusiasm is likened to a vicarious wish fulfilment. Worse of all, this enthusiasm stems from a need of not to lose out to other children or for the associated prestige element. As all of us wish for the best for our children, these activities should be opportunities for us to enhance our bond with them, to share, to enjoy, and to treasure.

Temper tantrums and aggressive behaviour

The 'terrible twos' — a time when a child realizes that he is a separate individual and wants to assert his rights or tests his boundaries by refusing to always obey authority figures, is familiar to all parents. However, with proper supervision and support, most children do grow out of temper tantrums and engage in more fulfilling exchanges with their parents regarding what they can or cannot do. However, in some families, temper tantrums are not resolved. Instead, it gets escalated and the child becomes aggressive. Coercive family processes come into play when the child refuses to obey and the mother, after a period of screaming, shouting or even hitting, gives up. In this process, the child finally gets his own way. He is inadvertently reinforced with the idea that in order to achieve his goals, he needs to continually refuse to obey and to escalate his screaming or shouting. After a period of time, he assumes that others will give up and he will succeed.

In other families, the mother would persistently scream, shout or even hit the child until he finally complies. This sets up a pattern of undesirable family behaviour where screaming and physical punishments are always needed before rules are adhered to. Once these dysfunctional patterns of family behaviour are fully established, it is much harder to change. The main focus would be to set out in place, from the very beginning, a warm and positive relationship with the child where he is loved for his own sake, and yet establish certain firm rules of behaviour which are to be adhered to.

Parents should provide positive attention to the child when he is behaving well and not only pay attention when he is naughty. To establish certain norms of behaviour, parents need to be consistent in their reaction to the child's behaviour. The way to bring up an aggressive delinquent is to be inconsistently aggressive towards the growing child. The child does not know to what extent his misbehaviour would be punished, except that it will be physical. The amount of physical pain inflicted, in these instances, does not depend on the child's misdemeanour, but rather on the parents' mood at the time of punishment. These unfortunate children learn that they have no control over their punishment level and that aggression is not only tolerated, but that it should be modelled upon. Care givers, hence, need to discriminate which misbehaviours are mild and can be ignored and which misbehaviours need to be punished.

Similarly, the extent of reward for good behaviour needs to be set out and the child told of these family rules. Here, it is crucial that parents must discuss among themselves a joint view on the punishment or reward level before instituting it. If not, the child senses this discrepancy and may be used to manipulate one parent against the other. To ensure compliance, parents may need to decrease, initially at least, the number of demands. The aim is to achieve an early successful experience for the child. The child then feels that he can master the tasks assigned and feels good when he is rewarded or praised. This encourages him to continue to comply, as he knows he can not only do it, but that it can be done quickly and rewarded accordingly.

When the child deliberately disobeys, parents need to set clear boundaries of what is unacceptable. If the undesirable behaviour is dangerous, some feel that it is acceptable to shout or even smack the child. For most part, an extreme form of ignoring or 'time out' is deemed more appropriate. In this instance, the child is put in a room, corner, or 'naughty chair' for a certain duration. Despite his crying or shouting, the child stays in this confined area for a fixed duration of time, usually for 5–10 minutes. When the time period ends, the child should go back to the situation that evoked the outburst and behave appropriately. When initiating 'time out', parents should not lose their temper or give up when the child cries. The aim of this management is that the child is placed in a quiet, unstimulating environment when he is naughty, with his parent(s) ignoring him totally. There is no inadvertent reinforcement for his shouting or crying. After a suitable period, he must return to the original scene and relearn appropriate behaviour so that the 'time-out' period is not an escape from a chore or situation.

This firm method of establishing desired behaviour is only successful if the overall relationship between the parents and the child is a warm and positive one. The child is told that he is being punished for his misbehaviour and not because he is inherently bad. Consistent firm discipline in a background of a caring relationship develops in a child, a sense of security as well as an appreciation of the boundaries of his behaviour. A child who does not know boundaries in his life, lacks self-discipline and security even if he is brought up in a warm but extremely permissive environment with no set limits.

Socialization and friendship

As children develop physically and emotionally, they engage more with their peers. They are more interactive as their prosocial behaviours begin to bloom. Even as early as at infancy, vocalization, smiling and touching would be seen when babies are close together. At the toddler stage, cooperative play, turn-taking and imitative behaviour begin to develop. At nursery school, improving language skills allow for more complex interactions and the subsequent development of friendships.

Interactions with friends not only serve as sources of enjoyment, but also allow opportunities to learn social skills such as sharing, turn-taking, dealing with conflicts, and exploring the boundaries of acceptable social behaviour. Having a friend also means that one has desirable qualities as a companion. It enhances one's self-image and sense of personal worth to be selected by someone else to be their friend.

Socialization and friendship form the nidus from which the child builds upon his emotional intelligence. He needs to empathize with his peers, know how to initiate engagements and enter into group play. Mixing with peers allows him to develop the skills to recognize emotions in others as well as how to deal with rejection. A child who is able to socialize well would gain greater acceptance and achieve higher liking amongst his peers. Such socially gifted children would grow up with higher self-esteem and confidence. Low-accepted children, on the other hand, when faced with social rejection, would tend to blame themselves for their poor social incompetence rather than on any external factors.

For parents who want to enhance social competence in their child, the good news is that it can be taught. Children can be trained to empathize with their peers, to show more cooperative behaviour and patience during turn-taking. Social skills for initiating oneself into a group already engaged in play can be taught. Low-accepted children tend to barge into groups, demand a dominant position in a game and become either aggressive or tearful when rejected. More skilful children know how to quietly introduce themselves to an established group, adopt a non-threatening posture, be willing to take on a more passive position initially at play before becoming more directive. Such children are able to take the occasional rebuff in their stride as they have had many successful experiences before.

Children can also be taught to control their emotions. Some children are naturally more domineering or aggressive and must be taught to check themselves before launching onto unsuspecting playmates. Teaching these children a 'stop, think, go' programme where they need to mentally halt to evaluate their actions and future plans before engaging others is a useful way to control their natural enthusiasm or threatening behaviour. Here, these children are trained to visualize an image of a traffic light in their mind where red, amber, green represent the need to first check their natural exuberance, and then to evaluate their options before finally implementing their plan of action and monitoring the consequences.

Starting preschool and primary school

The commencement of schooling, be it in pre-school or primary school would mean a change of environment for the child. From a typical small family structure, the child is now mixing with a large number of his peers in a more formal and structured setting.

The child's temperament and previous experiences of mixing with friends in his neighbourhood would determine the ease in which he makes this transition. Especially in the preschool transition, it is important for parents to see the venue with their child before term starts, in order for him to reduce anticipating anxiety. If possible, it would be ideal to start half-day placement before going on to full-day school. Parents may stay for a while at the initial period of school, but would need to leave once the lessons begin. At the preschool level, it is especially useful if there is an orientation programme for the children to familiarize themselves with the facilities and be introduced to their friends. It would also be good if children are loaned a book or a toy at the end of the first school day to gently remind them that they are expected to return it to school the next day.

The choice of preschool is also important. Some preschool programmes are modelled closer to primary schools where there is more emphasis on a formalized time structure with higher expectations of adherence to a fixed curriculum. Others are based on a more *laissez-faire* philosophy where children are expected to learn only if they feel like learning at the moment. These schools provide an enriching environment prepared for the optimal stimulation of learning. However, there is much less adherence to any timetable or fixed curriculum. Children are encouraged to question more with less obligation to conform to a structured learning programme. Thus, it would be much less traumatic for children to initially enter such a setting. However, towards the kindergarten level, parents should ensure that the preschool environment becomes more formalized and structured. If not, they may have to change kindergartens because children in Singapore would enter primary one in the national curriculum where a much more structured environment exists with larger classroom sizes. Most children do adjust and continue to perform well in our schools. Surveys have shown that our average grades in science and mathematics are superior to those in the West. This reflects not only an increase in cognitive ability of our children, but rather, higher parental and teacher expectations of better academic performance coupled with higher emphasis on homework and tuition.

Nevertheless, it must be accepted, even in our competitive society, that not all children would perform equally well academically. While we must ensure that our children strive for the best, it must recognize that everyone has different levels of abilities and thus, each child's best would need to be set at different levels. Children have different talents; even in the gifted class, children may not be globally superior in all subjects. Compounding this issue is that talent and abilities may also develop at different stages. Some children, being the classical late bloomers, take a longer time to develop their superior abilities.

Having understood the process of bonding and the importance of emotional development, we hope to bring up confident children, secure in the knowledge that they are loved. Academic excellence, while important, is but one facet of a child's abilities. Children are unique and precious, each representing a special potential to be realized, entrusted to us for our care and nurturance. Childhood is fleeting and we, as parents and care givers, should both honour our responsibilities as well as treasure our many joys in raising our children.

8

Toilet Training

YAP Hui Kim

Bladder control

A normal baby has no control over bowel and bladder movements, as these are entirely reflex activities. Over the age of 12 months, he still has little control until the age of 18–24 months, when he begins to show signs of readiness for toilet training. Some children may not be ready till they are at least 2½ years or more. Most babies will attain bowel control first, as a 'full rectum' is easier to control than a 'full bladder'. Daytime control of the bladder is attained first, as a child of 2–3 years old can only control voiding for up to 4–5 hours. Night-time control is the last to develop.

In the development of bladder control, a child first learns to control voiding with voluntary contraction of the pelvic floor muscles. This forms an 'emergency brake' to prevent him from accidentally wetting his pants when an urge is felt. This feeling of urge can only be recognized by children from the age of 2. Some children only develop this cognitive ability when they reach 4–6 years old. Development of central inhibition and facilitation of voiding is slower and is subject to socio-cultural influences. For example, in the farmlands of China, India and rural Africa, young children may not wear underpants and they can then urinate outdoors whenever they have the urge — girls squatting down and boys standing up. Whereas in our urban society, children have to wear clean underpants, and whenever they have to void, they have to close themselves behind a toilet cubicle.

Toilet training

Toilet training is an integral part of growing up. Your child should never be hurried or pressurized to begin toilet training before he is ready to do so.

When do I begin toilet training my child?

You should begin toilet training your child only when he is **ready**. This usually occurs between the age of 15 and 18 months. Signs which indicate that your child is ready include the following:

Awareness of being wet or soiled

This is one of the first promising signs that your toddler is ready to be trained. Your child will indicate this awareness by making some noises, showing facial expressions or gesturing. He appears to feel uncomfortable with soiled diapers and wants to be changed. Changing nappies rather than leaving him wet will enhance his desire to stay dry.

Regulating bowel movements

Most children will have regular and predictable bowel movements every day. This is especially so if you have been placing him regularly on the potty at a fixed time daily such as after breakfast (this is a good time as it utilizes the gastrocolic reflex which occurs after meals to help move the bowels for defaecation to occur).

Awareness of the need to let go

Another useful indicator that your toddler is ready for toilet training is when he articulates some words, points or signals, or assumes a certain posture, whenever he is about to urinate. At this stage, control is poor, and he will probably wet himself if he does not get to the potty immediately. Even when he has the awareness of the need to urinate, your child may be to engrossed in play to pay attention to the urgency and ends up wetting himself.

Increasing periods of dry spells

As your child matures, he is able to stay dry for 2-hour periods at least during the day, and is sometimes dry after a nap.

Good dexterity in using the potty

Your child will be able to pull down his pants, sit on the potty and put on his pants after urination. At this stage, he can follow simple verbal instructions such as 'use the potty before going for an outing'.

Refusal to wear diapers

Your toddler may indicate that he prefers to wear 'adult' underwear. Wearing diapers may be a sign that he is still a 'baby', especially if he has older siblings to emulate.

How do I toilet train my child?

Toilet training can be easily divided into five steps:

Getting used to the potty

Introduce your child to the potty from the age of 15–18 months when he begins to show signs that he is ready. Begin with bowel training by encouraging regular 'potty' times after a meal, especially if he tends to move his bowels at that time into his nappy. Explain to him the purpose of the potty. Praise him for every success. Clean up after he has finished, and encourage hand-washing to follow.

Weaning of the diapers during the day

Once he shows signs of long periods of dryness during the day, leave the diapers off for prolonged periods, and only use them at night initially, or when going on trips such as shopping. Encourage him to wear regular underwear that is easy to pull off and put on for easy use of the potty. Change his underwear quickly whenever 'accidents' occur.

Stopping the need to use the diapers at night

When your child is able to stay dry during naps, you can try to wean off the diapers at night. Encourage him to empty his bladder before going to bed every night. If he has more than three wet nights per week, then it may be better to leave the diapers on and try again later, otherwise his sleep may be disturbed and he will be fretful and tired in the daytime. Leave the potty near the bed and encourage him to be independent.

Learning to use the toilet

When your child is using the potty regularly throughout the day, encourage him to sit on the toilet bowl during the day. Children need to develop confidence sitting on the toilet bowl, and some may be afraid of falling in. In Asian societies, the child has to be taught how to use the squat toilet. Flush the toilet only when the child is out of the toilet, as some are frightened by the sound of the water. Others may enjoy flushing the toilet themselves, especially when they are over the age of 3.

Training boys

Boys need extra training in standing and aiming at the toilet bowl before passing urine. They should be taught to lift the toilet seat before passing urine. A piece of toilet paper could be placed in the bowl for him to aim at.

What should I not do about toilet training?

There are a few things which parents should note:

- Do not start toilet training your child during a time of change where there is a possibility of psychological trauma, such as starting child care or nursery school, change of babysitters or arrival of a new baby.
- Do not force if your child is not ready. Let him set the pace. Do not nag him to use the potty, otherwise, he may feel that it is easier to use diapers. This may delay his development of full independence from using diapers.

■ Do not scold your child if he has 'accidents' during potty-training. Just clean up and do not make a fuss. 'Failures' are inevitable, as children urinate many times a day, especially when they are engrossed in some form of activity. If you make a fuss, he may think that you are angry with the urination or bowel movement, and refuse to oblige when made to sit on the potty the next time.

■ Do not expect your child to wait when he asks for the potty, as children cannot control their urge to urinate.

■ Do not expect your child to be able to urinate when he does not feel the urge to do so. Sitting him on the potty before going for an outing so that he would not wet his pants will not achieve its aim unless he is ready to urinate. Only children around 3 years of age will be able to voluntarily urinate when there is no urgency.

■ Do not try to induce bowel movements at convenient times by using laxatives. This will cause more harm than good, as your child may develop a phobia of going to the toilet.

■ Do not worry if there are setbacks as newly achieved control can be broken by any upset such as illness and psychological stress including going to a child care or nursery and a new baby in the family.

Persistent bedwetting

Many parents are worried when their school-going child continues to wet his bed at night. The skill of being dry at night is inborn and does not depend on training. Most children become dry by the age of 5, a time when societal contact with friends becomes important. Depending on socio-cultural circumstances, persistent bedwetting at night or the medical term, nocturnal enuresis, is usually viewed with concern once the child starts school. Among school starters, approximately one or two children in each class will be bedwetters. The prevalence of bedwetting at age 5–6 is 8–10 per cent. Between the 7 and 10 year olds, the reported prevalence is 7 per cent. Up to this age, it is more common in boys than in girls, with a ratio of 2 : 1. This difference is not seen after the age of 12. Approximately 15 per cent of children with nocturnal enuresis resolve their symptoms each year (Figure 8.1). However, the problem is persistent in 1–2 per cent of adults.

Figure 8.1: *Prevalence of persistent bedwetting in children*

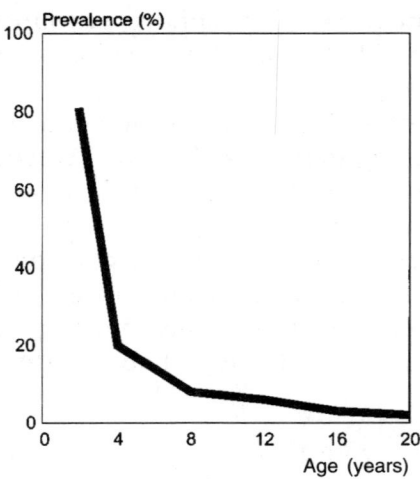

What is the underlying cause of nocturnal enuresis?

Bedwetting was a problem as far back as 1500 BC (Ebers papyrus). Since then, bedwetting has been recognized as a significant social problem. George Orwell, in his essays on his experiences between 1945 and 1950, describes his struggle with bedwetting, *"I knew that bedwetting was a) wicked and b) outside my control ... It was possible therefore to commit a sin without knowing that you committed it, without wanting to commit it, and without being able to avoid it ... ."*

In a survey conducted in Singapore, today's Asian parents also view nocturnal enuresis as a social stigma, and many are too embarrassed to discuss the problem. Up to 37 per cent of parents prefer to seek traditional folk remedies to address the problem. The Chinese perceived nocturnal enuresis as a 'weakness of the bladder', requiring a brew consisting of pig's bladder and hot pepper or soup with ginko nuts. Some Malays and Indians believe that certain 'spirits' can cause nightmares resulting in bedwetting, and preventive measures include special prayers to drive away the 'spirits' and wearing of special bracelets or herbal remedies to 'cleanse the body from all evil'.

Hereditary factors may play a role in nocturnal enuresis. When one parent of a child had a history of bedwetting in childhood, there is a 50 per cent increased likelihood that the child will be enuretic. When both parents had the problem, this likelihood increases to 70 per cent.

In the past, behavioural or emotional disturbances were thought to play a role in this condition. This is not found to be the case. On the contrary, nocturnal enuresis occurs in normal children, and this may induce reactive emotional or behavioural symptoms if they are punished inordinately, or the child is made to feel ashamed because he is still wetting his bed. George Orwell, in his treatise, continued that, "*And the double beating was a turning-point, for it brought home to me for the first time, the harshness of the environment into which I had been flung... . I had a conviction of sin and folly and weakness, such as I do not remember to have felt before.*"

In a survey of parental beliefs in Singapore, 43 per cent felt that bedwetting was due to the child being lazy, difficult or defiant, with 20 per cent resorting to corporal punishment as treatment.

Sleep disturbance has been offered as an attractive hypothesis for explaining bedwetting. Both children and parents often feel that deep sleep was the problem, resulting in the inability to wake the child to void. Even bedwetting alarms have not been successful as the child does not wake up, whereas the rest of the family members are aroused by the incessant ringing! Studies in sleep research have not confirmed the hypothesis that nocturnal enuresis is an 'arousal disorder'. The earliest studies indicated that bedwetting occurred during light sleep. More recent studies have shown that wetting can occur during both deep as well as light sleep.

Bladder muscle instability and other organic causes such as urinary tract infections are not a cause of isolated nocturnal enuresis, in the absence of any other daytime symptoms. However, another circadian phenomenon has been put forward as a possible causative factor for bedwetting. Some children (20–30 per cent) lack the normal increase in endogenous production of antidiuretic hormone (ADH) during sleep. This hormone is important for concentrating the urine and hence decreases the urine volume. This forms the basis of one of the recommended treatment modalities for bedwetting.

Is investigation of bedwetting necessary?

A good history-taking is of primary importance when evaluating children with persistent bedwetting. Children with isolated primary nocturnal enuresis are normal and do not have any kidney or bladder abnormalities. Enuresis is defined as normal voiding at a socially unacceptable time and place. Primary nocturnal enuresis is persistent bedwetting at night without a period of dryness since the child is toilet-trained. Thus, if the child does not have any daytime wetting or other urinary symptoms, and only wets his bed at night, then his condition is entirely benign and he does not need to undergo any special investigations. On the other hand, if the bedwetting occurs after a period of dryness, that is, secondary nocturnal enuresis, then conditions such as urinary tract infection and psychological stresses have to be excluded. Examples of such stresses include starting of primary school, a new baby in the family, and parental discord.

What is the treatment for bedwetting?

Is there a rationale for the treatment of bedwetting? In most instances, bedwetting is a self-limited condition due to maturational delay, with no physical complications. However, persistent bedwetting has psychosocial side-effects on both the child and his family. Many parents in Singapore sought treatment for their children as they wanted a break from the fatigue of constant laundry and cleaning of bed linens, soiled pyjamas, and plastic drawsheets. Disrupted sleep was another complaint, as many parents had to wake up periodically to wake and bring the child to the toilet to urinate.

On the other hand, about 80 per cent of school-going children with persistent bedwetting felt that it was a social stigma. One-third of children felt tired in the mornings, and some even felt that their school performance was affected. In child development, significant social interactions are provided by parents initially, and later, by siblings and peers. There is evidence that bedwetting is stressful and aggravating to many families. Punitive measures are not the answer for bedwetting. This will only lead to poor self-concept, with the possibility of development of behavioural or psychological disorders as the child grows up. In recent years, more parents have been concerned about bedwetting, as many schools now include overnight camps and overseas field trips in their extra-curricular activities. Hence, in the local context, most parents will seek medical help when the child starts primary school. By then, most parents would have tried restricting their children from drinking fluids after dinner, with little success.

Most therapeutic strategies are aimed at teaching the child to recognize the sensation of a full bladder, and to feel that it is important enough to wake up. There are three strategies that are generally recommended by most doctors:

Conditioning with urine detector and alarm

The highest success rates have been reported with the use of the enuresis alarm. This basically consists of a urine detector, worn as a pad in the underpants, and is triggered by a change in resistance to an electric current when urine comes in contact with the detector. This sets off the alarm, which varies from a bell, beeper or buzzer to a vibrator. The child has to monitor his progress with a 'star' chart. Once he has been dry for at least 3 weeks, a useful strategy is to encourage him to drink water before bedtime, and if he can remain dry with this strategy, there is a higher likelihood for cure. The cure rate with the use of an enuresis alarm is in the region of 60–70 per cent, with a relapse rate of 5–10 per cent.

'STAR' CHART

Date										
Nights	Wet	Dry	Dry							
Treatment	Alarm	Tablet								

Desmopressin

There has been evidence that some enuretic children lack the nocturnal rise in ADH, resulting in a relatively high overnight urine production which exceeds their bladder capacity. The drug, desmopressin, is an analogue of ADH and can be given either intranasally or as a single dose orally before going to bed. The oral formulation is useful for those children who have rhinitis, a condition common in Singapore children. An important precaution for these children using desmopressin is to avoid drinking water before bedtime especially after administration of the drug so as to avoid problems of water retention. Most side-effects reported are minor, consisting mainly of headache, loss of appetite, and abdominal cramps. Very rarely, seizures have been reported. On the whole, however, intranasal or oral desmopressin usage in children with persistent bedwetting has been safe as shown in various controlled trials where objective measurements of significant water retention, that is, body weight, blood pressure, serum sodium or serum osmolality, do not show any changes. Use of the intranasal form has also been associated with nose bleeding and local discomfort in some children.

The dose of intranasal desmopressin should be titrated from 10–40 mcg and maintained for 3 months. The success rate using this preparation is about 70 per cent. However, discontinuation of the drug may result in recurrence of the wetting, in about 70 per cent of children. The oral dose ranges from 400–600 mcg, and this has been shown to decrease the number of wet nights by at least 65 per cent, with 20–50 per cent being full responders. In children who relapse after 3 months of treatment, a second course of desmopressin can be attempted. Desmopressin can also be used as a short-term measure for children going to school camps or travelling overseas.

Changing sleep with central stimulants

Central stimulants have been used traditionally in the treatment of children with bedwetting. Imipramine, a tricyclic antidepressant, has been recommended in a dose of 25–75 mg nightly. It acts by altering the sleep pattern to such an extent that the child is able to perceive the urge to void and is able to wake up to urinate. A 'star' chart should be kept by the child, as this will encourage him to succeed. Initial therapy is for 2 weeks, as this will give an indication whether imipramine is useful in a particular child. It can then be continued for 6 weeks, with gradual reduction in dosage subsequently for a total treatment period of 3 months. Abrupt cessation of the drug will result in a high relapse rate. This drug should only be used for children above the age of 7. It is potentially hazardous to young children who take an overdose. Fatal accidents have been reported, and it is important that if any child is on this drug, his parents must be warned to keep the drug out of reach of toddlers and young children. Side-effects to therapeutic doses of the drug are rare and include erratic behaviour at onset of medication. This side-effect disappears once the drug is discontinued.

In children who are on the enuretic alarm and who have a problem waking up at the sound of the alarm, imipramine is a useful adjunct to alter perception during sleep.

Consulting a doctor

Children with urinary tract infection or functional incontinence can have problems with daytime wetting. Hence, when bedwetting at night is not isolated, but is associated with wetting during the day, then a doctor should be consulted. Other important symptoms to note include the following:

- Pain during urination
- Frequent urination at least more than seven times a day
- Urge symptoms
- Straining on urination
- Poor urine stream
- Recurrent bedwetting after at least a 6-month period of dryness
- Abnormal posture such as squatting on heels

Conclusion

Parents look forward to their children gaining each developmental milestone. Their eagerness in many cases is as much for their own sake as it is for their children's well-being. However, there is no fixed time in a child's growing years that the diapers can be packed away. Bowel and bladder control cannot be hurried, and each child has his own timetable for development. Too much pressure before the child is ready can effectively delay rather than hasten the achievement of this important event. Parents must understand that toilet training is a phase that may seem terribly important at the time, but it will eventually pass, and should not be magnified into unrealistic proportions that may leave some emotional scars on the child.

Belinda MURUGASU

Introduction

In the days before parenthood, any reason can be a reason for a trip. One can pack up on the spur of the moment and go, but such a rushed task ends abruptly with the arrival of a child. Although vacations with young children are rarely restful, they can be both feasible and enjoyable for the whole family.

Planning

Time spent in planning a trip, and taking sensible preparatory steps is very important as this will result in a more enjoyable holiday all round.

Realistic schedule

Forget whirlwind itineraries and instead set a modest pace with plenty of unscheduled time — an extra morning/afternoon or even an extra day. With children, you will need it.

Valid passports

Update all passports. It is important to enquire from your travel agent about visa requirements. Some countries require passports to be valid for at least the next 6 months.

Careful choice of destination

If you have young children, it may be best to avoid places where the hygiene of water is questionable. If you really have to go to such a place, equip yourself with a heating coil and utensils for boiling, and confirm the voltage of power supply. Chlorine tablets are another option.

Timing of the trip

For a young child, especially a baby, the hour of travel will depend on his schedule and how long it takes to get there. It is nice to travel at off-peak times as there is a better chance that there will be empty seats to use and less disturbance to the fewer fellow passengers. If your child tends to fall asleep while travelling in a car, travel at night or during nap times. But beware of the potential problem of 'sleep all day and ready to play all night'. In those who are usually too excited to sleep, the opposite may be better, that is, travel after a nap to avoid crankiness. Remember too that trying to arrive as quick as possible via a non-stop route is not always the best as children need a break from the monotonous travelling.

Food order made ahead

Airline food, including different types of baby food, can often be pre-ordered. At the same time, ask if bottles and diapers are available. Nevertheless, it is always a wise move to bring your own snacks. Ready-to-feed milk is convenient but bulky and heavy to carry.

Practical seating arrangements

Arrange for suitable seating such as aisle seats so your child can walk about without disturbing others. The seats at the front row often have more leg space where a little one can play. Request to have an empty seat next to yours if the plane/train is not full. Make sure that the whole family is seated near each other.

Seat confirmation

It is important to confirm reservations in advance and departure times just before you leave home. It can be exhausting trying to entertain a child for hours because a flight is delayed. Always bring an extra storybook or other toys to entertain your baby as some waiting is ineviable.

Movement gadgets

Free your hands if you have a baby by using a carrier. Lightweight, compact umbrella strollers are easy to manage and you can hang totes from its handles. Although many do not like the idea, a wrist-to-wrist leash keeps your child from wandering too far. Portable car seats are useful for rent-a-car holidays and may be accepted in some planes.

Hotel reservation made ahead

Do not assume that all will go well but reserve rooms in hotels even during off-peak seasons. Choose a helpful hostelry if you want the option of a cot and babysitting services. From a phone call, you can usually tell if that hotel/motel is child-friendly. You can also find out about the hotel/motel by asking your friends who had visited the place previously.

Medical precautions

Check-up

A well-child check-up before an extended trip is a good idea to assure good health and an opportunity to ask your family doctor any questions. A child with congestion of the nose, sinuses and blocked tubes in the ears can experience bad ear pain when a plane takes off and lands. Those with long-term disorders such as bronchial asthma or congenital heart disease should be adequatley treated. Ask your doctor for adequate medical supply. It is wise to let your doctor know that you are travelling with your baby. Your doctor may be able to offer valuable advice.

Immunizations

Routine immunizations should be up-to-date and specific immunizations for typhoid, cholera, yellow fever and hepatitis A may be necessary (Table 9.1). Further information is available from the travel agent or from the Centre of Communicable Diseases. Your family doctor can help you decide about your baby, that is, the side-effects of the vaccine and whether a brief vacation should wait till your baby is older. Certain vaccines have to be given some time earlier before immunity is achieved. It is also good to allow a few days for vaccine-related problems such as fever to settle before travelling.

Prophylactic medication

This may be needed, for example, in malaria endemic places (Africa, South America and parts of Asia) when prophylaxis should be started 1 week before arriving at

the destination. Certain antimalarials cannot be taken
by people with G6PD (an enzyme glucose-6-phaphate
dehydrogenase) deficiency.

Table 9.1 Vaccinations required by various countries

Vaccine	Administration	Country
Cholera	Injection/Oral	Africa, South America, Asia, e.g. India, Vietnam, Thailand, Indonesia Areas with outbreak
Hepatitis A	Injection	Rural areas in developing countries
Japanese B encephalistis	Injection	China, India, Japan, Korea, Laos, Myanmar, Nepal, Philippines, Sri Lanka, Thailand, Vietnam
Yellow fever*	Injection	South America, Africa
Meningococcus A+C	Injection	Middle East
Influenza	Injection	Areas of outbreak
Typhoid	Injection/Oral	Africa, Asia, e.g. India, Latin America

Vaccinations can be divided into three main categories:

1. Routine — diphtheria, tetanus, poliomyelitis, mumps, measles, rubella, hepatitis B. Most children in Singapore have been vaccinated with these.

2. Recommended for high risk travellers — Japanese B encephalitis, meningococcus, typhoid.

3.* Required for entry — Yellow Fever.

The World Health Organization (WHO) publishes an annual guidebook entitled International Travel and Health. The Centres for Disease Control and Prevention (CDC), Atlanta, United States, publishes a bi-annual Health Information for International Travel. The Internet and electronic media offers a wide range of information, e.g. the Tan Tock Seng Hospital's "Traveller's Health and Vaccination Clinic" at http://www.ttsh.gov.sg/, the WHO's at http://www.who.ch/ and the CDC's at http://www.cdc.gov/.

Regular medication

If your child is taking any regular medication for a known illness, make sure that there is more than enough supply for the entire duration of the trip. In less developed countries, medication may not be readily available. Some drugs which are available over-the-counter in some countries, may be prescription drugs in others. In case of spillage or loss, separate the medication, especially liquid preparations, into a few lots and also, get an extra prescription. Ideally, all medications should be stable if left unrefrigerated.

Useful medication

Bring these along — acetaminophen (Panadol, Tempra, Calpol) for fever and decongestants for a cold, diarrhoea medication. If you have never used them before, find out the safe dosage for your child, when it should be given, and the possible side-effects.

Additional health insurance

This may be advisable if there are any ongoing or chronic health problems. Discuss your holiday plans with your own doctor and determine what health care resources are available *en route* and at your destination.

Name of a doctor

The name of a doctor or paediatrician at the destination is useful in extended trips or if your child has a chronic illness.

Avoidance of unnecessary changes before a trip

If your baby is breast-fed, do not wean him off at this

time. Breast-feeding is also convenient, and hygiene is less of a problem. If solids have not been introduced yet, hold on. Nevertheless, finger foods are useful when travelling, so if your child is ready, introduce it a few weeks in advance. Expect some regression during the trip, for example, night-waking. It is also not the time to train your baby to 'sleep through the night' and definitely do not try the 'cry it out' technique in a new place and where you will disturb the peace of others.

Packing

Decide what you absolutely need, then pack some extras in case of emergencies. Be prepared that the final load may be heavy. Always have a checklist of essential items for each child. It is best to avoid last-minute packing as you are likely to forget one or two important items.

Small and disposable items

Use sample-size liquid baby soap, toothpaste, and acetaminophen. Depend on disposable diapers which are ultra-absorbent and ultra-thin.

Baby's diaper bag

It should be lightweight, plastic-lined, with outside compartments for storing tissues, wipes, bottles, and other need-in-a-hurry items and should have a shoulder strap. Some baby's clothings must be kept handy for a quick change. Make sure that all the items are easily retrievable.

Clothing and useful items

Items that may be used during the journey must be easily accessible. A light jacket is a must for children — the ideal would be water-proof nylon with a hood to double up as a raincoat. If travelling to a temperate/cold country, pack enough warm clothing and ensure that a change of warm clothes/coat is within easy reach upon arrival. Other useful items include diaper rash ointment, water-proof or disposable bibs, a pair of socks, re-sealable plastic bags to hold leaky bottles, dirty clothing and soiled diapers, a light blanket to nap or play *en route*, and a water-proof changing pad. For the holiday, pack lightweight fabrics that dry fast and coloured bright clothes that can hide stains. Bring enough diapers for the first leg of the journey and in case of delay or diarrhoea. Plan to buy unless you are travelling in a car with room. A plastic sheet to protect rugs and furniture is useful to carry.

Toys: Something old and something new

Bring something old treasured by the child for comfort and something new for entertainment, for example, an activity board, a bright book or a musical stuffed toy. If your child is used to having a night light bring one along.

Food and drink

Bring along a generous amount of snacks and beverages such as crackers, small containers of cereal, ready-to-use formula in disposable bottles, juice in bottle/cup with lid, and baby food (dehydrated form or in small ounce jars to provide variety and avoid waste). Plastic spoons and paper towels are essential. Do remember to bring your baby's most favourable cup, spoon, bowl or plate. This will help a lot when feeding him. Obviously, you should not forget to bring his most favourite food and drink.

Medical and toiletry bag

The bag should be locked. Medicines may include vitamins, acetaminophen for fever, a decongestant, an antiemetic, an anti-diarrhoeal, and oral rehydration salts. Medical insurance information can be kept in this bag. Other useful items are sunscreen, insect repellent, calamine and bug-bite lotion, a first aid kit with plasters, antiseptic, creams, a thermometer, a nail clipper, and a pocket knife. Remember your child's toothbrush and toothpaste.

Car/Train/Plane

A car allows more freedom and flexibility while a train may be slower than a plane but allows more mobility for a child. It is worth paying for an extra seat for your baby as it gives you more flexibility.

Driving

Going by car allows you to travel at your own pace and short stops are welcomed by children. Frequent breaks like every 2 hours allow them to crawl and walk around and get some fresh air. Parents can also alternate roles of being the driver and entertainer. A small baby travels well if kept dry, fed regularly, allowed to sleep, and given warmth and attention. If you are a nursing mother, have adequate food available. Ice packs in well-insulated containers are extremely useful.

Checking in

Try to arrive early for checking-in of luggage, and choice of seats if not pre-booked. Request for seats in the non-smoking section as far away from the smoking area. Pre-boarding allows the family to settle in and stow luggage in overhead compartments. However, it may be preferable to board last if your child is fidgety and prefers open spaces; one adult can pre-board while the other supervises the last run-around. Take the opportunity to exercise before a long ride or flight.

Up and away

It is good to coordinate feedings with take-off and landing times as children are sensitive to cabin pressure changes during ascent and descent and might complain of ear ache or pain. Frequent swallowing with nursing, bottle-feeding, finger foods, or using a pacifier can help prevent pain. An older child may appreciate a sweet to suck on. Travel in a plane can be dehydrating, so offer a lot of fluids to drink. If you need to warm food, always stir and check the temperature as microwave gives uneven warming. Remember that flight attendants can help especially if you are travelling alone with your child. Be the last to leave the plane to avoid the squeeze.

Comfort

Travel clothes should be comfortable and compatible with the ambient temperature. Provide each child with a sheet or blanket and pillow to sleep with when he feels like it. In a car, it helps to define shares of the back seat with these rolls of blankets/pillows between children. Ensure that there are paper towels and plastic bags for motion sickness. Sedating children for long trips is usually unnecessary and actually counter-productive as taking of drugs may result in hyperactivity.

Safety

Safety must come first whether in a car, train or plane. Each child should have his own safety seat. Safety lock devices for doors and driver-controlled doors and window locks are important safeguards when young children are in the car. Use the appropriate seat belts, car seats/booster seats, and head rests.

Long distance travelling

Be prepared with games and toys when you go on a long journey as bored children often end up squabbling and fighting. Playthings attached to car seats are fun and a play table of his own with his own cuddly toy can keep a child happy for a considerable length of time. A surprise bag can contain small cheap treasures (a balloon, a notebook and crayons, a small car, a doll, a toy animal, some plasticine, a bubble-blowing kit which can work wonders through a partly-opened window, a new comic or puzzle, a colouring book, a kaleidoscope/ telescope, and some favourite snacks).

Other articles that keep children happy include pocket puzzles, pinball games, and computer games. Side windows can be well used when a felt-tip pen and damp sponge for side windows, re-usable stickers are provided and even a toy gun to shoot motorists. You can also occupy time with spelling games, story telling, and rhyme chanting. A tape recorder can perform wonders;

a tape can be prepared in advance and can contain stories, songs, jokes, riddles read by different members of the family.

It is always a difficult job to keep children occupied. Sometimes, it may be necessary to have another adult to help you entertain your baby.

Travel/Motion sickness

Travel/Motion sickness is thought to be associated with upset to the delicate balance mechanism of the inner ear. This mechanism is more sensitive in children than older people. If your child has motion sickness, it usually becomes obvious between 6 months and 2 years of age and is likely to last till puberty. It can cause misery to the whole family but fortunately, it tends to improve with age. The exact form of motion that causes this problem varies, for example, rough choppy motion may be more tolerable than smoother rolling motion. Heavy traffic and stop-start driving are particularly nausea-provoking. Night-driving and highway motoring are better tolerated as traffic is less heavy and smoother. The child's own motion also aggravates the condition, so keep the seat belt firmly fastened, and active play and back seat scuffles.

Reading in the car makes things worse and it is better to listen to a *Walkman* or tapes in car. Large greasy meals and hunger makes one feel worse, so it helps to take a light non-greasy meal beforehand and to have a ready supply of candy, plain crackers, and iced water. Drugs are effective but have unpleasant side-effects including dry mouth and overwhelming sleepiness. Try it out before the trip and if you do decide to use drugs, give it at the recommended time in advance of the journey for it to work. On the whole, most children sleep on long trips with or without drugs.

Jet lag

Like adults, some children suffer from jet lag and others do not. Young babies usually have their own schedules and are not amenable to change. It is possible to help preschoolers adjust their biological clock. Sleeping during a long flight should be encouraged if the time corresponds to night at destination. Most children will adjust according to bright light or sunshine. Upon arrival, keep the children active in the day and avoid long naps until it is bedtime. As far as possible, try to follow the day and night hour of your destination. You may need an extra day for catching up with the effect of jet lag.

Upon arrival

There is often a sense of relief and achievement upon reaching the destination. Nevertheless, there are some preparations and precautions that should be observed as the children settle in to some sort of routine.

Rooms

Always do a safety check on rooms at hotels, motels, or other homes. Pay attention to the crib/cot provided, the windows, electrical sockets and cords, and any glass items. Allow babies and toddlers to explore the room under supervision. Enquire if there is a babysitting service in case you need one.

Restaurants

If your family is used to eating out, you have probably learnt all the restaurant survival skills. Lingering over dessert and coffee is a pleasure of the past. A parent has to dine on his baby's schedule, eat early and quickly, and preferably go to a place where no waiting is needed. It helps to call ahead for a high chair or bring a portable one. Request for a table at the back or in a corner to avoid getting in the way of waiters and other diners. Bring a bib and a piece of clear plastic to line the carpet under high chair in case your child makes a mess. Toys and books are good for diversion, but should be used only when needed. Fingerfood snacks can tide an empty stomach but again, they should be used only when needed. Never let a young child walk or crawl around for it can be dangerous. Order promptly and one adult can keep your baby busy out of doors or in the lobby till the food arrives. Even if it is not on the menu, ask for food that you know your child can take, that is, bread, cheese, chicken, potatoes, well-cooked carrots and peas, pasta or noodles which are often available.

In places where hygiene is questionable, use bottled water/juice and avoid ice and dirty glasses, raw vegetables, and unpasteurized dairy products. Remember 'cook it, peel it or leave it'. Be sensitive to diners and recognize when it is time for a stroll. You may have to take turns eating or walking with your companion.

There and then

Babies of 6–8 months old are aware of their surroundings and need time to settle in unfamiliar surroundings. Bring along a few favourite toys and avoid too many change in locations. Toddlers love to discover, so explore the world anew with them. Give allowance for extra soiling, wetting, and spillage. They will prefer small simple meals and you can always count on the familiar cereal and powdered milk. Preschoolers will look at travel as a wonderful family adventure and tend to adjust more quickly to surroundings. In order to have fun, stick to a realistic itinerary and do not over-schedule. Be flexible as you may have to add overnight stops or postpone a site visit. Stick to sites where your child is not confined to or where they are not required to keep silent for long periods — the outdoors, parks, ruins, zoos are good places. If you really want to go to the opera, concert or theatre, use a babysitter.

Temperature and altitude

In hot weather and when there is no refrigeration, feed formula immediately after making it. When travelling, do not store milk in a thermosflask. Ultra-heat treated (UHT) formulae are ideal and can be stored in a cool place safely. All foods must be handled with extra care during hot weather. Humid hot weather is particularly hard on babies; they perspire and need more water but cannot ask for it. Offer it frequently. Dress according to the weather and feel his body to make sure he is comfortable. Extra baths may be needed. Think of how you dress yourself; if you do not need a sweater or blanket, neither does he.

If mosquitoes are a problem, put a net over his stroller or sit out in a screened porch. Flies carry germs, so look out for them near food. Some children have a pronounced reaction to mosquitoes or other insect bites. Calamine or a soothing lotion may help. Sun rays have a damaging effect especially in those under 1 year of age. Use light weight clothings that cover arms and legs, and a sun hat. Choose areas of shade for play and sleep. Avoid direct rays in the middle of the day when rays are strongest and plan indoor activities instead. Always apply sunscreen with a protective factor between 15 and 30 when in sun. If the safety of drinking water is questionable, always boil before use. Wash raw fruit and vegetables carefully and peel before eating. Offer only peeled bananas or apples and cooked vegetables or fruit to toddlers. If your holiday includes going up to a high altitude, remember that sun rays are more intense, so exposure to the sun should be limited and sunscreen liberally applied. Fluid requirements are also increased.

Conclusion

A child who has the opportunity to visit different countries will be enriched by the experience and learns to meet changes in climate, food and culture. More and more restaurants, hotels and travel agents are catering to the needs of young families. Nevertheless, if anyone is to have a good time, remember the needs of those who have to come first. Of course, if your baby adjusts easily, 'do as the Romans do' while you are there. Travelling with young children will always be a challenge. So, keep your sense of humour and have fun.

10
Special Circumstances:
The Premature and Small Baby

I MALATHI & LIM Sok Bee

Introduction

A premature baby is born before 37 weeks (or 9 months) of pregnancy. Most parents imagine a premature baby to be small and vulnerable, with some comparisons being made — 'like a little rat' or 'smaller than the palm of an adult'. Not all small babies are premature. Some babies do not grow well in the uterus due to various reasons and may be born with very low birth weight. There is one such baby classified as Very Low Birth Weight (weighing less than 1.5kg) in every 100 births.

Certain illnesses in the mother can result in a premature birth — conditions such as severely raised blood pressure in the mother, certain infections, or a lowly placed placenta with severe bleeding. In some mothers, the cervix or the opening of the womb, opens up too early, resulting in a premature birth. Multiple pregnancies (twins, triplets, etc.) are also at a higher risk of being born prematurely. In some cases, labour pain begins for no apparent reason — the baby probably 'decides' that he wants to be born early.

Diabetic mothers are more likely to have premature labour. The babies may be born with good birth weight, but they are physiologically immature and should be treated like any other premature baby.

Anticipating a premature delivery

Although not all premature deliveries can be anticipated, certain precautions can be taken when one is expected.

How will I know if my baby is coming early?

The presence of a blood stained discharge, associated with frequent cramping pains, usually signals the onset of labour. If these symptoms (or when there is severe bleeding or early leaking of the 'water bag') are present, you should get admitted to hospital immediately. The chances of survival for a premature baby will be better if he is delivered in a hospital where the full medical facilities for resuscitating and managing premature babies are available.

What happens after my admission to hospital?

If you are in premature labour, you might be given medication to inhibit or reduce the contractions of the womb. You will be advised to rest completely. You may also be given some medication to improve the maturity of your baby's lungs. In some cases, such as in massive bleeding in the mother or if she has severe hypertension, the delivery cannot be delayed for long. Every extra day spent in the womb is a 'bonus' for the baby as the chances of surviving increase with each day.

Looking after a premature baby

A team of doctors, known as neonatologists will be on 'stand-by' to manage the preterm baby upon delivery. The baby will be revived, given oxygen, and when stable, sent to the Neonatal Intensive Care Unit (NICU).

The Neonatal Intensive Care Unit (NICU)

The Neonatal Intensive Care Unit (NICU) is a special unit where a premature baby may have to spend the first few months of life. Specially trained doctors (neonatologists) and nurses look after the baby round the clock. Most parents are initially apprehensive and upset by the equipment and the technology used to keep their baby alive in the NICU.

The following shows a list of common equipment in the NICU and their uses:

The incubator

A premature baby is nursed in an incubator which may be of two types — the 'open-care incubator' or the 'closed' incubator. The incubators basically serve to provide warmth for the baby. The 'closed' type incubators also provide humidity for him and prevent loss of water.

The ventilator

The ventilator is a machine that 'breathes' for a premature baby. It delivers mechanical breaths at a certain rate and at pressures suited for him via an endotracheal tube (ETT — a tube placed into the baby's windpipe).

The monitors

A premature baby needs constant, second-to-second, minute-to-minute monitoring of his 'vital' signs — the heart rate, blood pressure, temperature rate of breathing, and the amount of oxygen present in his blood. This is made possible by the various monitors, connected to him by means of probes and placed on his skin. If there is any disturbance in his breathing or if his heart rate suddenly drops, these monitors will pick up the signal immediately and an alarm sounds. This is why the NICU can sometimes be a very 'noisy' place.

The infusion pump

A premature baby often has several intravenous lines necessary for the infusion of the vital glucose and electrolytes for his needs. In the first few days, the infusion lines may be set in the umbilical cord. The infusion pump ensures that the infusion fluids run at a set rate.

The phototherapy unit

As jaundice is a common problem in a premature baby, the phototherapy unit is a common sight in the NICU. The phototherapy unit consists of a bank of fluorescent to blue lamps arranged to deliver light waves of a certain frequency so as to reduce the jaundice level.

The cranial ultrasound machine

A premature baby receives frequent scans of his head in order to detect bleeding in his brain. The portable scanning machines enable the neonatologists to perform these scans with the baby in the cot.

Common problems in a premature baby

As a premature baby is born too early, he is at a high risk of facing many problems related to the lack of maturity of the major organs. These include the following:

Lung immaturity: Breathing problems

Normal lungs require a chemical substance called **surfactant** to keep the small air sacs (alveoli) open, thus allowing the normal exchange of gases. Immature lungs are unable to produce this substance in the first few days of life. This results in severe difficulty in breathing and impaired gas exchange. A premature baby requires special breathing machines (the ventilators) and additional oxygen. Artificially produced surfactant may be instilled into the lungs of some babies as a replacement. As the premature baby grows, his lungs mature and he is able to breathe on his own after a few days.

Skin immaturity

The skin of a premature baby is thin, without much fat underneath. This causes him to lose heat readily. The thin skin also allows the loss of fluids and entry of germs into his body easily, causing higher risk of infections. He is usually nursed in an incubator to overcome these problems.

Risk of infections

The immune system of a premature baby is not well developed and he is unable to fight infections easily. This, in addition to the thin, immature skin and the presence of various tubes and lines in him, leads to a higher risk of infections in him. Precautions such as careful attention to hand washing, close monitoring of the baby and the use of antibiotics when needed, help to reduce this risk.

Low blood pressure

A premature baby is sometimes unable to maintain a normal blood pressure due to inadequate pumping function of the heart. Medications may be given to bring up the blood pressure, as otherwise, there may be inadequate circulation to the important body organs such as the brain, heart, and kidneys.

Cardiac problems

A common condition called Patent Ductus Arteriosus (PDA or duct) occurs. This is a blood vessel present in all babies connecting the venous (carrying blood to the lungs) and the arterial (carrying blood to the body) vessels leaving the heart. This vessel normally closes by the 2nd day of life, but in some babies, it remains open. This condition can sometimes result in cardiac failure or bleeding from the lungs. Most premature babies with this condition are treated with low fluid intake and a medication known as **indomethacine**. In some cases, surgery may be necessary to close this duct.

Low blood sugar/salts

This problem occurs because of inadequate stores of sugar in a premature baby. Low blood sugar can possibly cause brain damage. He is, therefore, monitored carefully by frequent measurements of the blood sugar levels. Similarly, disturbances in the salt balance (sodium, potassium and chloride) may occur, and their levels are frequently monitored.

Feeding problems

Due to immaturity of the digestive system, a premature baby is not able to take feeds by mouth initially. He receives the necessary nutrition and fluid by means of intravenous drips. Oral feeds are commenced slowly as there is a risk of developing Necrotizing Enterocolitis (NEC) which is inflammatory/infective process of the intestines. The mother is encouraged to express the breast milk (EBM) as the baby is able to digest it better, and it is also protective against infections.

Immaturity of the brain

Because of multiple factors including structural immaturity of the brain, low blood pressure and the PDA, a premature baby is more prone to develop a haemorrhage in the brain, known as intra-ventricular haemorrhage. Ultrasonographic scanning of the brain is performed at frequent intervals to detect such haemorrhage. Some babies may develop cysts in the brain, following a period of lack of oxygen to the brain. Such haemorrhage or cysts have long-term implications as these babies are more likely to develop developmental behavioural problems in later life.

Apnoea of prematurity

The centres in the brain responsible for controlling breathing are not fully developed in a premature baby. He is, therefore, more prone to irregular breathing or may even stop breathing. This condition, known as apnoea of prematurity is treated with medication (such as caffeine) to stimulate the breathing centre. He also requires monitors which sound an alarm once he 'stops breathing'. As he becomes older, the respiratory centre matures and he 'outgrows' this problem.

Jaundice

A premature baby develops some degree of jaundice in the first few weeks of life. Most respond well to photo-therapy treatment.

Retinopathy of prematurity (ROP)

This condition which affects the eyes of a premature baby is caused by multiple factors, including the immaturity of his eyes, treatment with oxygen and infections, among others. All preterm babies less than 34 weeks are routinely examined by the eye doctors for this condition. If left untreated, this condition can sometimes affect the vision of the child.

Anaemia

A premature baby grows rapidly in the first few months of life, once his condition stabilizes. The bone marrow (where red cells are produced) may not be able to keep up with this rapid growth, and this can result in anaemia. All premature babies are given iron and vitamin supplements. Some may require blood trans-fusion if the condition is severe.

Coping with a premature baby

Having a premature baby in the Neonatal Intensive Care Unit (NICU) can be a very stressful experience for the mother. Most parents go through an emotional turmoil when they see their tiny baby, for the first time, hooked on to various tubes and machines. They, especially the mother, feel helpless and guilty at being unable to carry him to term. Conflicts may arise within the family or between the couple. Well-meaning family members might aggravate the situation. The mother may go though a phase of initially blaming herself for her baby's condition, or blaming others for the situation. The next phase will be one of denial, followed by gradual acceptance.

The best way to go through this difficult period is to visit the baby often. Most NICUs have an open visiting policy and parents are allowed to spend as much time as possible with their babies. It is good to speak with the doctors and nurses and find out about the baby's condition.

You can touch your baby — hold his tiny fingers, stroke his hands and head. As a parent, you may initially feel afraid to do this or worried that you might dislodge sometimes. As long as you take the proper precautions such as good hand washing and gentle handling of the baby, he will not be harmed.

You can talk or even sing to your baby. He can recognize your voice and can get 'calmed down' by your presence. You can express your breast milk and give it to him as your milk is best for your premature baby. A premature baby can digest his mother's milk much easier. In addition, your breast milk also contains important antibodies which can help your baby fight infectious disease.

As your baby grows, you can be involved in taking care of him. You can learn to feed him by his gastric tube. You can be involved in changing the nappies and even learn to clean him. Once he is taken off the ventilator, you can look forward to the day when you can carry him for the first time. You can also be involved in early stimulation of your baby under the supervision of the rehabilitation team.

Do not neglect yourself and your family while you are involved with your baby. If you have other children, let them come and visit him too. Explain to your friends and relatives about his condition and allow them to help out with domestic arrangements — for example, babysitting your older children help with meals or household chores.

Make sure that you get sufficient rest and good food. You can have normal confinement diet when you are breast-feeding, provided there is no excessive herbs or other medication used. It is good to check with your doctors if in doubt.

Going home

After a long period of hospitalization and much anxiety, the prospect of taking a premature baby home raises further questions and concerns. There is also much excitement at the home coming of the precious little baby.

When can my baby go home?

Most parents await anxiously the homecoming of their premature baby after a long period of hospitalization which usually ranges from 3–4 months on the average. Your premature baby is ready to go home when his condition is stable and his body weight is generally close to 2 kg. He must be breathing well on his own, needs no supplemental oxygen, is free from apnoeas, and is sucking his oral feeds well.

How can I get prepared to bring my baby home?

Parents are encouraged to visit their baby frequently, spend as much time with him as possible, and learn to be comfortable in taking care of him, while still in hospital. This includes learning the basics of baby care — feeding, burping, changing nappies, bathing, giving medications, and also learning ways to comfort or calm the baby.

Parents are also taught the basics of Cardio-Pulmonary Resuscitation (CPR) before their baby's discharge from the hospital.

You need not make any special preparation at home for your premature baby. Once he is home, he can be treated as a normal term baby. He can take normal milk feeds (breast milk or infant formula), be dressed in normal infant clothes and can sleep in a normal cot.

What happens after my baby's discharge from the hospital?

After discharge, your premature baby will be followed up by the hospital at regular intervals for the monitoring of his growth and development. You will also be given appointments for an eye examination and a hearing assessment. If your baby is already on the early intervention programme for stimulation, you will be given an outpatient appointment to continue therapy at the rehabilitation department.

Your premature baby will be immunized according to the normal schedule for all babies. You will be given a discharge summary and a referral letter to your family doctor or the polyclinic for immunizations.

Caring for a premature baby at home

Care of a premature baby at home is similar to that of any normal baby. Most premature babies who have spent a long time in the hospital may have the same problems in the first few days at home while settling down to a routine.

Some concerns that parents of premature babies may have include the following:

Feeding

Your premature baby can be fed normal term formula or breast milk at home. The amount taken varies. Most babies take about 50–60ml initially, approximately every 2–3 hourly. It is best to feed your baby on demand. The usual precautions about hand-washing and sterilizing of bottles should be adhered to strictly. Feeds can be increased according to your baby's appetite as he grows older and there is no strict schedule to adhere to. It is usually not necessary to give any extra water in the first few months.

Weaning

It is best to introduce a weaning diet to your baby at 4 months of corrected age (i.e. not the actual age in months, but rather the age calculated from the time when the baby reaches 10 months of pregnancy, e.g. a baby born 3 months prematurely would, at the time of 6 months after his birth, be considered to be only 3 months old). By 4 months of age, your baby would be ready to take solids. You could use commercially prepared rice cereals or make your own rice powder in the traditional manner. You could try feeding the cereals by spoon rather than by bottle, as by this stage, your baby would be able to accept and swallow spoon feeds. Gradually, you could add on fruit, vegetables or egg yolk (after 6 months).

Immunizations

Your premature baby would normally be able to follow the immunization schedule as per any normal child. The BCG injection is given only when your baby reaches 2.5 kg in weight. The DPT and Polio vaccinations can be given at 3,4 and 5 months after birth. The oral polio vaccine is usually not given while your baby is still in hospital, but can be given at monthly intervals after discharge from the hospital. The hepatitis B injection can be given soon after birth at 1 and 6 months of life. Other vaccinations should be given at the appropriate time and in general, this will not be different from those born at term.

Visitors and going out

Most relatives and friends would be anxious to visit your baby at home. Although a premature baby, at the time of discharge is stable, he can catch an infection readily, as any other newborn baby. It would be wise to inform your friends and relatives not to visit you and your baby when they are having a cold or flu. Also, avoid exposing your baby to cigarette smoke.

In the first 3 months after bringing your baby home from the hospital, avoid taking him out to crowded public places such as supermarkets, cinemas, shopping centres, schools, or buses. It is also advisable for him to be in a smoke-free home environment. Once he is older, he can do all the things a normal term baby can do, including swimming.

The unwell child

Most parents usually learn to tell when their baby is 'not right'. Some premature babies show changes in their behaviour or response when sick. It may be one or more of the following:

- change in the breathing pattern or coughing
- excessive crying or irritability
- change in the feeding pattern or vomiting
- lethargy or difficulty in waking up
- frequent watery stools
- fever
- blue or pale coloured skin

It is advisable to bring your child to the doctor if he has any of the above symptoms. Invest in a good thermo-meter and learn how to take your baby's temperature (by placing the thermometer under the armpit, rather than the mouth or use an infra-red thermometer). There are newer thermometers such as the electronic or ear instant thermometers. You must read the instructions carefully and make sure you know how to use them correctly.

Minor problems causing concern

A common problem that worries parents once their baby comes home, is that of 'noisy breathing'. Most babies have some congestion of the nasal passages, which may result in noisy breathing. It is not necessary to treat such nasal congestion as long as the baby is sleeping comfortably and is able to feed well.

Hiccups and sneezes are normal and will normally just settle by themselves. Frequent sneezing, associated with running nose, could mean that the baby has caught a cold.

Growth and development

Your premature baby will be followed up closely by the hospital at regular intervals where monitoring of your baby's growth and development will take place.

Your premature baby should 'catch up growth' in the first few months of life once the initial hospitalization problems have settled. By the age of 1, your premature baby has weight and length comparable to term babies. Some preterm babies, however, may lag behind in growth with poor weight gain. These babies include:

- those, who, at birth, were small for their number of weeks of gestation
- those who were sick for a long period of time, requiring mechanical ventilation or are oxygen dependant for a long time

- those with consistently poor weight gain while in the nursery

Your baby's weight, height and head measurement will be taken at each visit and these measurements will be compared with the established charts for normal babies. (Note that comparisons will be made for the 'corrected age' of your baby.)

Regular follow-up visits also monitor the rate at which your baby is developing. It is important that you attend all scheduled appointments. The close monitoring of your baby's development will ensure that any delay or abnormality in development is detected early and the appropriate referral for early intervention or rehabilitation effected early.

The child with special needs

Being born premature may result in a higher risk of disability requiring special care — motor, sensory, or cognitive. The hospital follow-up team have been trained to assess and refer your child to societal resources for special education.

Long-term outcome

Having a premature baby immediately raises concerns regarding the baby's possible survival outcome. The mother's womb is the safest place for him. However, at times when the inevitable happens, doctors and nurses together with all the technologies available to us, try their best to give these tiny babies the chance of a reasonably meaningful life. It is, therefore, important to understand the chance of survival and disability in these premature babies.

Survival

One of the first questions crossing the parents' mind on the birth of their premature baby is the chance of their baby surviving. Factors influencing an individual baby's survival include the following:

■ the degree of prematurity or the gestational age of the baby (the number of completed weeks of pregnancy). This is obviously an important factor in determining survival because it determines if the organs of the baby, particularly his lungs, have developed sufficiently to enable him to live.
■ the birth weight of the baby.
■ the condition of the baby at birth and the amount of resuscitation given to the baby.
■ the presence of severe disease — lung immaturity or infections.

Generally, as the practice of Neonatal Intensive Care Unit improves with the introduction of new technology and better trained staff, the survival of the smaller and more immature babies have improved. In Singapore, an estimate of the survival rates of premature babies from the Annual Statistics of babies born in Kandang Kerbau Women's and Children's Hospital in recent years is as follows:

Generally, the survival rates for babies weighing less than 1000 g at birth is about 70 per cent and for babies weighing between 1000 and 1500 g and above, it is more than 95 per cent.

Gestation at birth	Survival
< 24 weeks	0–30%
24 weeks	40–50%
25 weeks	50–70%
26 weeks	60–85%
27 weeks	> 85%
28 weeks	> 90%
29 weeks	> 90%

Risks of permanent sequalae

A premature baby is at risk of sustaining damage to his vital organs — including his brain, eyes, ears and lungs, as these organs have not fully matured at the time of delivery. While all precautions are taken while the baby is in the Neonatal Intensive Care Unit to minimize such injury, it may not always be preventable.

Sequalae

Brain injury may occur in the form of bleeding into the brain or in the presence of 'cysts' signifying lack of oxygenation to the brain. A premature baby who sustains such injuries has a very much higher chance of being handicapped, ranging from 5 per cent for minor bleeding to 90 per cent for extensive or major bleeding or cysts formation.

The incidence of **impaired vision** is higher in premature babies sustaining severe retinopathy of prematurity. Visual loss occurs in about 0.5–2 per cent of babies weighing below 1500 g. Milder degrees of visual disturbances such as astigmatism and shortsightedness, requiring the use of spectacles, occur in about 10 per cent of such babies.

The incidence of **deafness** ranges from 0.5–1.5 per cent of babies born weighing less than 1500 g.

Chronic illnesses

Approximately 20 per cent of very low birth weight babies (VLBW) (babies less than 1500 g at birth) may go on to develop chronic lung disease. Such babies require oxygen supplements for prolonged periods of time and may require hospitalization for several months. After discharge from the hospital, such babies are more prone to frequent chest infections and wheezing. They may require multiple hospital admissions for asthma-like symptoms. These children generally grow poorly, and may require long-term medication for their wheezing tendency. Most children with BPD, however, outgrow this tendency, and their symptoms settle down by the time they reach the age of 4–5.

Overall incidence of disability

What then are the chances of a premature baby being normal? In general, about 85 per cent of VLBW babies show normal development. Mental retardation is present in about 10 per cent, while about 5 per cent may develop cerebral palsy. The chances of disability are higher in the smaller and more immature babies.

Conclusion

Although having a premature baby can initially be a very traumatic and earth-shattering experience, however, with the support of your family and the understanding of the nurses and medical staff, you will be able to weather the early stormy days.

Initially, you may feel like being on a roller coaster but the situation will gradually calm down and you will begin to enjoy the company of your baby. Whatever the outcome of your baby may be, you have a very special child and you are a very special parent. Your love, care, and support will go a very long way in your child's growth and development.

After the first few years of life, most children who were born prematurely would have caught up with their growth and development. The majority of them can go to nursery schools just like other children.

11

Prevention of Injury/Harm

KHOR Sek Hoon Elizabeth

Introduction

One of the biggest threats to your baby's or child's life and health is accidents, and 73 per cent of all childhood injuries in Singapore are due to home accidents. Childhood accidents are the fourth most common cause of death in Singaporean children below 14 years of age. Often, accidents occur because parents are not aware of what their children can do.

Children learn very fast, and in no time, your little baby who has just started to lift his head will be wriggling off a bed or reaching out for your cup of hot tea or coffee. As he grows, he will suddenly be able to roll over and fall off everything. He may climb before he can walk and may grasp at almost everything. The baby and toddler will put anything and everything into his mouth as he explores the home. Your child does not understand what is dangerous, and he cannot remember the word 'No'. The active preschooler can fall off the play equipment and the bicycle, fall out of the window, fall down the staircase, and fall off everything he has climbed on to.

Your older child who is attending primary school is more independent and spends less time at home.

However, he can do more things that places him at risk for injury. He tries to prove to you that he has grown up, but he is not good at judging sound, distance, or the speed of a moving car. He is out of your sight more often, is more likely to drown or be hurt by his bicycle, or be hit by a car while crossing the road.

As a parent, you are in charge of your child's safety. With an active baby or toddler at home, you have to 'child-proof' your home so as to reduce his risks of injury from falls, burns, poisonings, and choking. You have to teach you older child safety rules to protect himself, and remind him that 'safe kids are smart kids'.

When are accidents most likely to occur?

Being a parent is a demanding 24-hour job, and the chances of an accident happening are increased if any of the following happens:

- Your child is tired or hungry
- Your child is sick or ill
- You are tired, pregnant or suffering from pre-menstrual tension
- You use unsafe baby equipment which do not comply with safety standards
- Your child is considered hyperactive or if he sleepwalks
- You and your spouse or close family members have emotional conflicts
- There is great excitement at home, like having a party or celebrating the arrival of a new baby
- Your child plays in an unsafe part of the house, e.g. in the kitchen or near the toilet or windows

How do I 'child-proof' my home?

When you 'child-proof' your home, you can approach the problem using the following:

- Home safety measures
- Room-by-room safety measures
- Age-specific safety measures

Home safety measures

After nine anxious months of waiting, your baby has finally arrived. If you have given birth to twins or triplets, you will have to take extra care and prepare your home earlier. Most of us would have 'inherited' baby equipment like cots or clothes from friends and relatives, and you would have bought some feeding and bathing equipment. Start preparing your baby's room during the second trimester of your pregnancy, as you will have no time to child-proof your home once your baby has arrived. Your newborn baby spends most of his time asleep, and you must make certain that the cot is a safe one. Newborn babies are at risk of 'cot death' or 'sudden infant death'. Babies sleep safer when placed on their backs/sides. If your baby is placed on a prone (face-down) position, he will need close supervision to ensure that his face is not buried in a pillow or cot bumper.

When you buy newborn equipment or if you are inspecting the equipment that you have 'inherited', pay close attention to the following:

Cot

The spaces between the cot bars should be 8 cm or less, so as to prevent your baby's head from getting stuck between the bars. This distance is approximately the width of an adult's three fingers. Also, check for defective cot bars. The mattress should be the same size as the cot, and a high density foam mattress is the best choice. Bumper pads are unnecessary as it prevents your baby from seeing out of the cot, and they can also be used to climb onto at a later stage. Paediatricians discourage the use of 'sarong cradles' as there is a higher risk of head injuries.

Bathtub

You can bathe your baby without buying an expensive bathtub. Round plastic bathtubs with a shallow depth of 15–20cm is good enough. These are readily available from neighbourhood sundry shops or supermarkets. You can place a small sponge lining or bathmat at the bottom of the tub to prevent your baby from slipping. Until the umbilical cord drops off, keep the water level below the navel.

Always remember to test the temperature of the water in the bathtub with your hand. The water should be lukewarm before you immerse your child into the bathtub. You should always pour cold water into the bathtub and hot water later to make it lukewarm. Never put hot water into the bathtub first as it may cause severe scalding if you forget to add cold water. Do not let your older child play with the shower howe or tap handles as he may scald himself with hot water. Never leave your child alone in the tub, even for a few seconds while you answer a telephone call or doorbell. As little as 2 inches of water can cause drowning.

Use a damp face towel to wipe your baby's head, neck, armpit, groin and the back of his knees while he is lying naked in the cot or changing table. It is difficult to clean these areas when he is wriggling in the bathtub.

Carry your baby by letting his back rest on your left forearm. Use your right hand to support his knees and lower him into the tub. Let his bottom rest on the base of the tub, so that his body is leaning backwards on your left forearm. Your firm grip on his left upper arm will prevent him from slipping into the tub. Use your right hand to scoop water over his body and watch him enjoy bath time.

Baby talcum powder

Remember that talcum powder can be dangerous if it spills on your baby's face, as he will breathe the talc into his lungs. Dust your baby's body lightly with talcum powder, and ensure that the powder container is placed a safe distance away from his face.

Safety pins

Cloth napkins are more 'eco-friendly' compared to disposable diapers. If you are concerned about safety, choose cloth diapers with velcro straps. If you prefer to use safety pins, it might be better to poke the sharp end of the opened safety pin into the mattress first, then place the cloth napkin and wrap it around your baby's bottom. In this way, you can reach for the safety pin easily when you need it, and he is not in danger of being poked by the sharp pin.

Pacifier

To prevent choking, the pacifier's shield should be at least 4cm or $1\frac{1}{2}$ inches in diameter, and the pacifier should be one single piece. Do not attach the pacifier to a cord as your baby may accidentally get strangulated.

Safety gadgets

Once your child is crawling, you will need electric-outlet safety plugs, cabinet door safety locks, plastic corner guards for sharp table edges, locks for window grilles safety barriers, and so on. You are encouraged to crawl around the house at the same eye-level as your child to look out for dangerous areas like dangling wires, nails, sharp edges, nooks and corners where your curious baby or toddler can hurt himself accidentally. The home environment takes on a different perspective when seen at a child's height.

Baby's walker

A baby's walker can be a lethal form of transportation. This wheeled device which allows babies to propel themselves with their feet before they can walk is responsible for many home accidents. It gives children access to things like pans on the stove or the electric cord of kettles. Keep your baby in a baby's walker away from staircases, stoves, and electric equipment.

High chair

A high chair can be used from the time your baby reaches 6 months, and for as long as your child fits into it. Look for safety belts at anchor points, and there must be a strap at your baby's groin to prevent him from slipping out from below. Never leave your child alone in the high chair as he may climb out and fall out. Traditionally, some Asian mothers buy the bamboo 'mother-baby-chair' which is a bamboo stool and baby chair built in one piece. The advantage is that your baby sits close to the ground, but you have to make sure that there are no sharp or rough bamboo edges. There are no straps available with this traditional baby bamboo chair.

Car safety seat

A child restraint seat is essential for transporting your baby in a car. Choose a model with standard safety feature.

Sibling rivalry

Older siblings can become jealous when a new baby arrives. The arrival of a new baby is stressful for the firstborn, and for those less than 3 years old. Your older child can be encouraged as a helper, but never leave the two of them alone. Some older siblings have been seen to use toys to hurt the baby. Your older child can touch and play with your new baby in your presence. You should not allow him to carry the baby until he reaches school age.

Room-by-room safety measures

The furnishings and fixtures in the rooms as well as the different kinds of activity in the area pose specific problems to a young child. Besides taking general child-proofing safety measures, it is important to go through a check-list meticulously to ensure that your child does not get involved in accidents in the bathroom, the kitchen, living rooms and bedrooms. Safety measures have to be taken too when staying outdoors — in the garden, the swimming pool, and the fish pond.

General

- Keep medicines out of the reach of your child in a locked medicine chest. Accidental poisonings include Panadol syrup or tablets, grandmother's diabetic pills and even contraceptive pills.
- Store all drugs and chemicals as far away from food as possible.
- Do not leave aerosol cans and rat poison around the house.
- Make sure that the cord of electrical appliances is kept out of the reach of your child.
- Fit safety socket covers to all unused power points.
- Screen and bar all windows, or lock the window grilles.
- Keep pins, needles, matches, lighters, sharp knives and scissors in a locked cupboard.
- Ensure that the furniture is solid and heavy so that your child cannot pull along.
- Keep scissors, medicine, usineties and razor blades out for your child's reach.
- Wipe up spilled liquid at once.
- Keep plastic bags away from your child.
- Never leave a hot iron around before attending to something else.
- Store away all cleaning substances like bleach and detergent and pesticides, plants sprays, and cleaning detergents.
- Fit a safety gate at the top and bottom of stairs.
- Ensure that stair bannisters are secure and have narrow gaps.

- Run flexes around the walls and keep the flexes on electrical appliances short.
- Ensure that anything breakable is out of your child's reach.
- Do not play with your child while carrying a hot drink in your hand.
- Ensure that your house plants are not poisonous.

The bathroom

- Make sure you can open your bathroom door from the outside.
- Never leave your child alone in the bathroom.
- Keep the bathroom floor dry and have a non-slip floor surface.
- Fit handles to the sides of bathtub or bath area and use a non-slip bath mat.
- Keep the lid of toilet seat closed.

The kitchen

- Never leave a boiling pan or wok unattended on the stove and turn the handles of all pans towards the back of the stove.
- Do not use table cloths as a crawling baby can reach up and pull whatever that is on the table on top of him.
- Do not cook with your toddler around you. Arrange a play area or place him in a playpen so that you can still see him and talk to him.
- Give your child plastic cups or bowls which are unbreakable.

The living room and the bedroom

- Keep the television set out of reach and do not place

hot or heavy objects on low tables. These items are potential 'killer litter' at home.

■ Store games and toys at a low level so that your child can reach the toys easily. Do not leave toys lying around on the floor.

■ Never leave your baby alone with the cot barrier down and on the changing table.

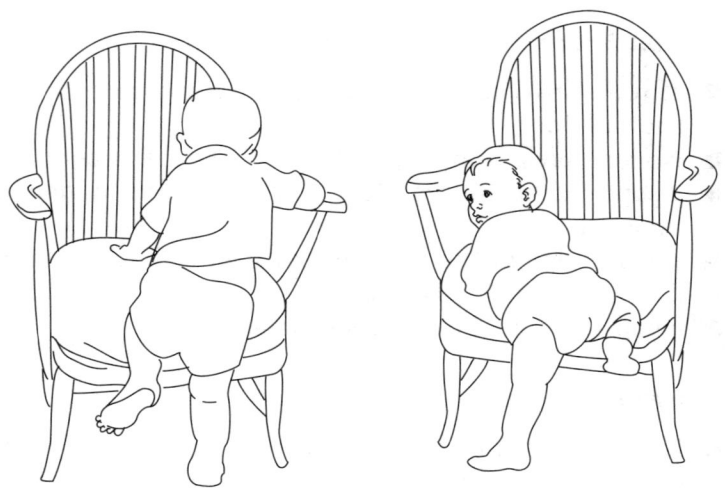

Watch it dear, lest you fall!

The garden, the swimming pool and the fish pond

■ Pull off any mushrooms or toadstools as soon as they appear.

■ Keep your children inside the house and shut all windows if the plants and shrubs need to be sprayed with insecticide.

■ Check that your swings or slides are safe.

■ Ensure that child-proof locks are used on all gates.

■ Never leave a paddling pool with water in it.

■ Fence off the swimming pool or 'koi' pond.

Age specific safety measures

As your child develops, he gains mobility. Coupled with the immense sense of curiosity and the bountiful energy level, he is continuously on the move and exploring his environment. The lack of appreciation of dangerous situations makes him extremely accident-prone. A child is vulnerable to different types of accidents at home during the different phases of development.

The active baby

A young baby will not keep still and does not remain in the same position even if he has not learnt how to get up from the lying position. Therefore, do not leave your baby alone on high places such as beds, sofa, chairs or changing tables as he may suddenly fall over. Unsupervised by adults, a baby who has begun to ambulate either by crawling or walking should be kept out of rooms where he might hurt himself. It is not advisable to hold anything hot such as hot food or drinks while you are carrying your baby at the same time. He will get scalded when you lose control of the active child.

Your baby will put any object he can grasp within his reach into his mouth. Leaving small objects within your baby's reach will put him at risk of choking on them when he puts them into his mouth. Similarly, feeding the young toddler with hard pieces of food such as peanuts will result in choking. A baby on a baby's walker and one who is only able to crawl can get on to the stairs or through the door quicker than you can realize. The use of gates on stairways and doors is a good safeguard to these accidents. A baby should never to be left alone in or near a bathtub, a pail of water, wadding or swimming pool, even for a moment. You cannot risk the possibility of your baby drowning under these circumstances. Knowing how to swim does not make the older child watersafe at this age.

The 'terrible two's or three's' /The active alert toddler

Your child can move at lightning speed and he can fall off any thing. The young toddler is characteristically energetic and curious. Nothing escapes his attention and curiosity. It is difficult to ensure that he is being supervised all the time to prevent him getting himself into trouble. It is wise to lock the door to any dangerous areas. The kitchen should be out of bounds to the toddler. Hot liquids, grease and hot foods can spill on him and cause serious scalds and burns. Kitchen appliances like toasters and irons remain hot for a long while after you have finished using them. A curious toddler can open any drawer and swallow any thing he finds. Choking or poisoning can result.

Trying to open the door

Trying to reach for things inside the drawer

The preschool or kindergarten pupil

Your child learns fast but does not know anything about safety. You must protect him and teach him simple rules in bicycle safety (e.g. wear a helmet while riding), not to play on the street and not to play with fire.

The primary school pupil

Your child has friends and he goes to school. Children at this age are still impulsive and have poor sense of judgement. He can learn safety rules but you have to remind him over and over again. Your child is not watersafe on his own, even if he knows how to swim. A child of this age must never play around any water, beach or swimming pool unless an adult is watching him. You should never let him swim in monsoon canals or any fast moving water. Teach him always to enter the water feet first at all times. Teach your child the 'rules of the road' and see if he knows how to cross roads and if he uses good judgement. If your child is active in sports like line skating, football and basketball, be sure that he wears the correct shoes and protective equipment.

Would I be able to help my child if he gets hurt?

Your child may sustain head injury from a fall. Head injury is serious and can lead to permanent brain damage. Therefore, you should consult a doctor if your child had a hard fall or has hit his head. When in doubt about how serious the fall has been, it is better to err on the side of safety and have you child checked by the doctor. A child who has become drowsy and not arousable or who vomits persistently after a fall and is unable to move his limbs, needs urgent medical attention as these symptoms may indicate that there is injury to or bleeding in the brain.

It is useful to have first aid knowledge on how to help a choking child and how to treat burns and scalds acutely. Your first aid knowledge may save a life. Courses on cardio-pulmonary resuscitation are regularly conducted by professional bodies such as the Singapore Paediatric Society. It is useful to learn the basic steps in resuscitation. You may be the only person around when your child urgently needs help.

It should be noted that this chapter serves as a guide for home safety and accident prevention among young children. It is not possible to be comprehensive and cover all possible circumstances where accidents may occur. You should be vigilant for possible accidents at all times and be aware that accidents will occur at any moment when you least expect them to occur.

12

Common Childhood Illnesses/ Conditions

QUAH Thuan Chong & QUEK Swee Chye

Common childhood illnesses

It is not uncommon that during the growing years, many episodes of illnesses are experienced. The relative lack of resistance to infection and the exposure to a wide variety of infective agents during childhood are important reasons. Fortunately, many of these common childhood illnesses are not serious, but they nevertheless cause considerable parental anxiety.

How are symptoms and diseases treated?

If your child is sick, it is a reflex reaction for you (and also many doctors) to give your child medicine — 'a pill for every ill'.

However, medicines are often unnecessary and may even be harmful. To help parents to understand the 'whys', 'whens', and 'wherefores' of helping a sick child (whether with or without giving medicines), we should understand the basics of illness — in particular, to distinguish between diseases and symptoms.

When your child, for example, has come down with fever, diarrhoea and vomiting, the disease is 'infective gastroenteritis' (an infection of the stomach and intestines) and the symptoms are what your child is 'suffering from' (in this instance, fever, diarrhoea and vomiting).

When we want to help the sick child, we hope to cure the disease — in this instance, by giving some medicine to kill the microorganism causing the infection. But most common infections ('flu', diarrhoea, etc.) are caused by viruses, and we do not have any effective drugs for most viral infections. Antibiotics are often used for infections, but they are effective only against another kind of microorganism (bacteria), which causes only a small percentage of common infections in children. Thus, we have no 'cure' for most common diseases in children. In effect, when we see children with minor illnesses (cough and cold, diarrhoea, etc.), we can only treat the symptoms.

Do all medicines have side-effects?

In most instances, if all we can do is to relieve symptoms (e.g. bringing down fever, reducing coughs), then we must realize that all medicines have potential side-effects because the side-effects can be worse than the symptoms we want to relieve.

For example, it is well known that antihistamines (the commonest type of cough suppressant) often cause lethargy and even drowsiness. What is less well known is that, they often cause irritability in young children. So, we can imagine a scenario in which a child is coughing away quite happily, and at the same time, eating and playing well. Then he is given a 'cough medicine'. After he has taken his cough medicine, he coughs a bit less, but becomes sleepy (and refuses to sleep) and irritable, upsetting everybody at home. Antihistamines also cause increased stickiness of mucus and may make it more difficult for the child to expectorate the phlegm, and thus the child may have to cough very hard to bring it out. In other words, the child may end up suffering more from the side-effects of the medicine than the actual effects of the 'flu' itself. Is this a price worth paying?

Except for identical twins, all of us have different genetic make-ups, and so everyone of us responds to medicines in different ways. Thus, some children become very sleepy with even a very small dose of antihistamine, but some are not at all affected. Thus, as parents, we should observe the child after he has taken his medicine, and decide for ourselves whether the side-effects are acceptable, or whether they are too severe to be worth continuing the medicine.

Fevers

Human beings are warm-blooded animals and we keep our body temperature constant so that our metabolic processes can function optimally. Fever is the most common illness that all children face as part of their growing up and may 'disturb' their body functions. It is for parents, probably the most vexing problem. Most fevers are due to innocuous viral infections but some serious illnesses may present with fever and parents like you, need to be very careful to look out for signs and symptoms that indicate a more sinister cause of the fever. There are a lot of myths and hearsay about fever and we shall dispel the rumours from the facts in this section.

How do I know if my child has fever?

Like many parents, you may depend on feeling your child's forehead using the back of your hands. This is, however, notoriously misleading — if you are in an air-conditioned room, your hand may be cold and hence if you feel your child's forehead, it feels warm.

To confirm that your child has fever, you need a reliable thermometer. Plastic strips that are placed on the forehead and changes colour according to temperature are unreliable. The classic mercury thermometer, electronic thermometer and infra-red thermometer are sufficiently accurate for general use. For the mercury and electronic thermometers, it is probably best for you to purchase one that measures the temperature under the armpit as children detest oral thermometers, especially when they are unwell. The infra-red thermometer measures the heat emission from the eardrum many times over a second and provides a rapid and accurate reading. It is, however, considerably more expensive, though not necessarily more accurate than the mercury thermometer.

Your child has fever if his body temperature is more than 37.3°C (99.1°F).

Fever: Friend or foe?

We may wonder to ourselves sometimes — why do we have fever at all? Our body reacts to foreign invaders with different defence tactics to try to expel or kill them. It is easy to imagine how production of phlegm and cough help us when we have a 'flu'. The phlegm may help in trapping the virus, and cough helps in expelling the phlegm and the virus at the same time.

What about fever? Does it help the body in any way? Is it a friend or foe? We want to have our fever lowered because we feel 'sick' when we have a fever. But before doing that, it may be worthwhile pondering on this: Why does our body produce fever? Is it good or bad for us? If it is good for us, then why should we bring the fever down? It is known that fever actually help our bodies to fight off the infection. There is some evidence that fever helps the body to kill microorganisms more effectively. So it is beneficial to some extent. But if the fever is too high (more than 38.5°C), the child would often feel very miserable and lowering of the body's elevated temperature does make one feel more comfortable. Fever can also a very unsettling signal to you that your child is sick. So it is no wonder that it is almost a gut reaction for us to want to bring the fever down.

When should I worry if my child has fever?

Most fevers are due to innocuous viral infections like common cold and diarrhoea. You should be careful about your child's fever if he:

- is younger than 2 months old as very young children are more susceptible to severe bacterial infections and have little tell-tale signs of something sinister
- has fever of higher than 41°C
- looks unwell or extremely irritable
- has known medical problems like cancer, immuno-deficiency disease, or heart problems
- has fever lasting more than 7 days as most viral fevers will have subsided by then

What are the myths about fever?

Myths about fever are abound; most of them being old wives' tales with little scientific basis and some may be even harmful. Some of these myths are discussed are as follows:

A child with fever must be covered with blankets to sweat it out

Covering your child with a blanket during fever is only useful when he is shivering. This occurs when his fever is rising, and the blanket is to be used until the shivering stops. When his fever is high, the blanket prevents heat loss and may cause his fever to rise further, which in turn may be more harmful.

Sponging your child may risk him catching a cold

Sponging, together with taking fever medications like paracetamol, is useful to help bring down your child's fever. Though common cold is a frequent cause of fever, sponging neither causes it or makes it worse. When your child is shivering, it is probably best to wait for the shivering to cease before you sponge him.

Fever causes brain damage

The fear of brain damage due to fever often can make you have sleepless night, religiously sponging your child and feeding them endless doses of paracetamol. You may be relieved to know that despite common belief, fever itself does not harm your child unless it is higher than 41°C. It is what causes the fever that may damage your child. For example, if a child has a brain infection, he will have fever and may later suffer some brain damage. It is not the fever that damage the brain but the infection on the brain itself. If a child has brain infection, he will have other symptoms like lethargy listlessness, disorientation, and disinterest in play or in the surroundings. He may even have fits. When these symptoms occur with or without fever, you should take him to see a doctor and not manage him at home.

Typhoid (more commonly known in Hokkien as Moh-tan) is a common cause of fever and Chinese medication is the only cure for it

With the excellent sanitation in Singapore and strict surveillance of food sellers, typhoid fever is rare cause of fever locally. Effective antibiotics are available and the 'moh-tan' powders are either useless or have too many unacceptable side-effects.

Medicine inserted into the rectum is better than oral medication

You may have heard — albeit mistakenly — that suppositories inserted into the rectum is necessary and better than the good old paracetamol administered through mouth. Suppositories like these often contain much stronger medications and may be associated with more side-effects than paracetamol. It is best to leave its use to trained medical professionals.

Antibiotics is crucial for treatment of fever

Most fevers are due to viral infections and do not require antibiotic therapy. Antibiotics is useless against viral infections and may be associated with side-effects like allergy, and is best avoided. Your doctor will balance the risk of bacterial infection when he examines your child, and the prescription of antibiotics is best left to his expertise.

Should fever be treated?

Fever should be treated as a symptom, that is, if the fever is harmful to your child (e.g. making him very irritable and miserable), it is reasonable to bring the fever down. However, if the fever is mild, and your child is happily eating and playing, it is not necessary to treat it. It would be ridiculous to chase after a child with a spoonful of fever medicine, to catch him after a big struggle, and to force the medicine down his throat! If he can run fast enough for you to have difficulty catching up with him, he does not need the fever medicine!

How is fever treated?

You can keep him in a cool, airy room and let him wear loose clothings as these will help the body to lose heat. Circulating the room air by switching on an oscillating fan on will also help. Make sure that your child does not shiver as this will cause his body to produce more heat. Encourage him to drink plenty of fluid to prevent dehydration which itself can cause fever. You can give him some antipyretic medication like paracetamol every 4–6 hourly.

You may use other antipyretic medication previously given by your doctor. You can also put him in a lukewarm bath for 10–15 minutes if the fever fails to subside with medication. As long as the temperature of the water is cooler than his body, his body will lose heat. Cold bath should not be used as cold water will cause constriction of the blood vessels in the skin. We lose our bodies' heat through the skin by dilating (opening up) the skin blood vessels. That is why we look flushed when we are hot or have a fever. If the blood vessels are constricted, heat cannot be easily dissipated and is retained in the body, causing a further rise in the body temperature although the skin feels cool.

It is tempting for you to sponge your febrile child because the results are rapidly visible, or rather, felt. It uses an entirely physical process (of conduction and convection) to remove heat, so it is more effective in removing surface heat than internal heat. Cold bath also causes your child to shiver and produce more heat. Cold compress should also be discouraged for the same reason.

Why are my child's hands and feet cold?

Very often, parents comment (and worry) that their child's hands and feet are cold, and may even turn blue, when their foreheads are so hot. Any paediatrician will probably inform them that the fever would go even higher very soon, and then the child's hands and feet would turn warm.

To understand this phenomenon, we would have to understand how our body regulates its temperature. There is a small area in our brain which acts as a thermostat. The normal setting is somewhere between 36.5 and 37.5°C (our body temperature is not perfectly constant throughout the day). When our body is invaded by, say, a virus, the thermostat setting may be raised to, say, 39.5°C. The thermostat then sends signals to the body to do two things to raise the body temperature — to conserve heat and to produce heat. The body conserves heat by reducing blood flow to the extremities — that is why the hands and feet are cold. This tells us that the thermostat setting is higher than the body temperature, and thus the body temperature will go higher soon. We also feel **chills**, a sensation of cold. We would then move to a warmer place, or put on extra clothings. However, young children cannot vocalize yet, and cannot tell us whether they feel cold. But we would know they have the 'chills' when their hands and feet are cold. It would be reasonable then to move them to warmer places and wrap them in extra clothings. However, if we do that, we have to monitor them carefully and often so that when their hands and feet turn warm again. When they begin to sweat, we should remove the extra clothings.

How about **rigors**? This is just like the shivering that we have when the weather is too cold. The muscle contractions help to produce heat and thus increase body temperature. Again, experiencing rigors also tells us that the thermostat setting is higher than the current body temperature, and the latter will go up very soon. It is then very cruel to **sponge** a child when his hands and feet are cold, and especially when he is shivering — even when he has a fever. We should learn to 'listen to our body' and 'follow its rhythm'.

Which are the common medications for relieving fever?

There are two main groups of fever medications available in Singapore. Paracetamol is, by far, the most commonly used and certainly the most useful fever medication. It is effective and has minimal side-effects if used appropriately. For young children, it is best to stick to the children preparations of paracetamol as its dosage is lower and so the risk of over-dosage is low. Over-dosage of paracetamol can result in death by causing irreversible liver damage, hence you should *always avoid* overzealous usage. The dose is 10 mg per kg of body weight per dose. One of the causes of accidental overdose is that paracetamol comes in different dose strengths (e.g. depending on the brand, 5 ml of paracetamol may contain 125mg or 250mg), and parents sometimes give the same volume of different preparations containing different dose strengths, thus inadvertently over-dosing the child. True paracetamol allergy is uncommon but it exists; allergy to syrup paracetamol may be due to the colourings or alcohol added. However, if you suspect that your child is allergic to syrup paracetamol, you should consult a doctor before you use it again.

NSAIDs (an abbreviation for non-steroidal anti-inflammatory drugs) form the second group of more 'powerful' fever medication. The trade names of the common NSAIDs include Voltaren® and Brufen®. Voltaren® is usually administered as a suppository into the rectum and is useful if your child's fever remains high despite syrup paracetamol. Allergies are more common with NSAIDs and its side-effects include bleeding and kidney impairment.

What is febrile fit?

About 3 per cent of children develop convulsions when they have fever. This is called **febrile convulsion** or **fit**. It occurs in a child between the age of 6 months and 6 years of age. The fits usually occur during the onset of the viral illness at the height of the fever. Parents are alarmed by the fit as their child may appear to be in great distress. However, 'febrile seizures' are rather benign. Children are unconscious during the fit but they leave no permanent damage unless very prolonged. The fit will usually last about 5–10 minutes. During the fit, the child will either stiffen up or be jerking all limbs and body, often with eyes rolling upwards. He will clench his teeth but will seldom, if ever, bite the tongue. Therefore, there is no need to force his teeth apart to prevent his tongue from being bitten. Forcing things into his mouth will only cause damage to the oral cavity.

All that need to be done during the convulsion is to keep calm and lie the child in the sideways position with his head slightly tilted backwards to maintain a patent airway. The child will stop fitting in a little while and he will not be worse off afterwards. He may fall off to sleep and then wake up a little later as though nothing dramatic had happened earlier. Extensive study has been done on the long-term effect of febrile fit in children and it is reassuring to know that it does not cause any damage to the child's brain. Fifty per cent of the children may have further attacks in future, but all of them will outgrow it by 5–6 years old.

Cough and cold

Cough and cold are some of the most common symptoms in children. They account for the numerous visits to doctors in the young, and frequently cause a great deal of concern. There is also a lot of myths surrounding these two symptoms, and treatment is often given incorrectly. Frequently, adequate explanation is necessary to prevent excessive use of medication in this young age group and allay the anxiety of parents.

Cough and cold are common as part of a viral illness commonly known as the 'flu'. Associated problems include fever, sore throat and poor feeding. Lethargy, muscle pain, and ache can also be frequently encountered. This period of illness may last from 3 days to a week before the fever subsides. Normalization of body temperature is usually accompanied by improvement in the rest of the symptoms, though the cough and runny nose can last longer than the fever.

How are cough and cold in a newborn babt treated?

In your newborn baby, cough and cold should be managed more cautiously as they are often symptoms of a more serious underlying pathology. You are, therefore, advised to consult your family doctor if these symptoms occur in the very young.

What is an allergic cough?

Allergic conditions can also account for a significant number of children with cough and cold. This is true in the asthmatic child. Cough in such circumstances may be prolonged and tends to be a more chronic or recurrent problem. There may be associated rhinitis or skin problem as part of the allergic process either in the patient or the family members. The skin problem is termed 'eczema'. This is a condition of dry, scaly skin frequently associated with itch. Typical sites include the elbows, knees, and neck. Treatment is usually topical; a moisturizing agent and steroid cream are very helpful, and oral antihistamines may relieve the itch significantly.

Cough and cold from allergy itself do not usually result in fever. However, asthmatic attacks are often triggered by a viral infection which are often associated with fever. The cough may progress to a wheeze and your child may experience difficulty in breathing. Under such circumstances, antiasthmatic medication given through a nebulizer is the treatment of choice. When there is chronic cough resulting from asthma, preventive treatment in the form of regular inhaled steroids may be useful in controlling the symptoms.

What kinds of respiratory tract infections can be expected?

Viral infections involving the respiratory tract are usually confined to the upper respiratory tract. However, occasionally they spread to the lower respiratory tract. This usually results in a more serious disease requiring antibiotic therapy. Your child may experience difficulty in respiration. In the young baby, this may manifest as an increase in the respiratory rate and in drawing of the chest cage. Diagnosis can be made after a careful physical examination, but occasionally the signs may be subtle and the diagnosis can then only be confirmed with a chest X-ray.

When the cough does not improve in a couple of weeks and becomes chronic, advice from the doctor should be sought. Further investigations to elucidate the cause of the chronic cough is then necessary to institute the correct treatment.

How are cough and cold treated?

It is necessary during this period to ensure that your child is adequately hydrated. You can expect your child to have some loss of appetite. Those children who do not feed well should not be coerced to do so as this can result in indigestion and vomiting. However, it is necessary to ensure that hydration is adequate. This means encouraging the intake of fluids and a light diet, for example, porridge.

If your child is very young, admission to hospital may be necessary if he is unable to tolerate fluids. Assessment of adequate hydration usually involves the doctor checking for moistness of mucous membranes (e.g. the tongue), skin turgor, and the amount of urine output. If your child is assessed to be dehydrated and he continues not to feed well (especially if vomiting occurs), hospitalization is required. Intravenous hydration in the form of a drip containing glucose solution and electrolytes is then useful. You might often worry about the pain and discomfort associated with drip-setting, but in fact, this is a relatively simple procedure, and your child tends to feel better with a drip running.

What types of cough mixtures are needed?

Medication for cough can be roughly divided into two types — the cough suppressant and expectorant. The former is frequently sought, but the latter may be a more useful medication depending on circumstances.

Cough is a reflex in response to some irritant in the respiratory tract. Of course, it is distressing to the care givers and the patient. It may be useful to suppress the cough so that the patient (and parents) get a good night's rest. However, it should also be stressed that suppression of cough itself is not treating the root of the problem but merely the symptom. If the disease resolves, so will the cough. Therefore, efforts should not just be directed towards the symptom, but more importantly, the underlying problem.

The expectorant has a place in the management of cough although it may cause an apparent 'worsening of the condition'. Production of phlegm is the body's response to an infection. Under these circumstances, coughing out of these secretions is important and desirable. It can be seen as preventing the accumulation of unwanted waste products from choking the respiratory tract.

Mucolytic agents are medications which make secretions less viscid, thereby loosening them. It is particularly helpful in a child who is 'chesty' with a lot of thick, sticky secretions.

Care must be exercised in the use of cough mixture for babies. Generally, cough medication is contraindicated in the young as side-effects are commoner in this age group. The term 'cough mixture syndrome' is used to refer to the complications arising from the use of cough mixture in babies. When cough is suppressed and the secretions pool in the lungs, the condition may worsen, with the patient literally 'drowning' in secretions. The sedative that may be present in the cough suppressant does little to help either, and in serious cases, it can depress respiration.

What is the medication for cold?

Medication for cold comes in two forms — oral and nasal spray or drop. The oral type is usually an antihistamine used to control uncomfortable and excessive nasal secretions. It may be sedative but newer medication claiming to be less sedative is now available in the market. The nasal spray or drop contains topical antihistamine and can be used as a temporary control for nasal stuffiness. Its use should be restricted to not more than a few days as a rebound in symptoms can occur if it is used for a prolonged period.

From the preventive point of view, a good deal of viral illnesses are acquired through spreading from person to person. While it is common for your young child to have several viral attacks in a year as his immunity is being built up, it would be prudent for you to avoid exposing your child to crowded environment with poor ventilation. This would increase his chances of picking up an infection. As there are innumerable viruses and since most of them cause rather self-limiting illnesses, there is at present no vaccine that is recommended on a large scale basis.

Stomach troubles

The diagnosis of stomach troubles in the young child who is unable to communicate may be difficult. Babies and children may not be able to say when they have a stomach discomfort but instead they present with irritability, excessive crying, and refusal to feed. This is often attributed to 'colic' where grandparents would advise rubbing of oil and other traditional therapy. Colic drops may be helpful, but careful observation and nursing is all that is necessary, as colic is transient and should resolve by itself.

What is gastroenteritis?

A very common problem is gastroenteritis resulting from an infection of the gut. This is usually due to viruses but bacteria and toxins may be responsible. Symptoms include diarrhoea and vomiting and are usually accompanied by fever. Although these symptoms are distressing to your child and you, adequacy of hydration is of prime concern. This is especially so if your child is unable to retain feeds at all due to vomiting.

How is gastroenteritis treated?

The ability to retain feeds in excess of losses needs to be checked. If your child continues to feed poorly or if losses are excessive, admission for intravenous hydration may be necessary. During the insertion of a drip in the hospital, a blood sample is usually sent to check for salt (electrolyte) balance. This may need replacement if a considerable amount from the gut is lost as a result of the vomiting or diarrhoea.

The use of antimotiliy or antiemetic drugs is generally not recommended in children because of potential side-effects. Some of these may cause sedation, drowsiness, depression of breathing, incoordination of gut motility, and retention of urine. Some children may be 'sensitive' to these antimotility drugs and present with a reaction known as the 'oculogyric crisis'. This is an involuntary action involving deviation of the eyes and limbs in an uncontrolled way, often very alarming to the parents.

With gastroenteritis, secondary lactose intolerance may develop. This would manifest as further diarrhoea and poor absorption of milk products. Diluted milk feeds, a change to a soy or semi-elemental (predigested) formula during the infective and recovery period, may circumvent this problem of lactose intolerance.

Other more serious but less common causes of stomach troubles may require surgery. Intestinal obstruction from a variety of causes can result in bilious vomiting (green vomitus from bile contents), abdominal distension, and pain.

These include acute appendicitis, telescoping of the intestines (intussusception), abnormal looping of the intestines (malrotation), absence of nerve cells (Hirschsprung disease), or gut narrowing (stenosis or atresia).

Management of stomach troubles is not always easy. When in doubt, the advice of a doctor should be sought. Even then, it is important to follow up the progress as your child may be seen in the early phase of the disease where the problem is not readily apparent. Being a child and not able to say what is exactly wrong or where the pain is, confounds the matter. As a general rule, a child who is not feeding well or whose condition does not improve following a close period of observation should be seen by a doctor.

Lazy eye

The medical term for lazy eye is **amblyopia**. This is a condition in which one eye assumes a more important role in vision than the other (which then becomes lazy). Sometimes, this is a result of a problem in the lazy eye, such as myopia, but it is not uncommon to find no predisposing cause to why one eye should dominate over the other. As this condition tends to be progressive, early detection is important so that the correct treatment be instituted early before permanent sequalae results.

This is often picked up by an observant parent as the child will have no complaints. The child may be observed to be not focusing at objects, or not establishing an eye contact. If this is suspected, the child should be brought to see an ophthalmologist. The trained doctor then checks the child's pupils with a light source to see if the spot of light is reflected equally onto corresponding sites of both pupils. A 'cover-uncover' test is usually carried out to confirm a squint. This test involves checking one eye at a time to see if there is a shift of the eye when the other is covered while maintaining focus on a distant object.

It is important to have the eyes of the child checked because Asian children tend to have a longer distance between the eyes. This may give rise to a 'false' squint. Whereas a false squint does not require treatment, a real squint needs to be picked up as early as possible. Treatment has to be started early, such as patching of one eye to encourage use of the 'lazy' eye and frequent reviews carried out. Severe cases may need surgical correction. The early pick-up in a child is emphasized because beyond a certain age, permanent loss of function occurs and further treatment may not be corrective where vision is concerned, but done only for cosmetic reasons.

As a general rule, babies should not have 'lazy' eyes beyond 6 months of age. You should consult your doctor if you notice that your baby is squinting his eyes after the age of 6 months.

13

Other Childhood Diseases

LOKE Kah Yin & YEOH Eng Juh Allen

Measles

Measles is an acute infectious disease which has become less common because of the nation-wide immunization programme. However, some children may not have completed the full primary immunization programme and may not have achieved adequate protection. This has resulted in a recent increase in the number of cases of measles. Measles is highly contagious, and is spread by droplet infection. An infected child becomes contagious by the 9th–10th day after exposure.

Measles is characterized by three stages. Initially, there is an incubation stage of approximately 10–12 days with no symptoms. This is followed by a prodromal stage which lasts 3–5 days, with fever, 'flu', cough, and conjunctivitis (redness of the eyes). There is also red mottling on the inner cheek and palate, with grey, white spots on the inner cheek opposite the lower molars which appear and disappear rapidly within 12–18 hours. These are the Koplik spots which are characteristic of measles. A final stage consists of a maculopapular rash erupting progressively from the neck and face and then the body, arms, and legs, accompanied by high fever.

If you suspect that your child has measles, you should consult your family doctor who can confirm the diagnosis, provide symptomatic treatment, and monitor for any potential complications of measles. It is important to keep your child well rested, with tepid sponging and medications to control the fever and cough, as well as to ensure that your child takes sufficient fluids, even if solid food is refused. Complications may occur and these include ear infections, pneumonia (infection of the lungs), and uncommonly, encephalitis, when the virus affects the brain. If any complications develop, your doctor can prescribe the relevant treatment and advise hospitalization, if necessary.

Otitis media

Otitis media, the medical term for middle ear infection, is a common problem that afflicts children. Almost every Caucasian child will suffer from otitis media and glue ear at least once in childhood. The cause for this high degree of affliction among Caucasian children is unknown but fortunately, among Asians, it is much rarer.

Otitis media may presents in a variety of ways. It usually causes earache or ear itch that makes the child constantly rub the affected ear. It may cause fever that may persist despite fever medications. In some children, the eardrum may perforate and foul smelling yellowish pus may flow from it. Otitis media may occur after a common cold as the latter may cause blockage of the Eustachian tube, preventing proper aeration of the middle ear cavity. A patent Eustachian tube is crucial as it airs the middle ear and prevents fluids from accumulating inside.

The treatment of otitis media consists of a course of antibiotics and nasal decongestants. The antibiotics will help eradicate the bacteria that causes the infection while the nasal decongestant will help unblock the Eustachian tube and air the middle ear cavity. Ear-drops may be helpful.

It is crucial to treat otitis media as the middle ear is separated from the brain by only a thin skull bone. A severe otitis media may spread to the brain coverings and cause meningitis or brain abscess. Sometimes, the fluids in the middle ear may not go away and requires an insertion of a little tube — a grommet — to help drain away the fluids. If left unattended, it may result in some degree of hearing loss. Hence, it is imperative that otitis media is adequately treated and normal hearing is restored. Hearing assessment may be necessary.

Acute tonsillitis

The tonsils are two large lymph nodes situated on both sides near the back of the throat. Tonsillitis refers to the swelling of the tonsils, usually caused by infection. Acute tonsillitis is very common and usually occurs in the common sore throat.

A child with acute tonsillitis will usually develop a significant fever (temperature of higher than 38°C) and may refuse to eat as food may irritate the swollen and painful tonsils. Sometimes, they may even vomit. There are a variety of viruses and bacteria that may cause tonsillitis.

Viral sore throats and tonsillitis do not require antibiotic treatment. If the child has runny nose, red eyes and hoarseness of voice together with his sore throat, viral tonsillitis is more likely. All he needs is fever medication like paracetamol and a lot of fluids.

Bacterial tonsillitis will usually make the child look sicker. The doctor may find that his throat is very red and the tonsils may be covered with a whitish coat. There may also be painful swelling of the neck glands as the bacteria may spread quickly to the neck glands. *Streptococcus* is the most common bacteria that causes tonsillitis, hence the common name of 'Strep throat'.

Bacterial tonsillitis requires antibiotic treatment as it will shorten the infection period and help prevent complications like an abscess and rheumatic fever. Rheumatic fever is very rare in Singapore due to improved nutrition and antibiotic therapy for children with *Streptococcus* infections. It is crucial to ensure that the child completes the full course of antibiotics to eradicate the bacteria. If his condition worsens despite oral antibiotic treatment, he may need to see a doctor to exclude an abscess that may develop from an inadequately treated tonsillitis.

Chronic tonsillitis refers to repeated infections of the tonsils, causing significant swelling and repeated sore throats. It is uncommon and the removal of tonsils (tonsillectomy) is not commonly done.

The tonsils are part of the defence mechanism of the body in the throat guarding and preventing severe infections from gaining entry into and harming the body. As children have sore throat frequently, it is common to find enlarged tonsils in children. In the absence of redness and pain, a big tonsil is harmless and will regress in size as the child grows up. On the other hand, a swollen tonsil may cause of the blockage of his airways at night, causing severe snoring and disturbed sleep at night. This condition known as **obstructive sleep apnoea** can be dangerous. Removal of the child's enlarged tonsils in such situation may provide the relief of the airway obstruction.

Chicken pox and herpes zoster infection

Chicken pox is caused by a highly infectious virus and the spread is airborne. The first time a person catches this virus, he has chicken pox which is characterized by fluid-filled vesicles over the face, trunk and spreading outwards to the limbs. Fever is always present with chicken pox. The fluid in these vesicles may range from colourless to a tinge of golden yellow. At times, the fluid may turn cloudy due to superimposed bacterial infection. When this happens, your child may look sicker and may have higher spiking fever. You should consult your family doctor as with this complication, antibiotic therapy may be necessary.

The fluid-filled vesicles in chicken pox appear in crops. New vesicles may still appear up to 3 days from the appearance of the first vesicle. The older vesicles may dry up quickly and become black scabs over the body.

Locally, misconceptions are rife about what may aggravate scarring in chicken pox. These myths include the need to avoid eating prawns because they are poisonous or consuming dark soya sauce as it may create more scars. There is no scientific evidence for these hearsays. Chicken pox does not cause much scarring albeit a few marks do persist but they are usually not unsightly.

You should let your child bathe when he has chicken pox. This will make him more comfortable and may decrease the risk of secondary bacterial infection setting in. During the bath, warm water and liquid soap will be very soothing. Avoid harsh soaps. Antiseptic soaps do not provide additional advantage. Liquid soap can be soothing as they do not cause painful contact with the vesicles. Pad dry the wet skin with a thick fluffy towel and avoid abrasive rubbing. Calamine lotion may provide additional relief if applied generously over the body.

Chicken pox tends to be more severe when it inflicts an older child. Young children are usually not much affected and they can usually continue to be active, eat well, and play even with the fever and the vesicles. Older children and adults usually have more vesicles and usually feel sicker.

Children with cancer and those on steroid or other immunosuppressive treatment are at risk of severe chicken pox infections. This is because they have impaired body defences against the virus. An otherwise innocuous infection in a normal child can be life threatening in these children. So, if your child has chicken pox, it is best that he should avoid school to prevent spreading the highly infectious virus to other children.

Vaccination has been the best strategy to prevent an infection. Recently in Singapore, the chicken pox vaccine is available at affordable prices. If your child has come down with chicken pox, antiviral therapy is available locally. Acyclovir, famciclovir and valiciclovir are specific antivirals that can decrease the severity of the chicken pox infection. For most children, these antiviral drugs are unnecessary as the infection is mild and self-limiting. Antiviral therapy is crucial in children who have cancer or are on regular steroids as they may have severe chicken pox infection. Older children and adults may benefit from antiviral therapy as well. The antiviral therapy is only useful if started early, within the first 2 days of the appearance of the first vesicles.

Lifelong immunity against chicken pox occurs after a chicken pox infection. Antiviral therapy does not affect this lifelong immunity.

Herpes zoster, more commonly known as 'snake' in Chinese, is due to reactivation of the chicken pox virus hiding in the nerve roots. Our skin is supplied on each side of the body by a nerve root, hence the reactivation of the virus follows the nerve, wrapping around the body and does not cross far beyond the mid-line in front.

The rash of herpes zoster infection resembles the fluid-filled vesicles of chicken pox, but is limited to a specific area as mentioned. The rash can be painful or itchy. It is uncommon for children to have herpes zoster, it may indicate underlying impaired immunity and it is wise to have your child medically assessed.

Chinese folk medicine may use joss sticks to burn the vesicles and various powders to apply onto the zoster rash. This may worsen the rash and cause more pain. The antiviral treatment for chicken pox is highly effective for herpes zoster as well. So, seek proper medical attention early to avoid severe problems that can persist due to inappropriate treatment of herpes zoster.

Heart conditions

Heart disease in children can be frightening to parents. However, there are many heart conditions which are mild, with minimal restriction to physical activities and lifestyle. Conversely, more serious heart conditions can be treated either with medications or surgery, and the paediatric cardiologists (heart specialists) will be able to advise on the necessary treatment and precautions.

Symptoms which may indicate the presence of significant heart disease include poor weight and height gain. Babies with heart failure may have breathlessness at rest, and this is worse during feeding. They may be sweaty and may take a long time to complete their feeds. The volume of feeds is less than that of a normal child of the same age. Such children should be seen by the paediatrician or paediatric cardiologist for an assessment as soon as possible. In addition, any child whose lips appear blue or less pink than normal at any time, must be seen by the paediatrician as soon as possible.

Children with milder heart disease may have mild symptoms of feeling tired easily on exertion or they may be completely asymptomatic and well, and only picked up on screening. One of the first indications of heart disease is often the detection of an abnormal heart sound called a **heart murmur**. This is not always abnormal as innocent murmurs are common in childhood. Innocent murmurs are due to turbulence of blood flow in the blood vessels or in the heart, and they are accentuated with fever, exercise, and excitement. They occur in normal hearts, and parents can be reassured that there is no need for any special precautions or restriction in physical activities. The paediatrician can advise whether the heart murmur is 'innocent' or not.

Common heart diseases include congenital problems such as 'holes in the heart' or abnormal valves which are essential for unidirectional flow of blood in the heart or blood vessels. Any of these conditions can result in inefficient blood flow, so that the heart has to work harder to maintain adequate oxygen delivery to the tissues of the body. If there are holes in the heart or if the heart valve is narrowed or loose and faulty, the primary function of the heart is impaired. The severity of these conditions can vary from mild, moderate to severe, and the treatment will depend on the severity of the conditions.

Some 'holes in the heart' will close spontaneously. Ventricular septal defects are holes in the wall of the heart separating the lower two chambers. Fifty per cent of small ventricular septal defects will close spontaneously. Most ventricular septal defects close during the 1st year of life, but closure does occur later. Occasionally, some holes fail to close. However, with the growth of the heart, the defect which remains the same size becomes relatively smaller. The paediatrician can advise about the follow-up of such problems.

Heart disease can sometimes occur in a previously normal heart. A viral infection can affect the heart and cause symptoms of heart failure, as described. Such cases of viral myocarditis or cardiomyopathy can be serious, and should be assessed by the paediatrician or paediatric cardiologist as soon as possible.

Apart from structural problems of the heart, there can also be rhythm problems when the conduction of impulses within the heart is abnormal. This can result either in a pulse rate which is too slow or too fast. Abnormal rhythm problems can cause palpitations (the sensation of a fast heartbeat), fainting spells, or heart failure. These must be reviewed by a paediatric cardiologist who will perform a rhythm strip to determine the exact rhythm abnormality and decide on the specific treatment.

Many parents whose child has a heart problem are worried whether their child is fit for physical exercise. The decision of exercise restriction will depend on the type and severity of the heart disease. Many children with heart disease can lead normal lives, and such children should not be over-protected. Children with mild heart problems are usually fit for normal, non-competitive exercise. Children with moderate heart problems may occasionally be allowed to join in some physical activities. Children with the same heart disease can pursue different activities, depending on the severity of their heart condition, and this must be appreciated. Discussion about the degree of exercise restriction of the child with the paediatric cardiologist is important.

It is important that parents should inform the school teacher, especially the PE (physical education) teacher, of the heart problem which the child has, and the exercise recommendations prescribed by the paediatric cardiologist. It is also very important to let the child's dentist know. This is because antibiotic coverage is essential for any child with structural heart disease in order to prevent bacterial infections of the heart. Furthermore, it is imperative to tell the dental officer if there are any known allergies to antibiotics, so that the appropriate antibiotics can be prescribed.

Kidney conditions

Kidney diseases can affect children, just as they can affect adults. The kidney is an important organ responsible for re-absorbing water and removing waste products. When the kidneys fail to function properly, there may be symptoms of facial swelling and swelling of the soft tissues around the eyes, swelling of the hands and feet, and increased or decreased frequency of passing urine. The accumulation of toxic waste to the body can adversely affect the growth of the child. Hence, children with chronic renal failure may not grow well and may be short and thin. They may also have non-specific symptoms of tiredness and lethargy. If in doubt, the family doctor can be consulted to perform some simple tests for the child.

Nephrotic syndrome is a common problem in childhood, in which the filtering mechanism of the kidney is damaged, and proteins in the blood can leak out into the urine. The resultant low blood protein fails to draw water from the tissues, causing swelling of the face, hands, and feet. If severe, the abdomen and the scrotum in boys may also become swollen. Since there is excessive loss of protein in the urine, the urine becomes very frothy. These children must be seen by the paediatrician, and treatment will be started as soon as the diagnosis is made. Most children with nephrotic syndrome will recover with medication, although some children will relapse and require further treatment. These children will need to be followed up by the paediatrician.

After a bad sore throat, some children may develop kidney damage, and this is called acute glomerular nephritis. Children with this problem may pass very little urine. They may become overloaded with fluids and develop high blood pressure. These children also have blood in the urine (called haematuria), which can be recognized visibly if the urine is red, and the red cells settle as a sediment after standing in a container. Alternatively, if there is only a small amount of red cells in the urine, the urine may only appear slightly cloudy or smoky. Cloudy urine, however, can be due to phosphates and can be normal. If there is any doubt, it is always good to consult your family doctor who can perform a simple test on a sample of urine to confirm the presence of blood in the urine.

Urinary tract infections can also present with fever, pain, and frequency of passing urine. The urine may be cloudy from the accumulation of white blood cells, casts or sediments, and may, on some occasions, be foul smelling. If these symptoms occur, it is best to see the family doctor who can test a sample of the child's urine and treat the infection with a short course of antibiotics such as amoxycillin and cotrimoxazole. Young children less than 6 years of age, may have a predisposing cause for recurrent urinary tract infections, and it would be prudent to have them investigated by the paediatrician.

Some malformations of the kidney may be asymptomatic, and often discovered only on screening. Single kidneys or abnormal kidney shapes such as horseshoe kidneys are compatible with a normal life, although the paediatrician will be able to provide necessary advice. However, some other malformations of the renal system such as ureteric strictures or posterior urethral valves may cause obstruction to urine flow, causing high backward pressure and large kidneys. These kidneys may be damaged by the high pressure system, and would need surgical correction of the obstruction. Children with these malformations may complain of pain felt deep in the abdomen or in the back because of the enlarged kidney. Alternatively, as described, they may also present with recurrent urinary tract infections, as infection is predisposed when there is stasis of urine in the enlarged kidney.

Childhood diabetes mellitus

Diabetes mellitus occurring in childhood is not common, although the number of children developing this disorder is increasing in Singapore. Most childhood diabetics require daily subcutaneous insulin injections (type 1 diabetes). However, obese children, like obese diabetic adults, can be treated with oral medications (hypoglycaemic agents), and dietary restriction (type 2 diabetes).

Diabetes mellitus is thought to be due to both genetic and environmental factors. Virus infections due to Coxsackie and mumps are known to be associated with type 1 diabetes. Epidemiological studies suggest that breast-feeding is protective against type 1 diabetes in childhood. The role of food factors causing type 1 diabetes is, as yet, unclear.

The symptoms which may suggest that a child has diabetes include excessive thirst, passing urine many times during the day and night, bedwetting, weight loss, and general ill-health. Sometimes, parents are astute enough to realize that there are ants in the toilet bowl. If a child has such symptoms, it is best to consult the family doctor or paediatrician for a check-up.

The initial diagnosis of childhood diabetes mellitus usually comes as a rude shock to the parents and relatives. It is quite common and natural to experience feelings of denial, distrust, anger, frustration, and guilt. However, it is imperative that the parents realize and accept that there was nothing that could have done to prevent the onset of diabetes, and nothing that could have been done to have caused it. This is the very first hurdle to cross, as it lays the path for them to learn all about diabetes. The more the parents learn about diabetes, the less fearful they are of it, and the better they can help their child achieve good control. The aim of good control is to keep the child in good health, and to prevent any long-term complications. These long-term complications such as problems with eyesight, heart and kidney problems, recurrent infections, and loss of sensation in the feet and hands, will only occur if there has been poor control for at least 5 years.

Diabetes mellitus in childhood is a lifelong disorder, and the diabetic child will not grow out of it. However, adjustments in lifestyle can lead to a relatively normal life. These include daily subcutaneous insulin injections for the type 1 diabetics, frequent monitoring of finger prick sugar levels using special monitoring devices. More importantly, attention to diet is important. All children like sweet foods and sugary drinks. These foods can also be taken, but the amounts need to be regulated. There are no forbidden foods, only forbidden portions. The paediatrician, paediatric diabetes nurse educator and dietician can help counsel the parents about this. Eventually, these lifestyle adjustments will become second nature to the parents and their child.

Diabetes mellitus occurring in different age groups will pose different problems. The toddler and preschooler can have a capricious appetite. Some children are fussy eaters, while others eat almost anything put before them. Parents of the latter may have some problems regulating the carbohydrate intake for each meal, and may have to deal with temper tantrums. Parents of the former should not be unduly worried if their child does not complete the meal. Reprimanding and forcing the child to eat may lead to food refusal. Successful parents have used a combination of firmness and discipline coupled with the art of distraction.

Injection times may be very stressful, as one parent will need to hold the child while the other parent administers the injection. It is important for the parents to experience a dry injection, so that they know that it is not painful. Injections should be performed quickly and with minimal fuss. It is also important to explain to the child that the injections are a means of helping him remain healthy and strong, and to emphasize that they are not a form of punishment.

The school-going child has greater autonomy and will experience more peer pressure. It is important for parents to maintain good communication with their diabetic children. At the same time, it is also important not to be overly protective. Diabetic children are first and foremost children who happen to have diabetes. They should be treated like normal children, and not be excessively restricted because of their diabetes.

Children with diabetes should be allowed to participate in physical activities, provided they know how to identify and treat low blood sugar levels. If there are recurrent symptoms of low blood sugar levels, the child can reduce the insulin level after his parents discuss with his paediatrician, or he can increase a portion of food before starting the exercise. It is important that the parents also speak to the school teacher or principal about the child's condition, and what to do when the blood sugar level is low. There should be no secrets, and it would be prudent for the child's classmates to be educated about diabetes, especially to know that it is not infectious.

The adolescent diabetic may encounter several problems which are a part of growing up for every child. Parents need to allow their diabetic child greater independence, and to try to understand his needs during this difficult transition phase. It is very important, during this time, for parents to continue to maintain good relationships with their adolescent diabetic child, so that he knows that their advice and guidance can be sought if needed. Certain rules pertaining to insulin injections cannot be violated, while it also helps to have another set of rules which allows for some flexibility, such as food exchanges. This allows the diabetic child to have some control over his life, instead of always being told what to do all the time. During this phase of growth, it is essential that the adolescent understands the rationale of the rules laid down, and the importance that good control will prevent the onset of complications of diabetes.

The most important principle to remember is that children with diabetes are primarily normal children going through the same stages of life as their peers, and should be treated with the same rules and discipline. Parents should try to focus on their child, and not on his condition. The goal of management is to let these children enjoy as normal a life as possible, and to set the scene for the gradual process of the child taking over the responsibility for his condition, within the framework of good family support.

The current treatment of type 1 diabetes is daily subcutaneous injections of insulin. There is no oral medication to treat type 1 diabetes as attempts to use an oral insulin (which is a protein) only result in digestion of the protein. However, there is always hope that ongoing research will result in novel modalities of treatment for type 1 diabetes.

Allergy

Allergy, one of the most common conditions that plagues children, often causes much distress to parents and grandparents alike. If your child is allergic to some food/ drugs, he is not alone; up to 50 per cent of children seen at clinics have allergy-related illnesses. Questions and misconceptions about this 'disease' are rife among concerned parents — 'Should my child avoid PE (physical education) in school?' or 'He took chocolates and cold drinks in school and these caused the asthmatic attack.' In this section, we will explore the extensive spectrum of childhood allergic diseases and discover the nuts and bolts of this troublesome problem.

An allergic child is unduly sensitive to many things. These, fondly known as **allergens**, include dust (house dust mite), animal fur, and pollens. A normal person may sneeze when exposed to large amounts of airborne dust while an allergic child, on the other hand, is sensitive to even minute quantities of these allergens. An allergic child is thus said to be hypersensitive and it is this 'hypersensitivity' that distinguishes an allergic child from the rest.

What is the spectrum of allergic diseases?

Allergy can manifest in a bewildering myriad of ways. Firstly, it may affect different parts of the body — the nose, eyes, lungs, and skin. Secondly, the severity and the trouble it incites ranges from an unnoticeable mildness to an extreme irritation that disturbs even a child's sleep. Table 13.1 lists some of the common medical labels for allergic diseases.

Table 13.1 Common allergies in children

Type of allergy	Other name	Description
Asthma	Hyperactive airway disease Allergic bronchitis Asthmatic bronchitis	Recurrent wheezing and frequent coughs especially worse at night or in early morning, precipitated by exercise, flu or sore throat
Eczema or allergic dermatitis	Atopic dermatitis	Sensitive, itchy, skin rash which affect the flexures especially the neck, elbow, and knee joints
Allergic rhinitis	Sensitive nose	Changes in temperature and exposure to dust cause a runny nose and may trigger a bout of sneezing
Allergic conjunctivitis	Sensitive eyes	Large amount of tears and itchy eyes that cause excessive blinking

Some children may just have allergy in one system, for example, asthma, while others who are less fortunate may have the full blown allergy affecting all systems.

Asthma

In Singapore, prolonged cough is a taboo feared by many. You may have heard of old wives' tales that chronic cough causes asthma or worst of all, tuberculosis; cough mixtures are very much sought after elixir — some apparently 'more powerful' than others — that when taken early, can prevent asthma. It is in the midst of these fears and misconceptions that you need to be calm and review the problem — what is asthma and what should you do if your child has asthma.

When do I suspect that my child has asthma?

You may suspect that your child has asthma if he has:

- recurrent episodes of wheezing
- cough that takes a long time to go away
- cough while exercising or when it is at night or early morning

Usually, he seems to fall sick easily since young, mostly with cough and 'chest infections', and there is often a family history of asthma or allergy.

How is asthma diagnosed?

If your child has recurrent episodes of wheezing and cough, and he has history of allergic skin or nose, he is most likely to have asthma. In many instances, there is no need for extensive medical tests to prove that your child has asthma.

However, when things are less clear, your doctor may perform a few tests to confirm that your child has asthma. A chest X-ray is recommended if your child is newly diagnosed to have asthma. This helps to exclude other more serious medical conditions like recurrent aspirations (where stomach contents are regurgitated down the windpipe causing irritation and wheezing) or bronchiectasis (where copious amounts of phlegm is produced by markedly dilated airways). Other medical problems like cystic fibrosis are extremely rare among Asians but should be considered in those from Caucasian descent.

What are allergens?

Allergens are seemingly innocuous substances that do not cause problems for normal persons, but may precipitate an asthmatic attack in your asthmatic child. Common allergens include the following:

- Dust that can precipitate an asthmatic attack due to the presence of house dust mite droppings. This is the most common allergen in Singapore.
- Second-hand smoking, where your child inhales the smoke breathed out from someone who has taken a puff of a cigarette, is well known to aggravate asthma. If you or your spouse smokes, it will greatly help your child's condition if you or your spouse quits smoking.
- Viral infections, like sore throats and common colds, may also precipitate an asthmatic attack. It is often difficult, if not impossible, for your child to avoid a viral infection. Good handwashing may help decrease the spread of viruses at home.

What is the underlying problem in asthma?

Asthma results from hypersensitivity to a variety of allergens. Extensive research has confirmed that the inflammation (medical term for swelling) of the airways causes the hypersensitivity in asthmatics. Hence, treatment of asthma has shifted from just treating the wheeze to treating the inflammation — the root cause of the problem — with considerable success.

Previously, treatment was directed only at reversing the wheezing during an acute asthma attack using bronchodilators which relax the airways. Currently, potent non-absorbable steroids are delivered directly into the airways by inhalation and this controls the underlying inflammation. You may have heard or read about the toxic effects of steroids; the steroids in inhalers are specially modified to convert it to be less absorbable, hence they are safe when used under doctor's supervision. Inhaled steroids are important medications that have revolutionized the treatment of asthma in children. With these inhaled steroids, many asthmatics can return to a near normal life, exercising and having no specific restrictions, albeit requiring daily puffs of the inhaler.

The hypersensitive airways go into spasm when exposed to allergens. This widespread constriction of the airways causes turbulence in the flow of air into and out of the lungs, generating the musical wheeze sound heard during an asthmatic attack. This widespread constriction of the airways increases the resistance to airflow, hence adding to the extra effort needed to breathe. Your child may appear to use more of his chest and neck muscles in order to breathe properly during an attack of asthma.

What happens when my child is diagnosed with asthma?

The diagnosis of asthma is feared by many parents. It seems to parents that their child is condemned to countless years of coughing, restricted lifestyle with no chocolate, cold drinks and physical exercise, and terrifying episodes of shortness of breath during an asthmatic attack. These distorted perceptions of the disease, asthma, are far from the truth. With modern asthma therapy, most asthmatics return to a normal, fairly unrestricted lifestyle, albeit with the help of inhaled medications.

How can things be set right?

It is extremely helpful to dispel certain fears and answer some anticipated questions that some parents may have. You may, initially, have the denial that your child has asthma — 'How could my child have asthma when I have taken great care to treat every cough with the best cough mixtures?'

Asthma is a genetic disease. It is not caused by a single gene like the ability to roll the tongue, but probably a number of genes interacting together with environmental factors. If there is family history of asthma, the risk of asthma in your child is greater. Changing the environment factors like getting rid of allergens and cessation of smoking, may help decrease the risk of asthma.

Before you start reproaching yourself for bad genes, the genes for asthma is extremely common — up to 10 per cent of Singaporean children have asthma. We cannot choose our genes — at least not at present — and the genes responsible for asthma are still unknown.

How is the severity of asthma assessed?

Different children suffer from different severity of asthma; some cough and wheeze only once in 6 months, while others may wheeze each time they run, or even as frequently as once a week. Doctors determine the severity of your child's condition and prescribe the appropriate treatment for that severity.

How is asthma treated?

The best treatment of asthma is to reduce the amount of allergens that your child is exposed to. Dust and cigarette smoke are the most common culprits which should be avoided at all cost. The way you can help to decrease dust at home is succinctly summarized in Table 13.2. The way to decrease cigarette smoke is to encourage people not to smoke at home.

Table 13.2 How you can help decrease dust at home

Keep your child's books in cabinets with a glass door so that little dust will settle on them.

Avoid using carpets and furniture with thick, soft covers that trap dust.

Avoid having fluffy soft toys — choose cloth and plastic toys that can be washed easily.

Avoid keeping a pets at home.

Mop the floor frequently (vacuum or sweep the floor stir up dust, so mop first).

Wash your child's bedsheets and pillow case frequently.

Sun your child's pillow and mattress to kill the house dust mites.

The treatment of asthma depends on its severity, the age of your child, and whether he is having an attack of asthma at present.

If your child is less than 5 years old and the asthma is mild, syrups are most helpful as it is easily administered. If his asthma is between moderate and severe, an inhaler is needed as he requires daily treatment with steroids, which are best delivered to the airways using an inhaler. There are many types of inhalers available, each designed with a specific need in mind and different devices (known as spacers) are created for children of different ages.

A **metered dose inhaler (MDI)** delivers a fixed amount of medication each time you depress the trigger. This ensures reliable delivery of the prescribed amount of medication each time. All inhalers in the market are MDIs.

The aerosol MDI has compressed gas inside which expels a fixed amount of medication in aerosolized form when it is depressed. These inhalers require a good hand-mouth coordination to depress the inhaler to inhale at the same time, so that the medication is sucked in and deposited in the airways. This is a difficult but not an impossible task for children less than 7 years old, and only children who use the MDI daily are able to flawlessly coordinate this hand-mouth action to ensure efficient and adequate deposition of the aerosolized medication into the airways.

To overcome this need for coordination, three types of devices are available — spacers which fit onto the conventional aerosol MDI, breath-triggered inhalers, and dry-powder inhalers. Breath-triggered inhalers and dry-powder inhalers do not require coordination as the medication is delivered into the lungs with inhaled air when your child sucks on the mouthpiece.

What are spacers?

Spacers are large volume containers with 1-way valves which allow medications to be drawn into the lungs during inhalation. During expiration, the valves snap shut and prevent the exhaled air from diluting the medications in the chamber. The spacers come with a mouthpiece where your child sucks in the medication through his mouth (e.g. Volumatic® spacer). If your child is younger and cannot breathe through his mouth alone, a mask that fits snugly over your child's mouth and nose will allow the medication to reach his lungs by simple normal breathing. Examples of the mask inhalers are Aerochamber® and Babyhaler®.

Medication via a spacer

How can myths about asthma be dispelled?

Misconceptions about asthma are abound — everyone around you seem to have something to say about asthma. You are probably as confused as anyone else about this common disease, so it is wise to distinguish between the facts and myths.

Inhalers are addictive — when you start your child on an inhaler, he will be an asthmatic for life

Many parents stare in horror when inhalers are prescribed to their child. They often protest that their child's asthma is not as severe as to require an inhaler. Inhalers help to deliver the asthma medication directly into the lungs so that only a small amount of medication is used and fewer side-effects are experienced. The dose delivered by an inhaler is a lot less compared to that taken by the oral route. Inhalers are not addictive; in fact, proper use of steroid inhalers can return a severe asthmatic to an almost normal lifestyle.

Inhalers are used only when your child is diagnosed to have moderate or severe asthma, hence the unfortunate perception that inhalers cause severe asthma. With modern steroid inhalers, good control of asthma with minimal side-effects can be achieved. Many patients find great relief from their crippling symptoms of asthma because of judicious use of steroid inhalers.

Avoiding cold drinks and sour fruit/food can prevent asthma

Asthma is a genetic disease; you cannot get asthma by drinking cold drinks or eating something sour. What cold drinks and sour fruit do is they may irritate your child's airway and trigger off an attack of asthma. This occurs only if your child has a predisposition to asthma. Avoidance of cold drinks and sour fruit may help decrease symptoms in mild asthmatics; in moderate and severe asthmatics, excessive restriction of food will only make your child think that he is sickly — reinforcing a sickly mindset — something which doctors and parents should painstakingly avoid. Judicious use of steroid inhalers can control your child's sensitive airways so that he can take all the food that he likes.

Eczema or allergic dermatitis

Skin allergy or eczema is very common. You may notice that your child's skin is unduly sensitive since young. If his diapers are not changed quickly, rashes will soon develop and they take a long time to go away. Eczema is a form of allergy; hence your child may have other forms of allergies like asthma or allergic nose in addition to eczema.

Eczema is worse in the skin flexures like the neck, the elbow, and behind the knee. It can be extremely itchy and it can be almost impossible to stop your child from scratching it, despite countless threats that you may hurl at him. The eczematous skin is usually thickened, red, and scaly. Scratching, though initially relieves the itch, will aggravate the eczema, further causing a viscious cycle of worsening eczema. The only way to treat eczema is to break this viscious cycle of scratching.

Firstly, you need to stop your child's scratching habit and change it to 'apply some cream' habit when he feels itchy. Steroid cream provides rapid and effective relief from the itch and help reduce the eczema. Depending on the severity and site of the eczema, your doctor may prescribe your child steroid cream of different potency. Once the eczema is controlled and the skin is no longer red and inflamed, you should change to a bland moisturizer instead as excessive steroid cream may thin your child's skin. From then on, if your child feels the need to scratch, you should encourage him to apply the moisturizer instead. If the redness appears again, revert to the steroid cream until it is better.

Eczema is also aggravated by strong soap and perfume. You should consider a bland and mild soap like baby soap or even soap with moisturizer like Dove®, as these will not irritate the skin and will not deplete your child's natural skin oils. A moisturizer is useful as it prevents the skin from drying and cracking; when the skin cracks due to dryness, it begins to itch and the viscious cycle of eczema starts again.

Except for young babies, food allergy is less likely to cause eczema, so you do not need to be very strict about restricting his food intake. With proper skin care, bland soap and judicious use of steroid cream, most eczema can be managed with ease.

Allergic rhinitis or sensitive nose

You may notice that your child's nose is extremely sensitive to dust, viral infections and changes in temperature, and he will sneeze and develop runny or blocked nose when he is exposed to these allergens.

As with all types of allergies, allergic rhinitis is extremely common. You may notice that your child seems to have perpetual blocked nose and breathes through his mouth instead of his nose. He may rub his nose so frequently that it is constantly red or a horizontal crease develops just above the tip of his nose. The problem may appear worse in the early morning or at night.

Allergic rhinitis, though an irritating problem, does not affect your child's health. Avoidance of dust and smoke will go a long way to decrease a lot of problems (see Table 13.2). Try to remove all carpets at home, change your bedsheets weekly and sun the mattresses frequently to get rid of house dust mite. Cigarette smoke will undoubtedly make things worse and should be avoided at all cost.

Antihistamines are commonly used to treat allergic rhinitis. Some of them like promethazine and chlorpheniramine, can cause your child to be drowsy, but may help provide the much needed rest. They tend to be more useful at night to help your child get a good night's rest. Prolonged daily treatment is not necessarily better and does not change the severity of the allergy itself.

Non-sedating antihistamines do not cause drowsiness but is usually less effective and may be more useful during the day. Your doctor may prescribe ketotifen for your child. Ketotifen must be taken daily (the syrup form is taken twice a day) and may, in some children, help decrease the allergic rhinitis. It is, however, quite costly and may not be effective in some children.

Steroid nasal sprays are more effective but its use may come with some side-effects. Young children do not like these liquid sprays as it has to be squirted directly into the nose. A dry powder inhaler may be less threatening, if you can get your child to cooperate.

Allergic conjunctivitis

Your child's eyes too may be sensitive to various

allergens like dust and dry air. This makes his eyes incredibly itchy and no matter how you try to stop him, he cannot stop rubbing his eyes. In less severe situations, he will tear and blink excessively to try to relieve the itch. Sometimes, the eyes may be red and congested.

Contact lenses, especially soft lenses with thiomersal preservatives, may cause the allergy to be worse. Protein deposits and thiomersal preservatives will accumulate on the soft contact lenses, making them less suitable for older children with allergic conjunctivitis.

Allergic conjunctivitis can be easily treated with topical eye drops. In milder allergies, cromolyn sodium eyedrops are extremely helpful with no major side-effects. For children with severe allergic conjunctivitis, steroid eyedrops are more potent and efficacious. Different strengths of steroid eyedrops are available; you should contact your family doctor for a fuller assessment.

LEE Woon Kwang

Introduction

Children often fall sick every now and then, especially after they are more than 6 months old when the antibodies which their mothers passed on to them during the pregnancy start to decline. Antibodies are substances in our blood which help us fight off infections and they are developed in our bodies each time we have an infection. Children do not produce antibodies themselves unless and until they get infections. However, during infancy, they get protection against infections from the antibodies their mothers passed on to them during the pregnancy.

In most instances, infections are due to viruses which cause illnesses like the common cough and cold (flu), diarrhoea (gastric flu), roseola (false measles), or mouth ulcers. At times, they are caused by bacterial infections such as tonsillitis, middle ear infection, pneumonia (infection of the lungs), urinary tract infection, or more serious infections like septicemia (infection in the blood) and meningitis (infection of the coverings of the brain). Each time a child gets an infection, he develops antibodies (immunity) against the particular infective agent. Slowly as time goes by, he will get more infections and hence develops more protective antibodies until he has encountered most of the common viruses and bacteria in the community he lives in. From then on, he will get sick less frequently as his immunity against these infections have developed.

It is not uncommon for parents to complain that their child always gets sick when they first send him to a day care centre or nursery. This is especially so if the child had not been sick often and hence has not built up much immunity. But once he gets all the viruses and bacterial infections which are going around in the day care centre or nursery, he will become sick less often as he builds up his immunity each time he falls sick. It may take 6–9 months after attending the day care centre or nursery for the child to get used to these infective illnesses. So, young children are expected to get sick every now and then until they are about 5–6 years old.

Teething has often been blamed for causing fever and diarrhoea in children. It actually does not cause anything other than some irritability. What actually happens is that teething often occurs at the age (i.e. from after 6 months old to about 3 years old) when a child is prone to infections. The two often occur at the same time and we wrongly blame teething for all the symptoms associated with the infections. Therefore, when your child is sick, always look for an infection somewhere rather than just blame it on teething.

Common illnesses

When a child has fever, vomiting, diarrhoea, cough or

runny nose, it is obvious that the child is sick. Sometimes, the sick child may not have many of these symptoms, but his parents will notice some subtle changes in his behaviour like decreased activity, loss of appetite, sleep disturbances, irritability, restlessness, or temper tantrums.

Recognizing that your child is sick

At times, you may not be able to pinpoint what is actually wrong with your child except to say that he is not like his usual self and this is enough to tell them that their child is not well. As you know your child better than the doctor, you are often in a better position than the doctor to know whether your child is sick or not.

The severity of the illness

When your child is sick, how do you tell how sick he is? Is it safe to observe him at home or should you bring him to see the doctor straightaway? Generally speaking, if your child's temperature is below 39.5°C and he is still quite active, can still play and is interested in the surroundings, it is quite safe to treat him at home. Make sure that he takes enough fluid to prevent dehydration (lack of water in the body) as it can make him quite sick. He may feel a bit dull when the fever has gone up, but if he brightens up and behaves quite normally after you have brought the fever down with antipyretic (fever medicine), you can be reassured that his condition is not that serious.

However, if your child is irritable, lethargic, drowsy, or listless with no interest in the surroundings or in play, you should consult a doctor even if his temperature is only low grade, as these symptoms would indicate that your child may have serious underlining illness which needs immediate medical attention. If your child has fever and his hands and feet are turning blue or dusky or he starts to shiver, he should see a doctor. So, it is not how high the fever is that is important, but how your child behaves when he has fever. You should also be concerned if his fever is above 39.5°C or if you are unable to bring down the temperature by the usual means. When his general condition has deteriorated suddenly, you should be worried even if you have brought him to see the doctor earlier.

The younger your child, the more concerned you should be when he is unwell. If your child is less than 6 months old, you should bring him to consult a doctor more liberally. Never 'wait till tomorrow morning' to see a doctor if your child is less 6 weeks and has fever. Consult a doctor straightaway as he may need urgent medical treatment. He will most likely be admitted to hospital for investigations, treatment, and observation. Your baby may not seem very sick initially, but he can deteriorate very fast and may become seriously ill within a few hours. That is why you must bring him to see the doctor straightaway. Newborn babies and infants can have normal body temperature as high as 37.5°C. Any temperature above this should be considered fever, although some people will argue that a normal baby's temperature can goes as high as 38.0°C. However, it is not worth the risk waiting till the temperature reaches that level before consulting the doctor.

Incidentally, the temperature should be taken by placing either a mercury or a digital thermometer under the armpit. Rectal temperature is seldom used these days. Do not use a thermal scanner applied over the forehead. It does not give an accurate reading. Infra-red scanner placed in the ear is accurate if used correctly.

At home

For a start, you can make him comfortable by putting the child in a cool and airy place. The clothings should be light, loose, and comfortable. Staying in an air-conditioned room is fine provided it is not so cold that it would cause the child to shiver. A room temperature of 24.0–25.0°C is ideal. If there is no air conditioning in the house, turning on an oscillating fan will also help. There is no need to restrict his activity, but strenuous exercise should be discouraged. Try to get him to rest as much as possible as this will help in speeding up the recovery of the illness.

Your child's appetite is likely to decrease and he may refuse to take any solids at all. This is all right provided he takes enough fluid to avoid dehydration. If your child does not eat much for a few days while he is sick, he will not be growing during this period of time. You should not be too concerned as he will start to grow again once he recovers and starts eating.

Meanwhile, he should not be allowed to get dehydrated as it can make him become more ill. Therefore, you must encourage your child to take fluids frequently to prevent dehydration. If your child is dehydrated, he will not pass much urine and it will be dark yellow or brown in colour (i.e. concentrated urine). If your child is a young baby, you will notice that his anterior fontanelle (the soft spot on top of the head) is sunken.

As long as he passes urine at least once every 4–5 hourly and the urine is colourless or only slightly yellow in colour, you can be certain that your child is reasonably hydrated. Nowadays, disposable nappies are commonly used among babies. You may not be certain about the number of times your babies passes urine. Generally, his nappies should at least be wet once in the morning, in the afternoon and in the evening to indicate adequate urinary flow.

It is important that each time you offer your child a drink, make sure that it contains some form of sugar or carbohydrate (starch) such as rice water, potato or pea soup, as the body requires energy to function probably. Normally, the body burns sugar to provide the energy. When the body's sugar decreases and is not replenished, it will start burning fat, the end product of which is acid production. As the body does not eliminate the acid easily, it will accumulate and make the body very sick. The symptoms of too much acid in the body are nausea, vomiting, rapid breathing, and lethargy. All these will make the child take in even less fluids and sugar, thus starting a vicious cycle of not eating and getting more and more acidotic.

Dehydration will also increase the temperature of the body, making the child more miserable. Therefore, you need to replenish the child's fluids and sugar at every opportunity. Flat soft drink (i.e. soft drink that has its gas shaken out), commercial packet drinks, milk, boiled rice water, potato or pea soup should provide adequate source of sugar if given frequent enough to prevent dehydration. Unless your child is taking some food, plain water should be discouraged as it does not contain any calories.

Children are often difficult to look after when they are sick. They are usually cranky and can be very demanding especially at night when the fever tends to be higher than that in the daytime. Many of them will actually 'regress' to a younger age and become more dependent on others. Some of them will stay up all night crying and moaning away. Others will want to be carried and rocked throughout the night. These can last for days until they recover from the illness. During this period, it can be quite tiring for the parents who not only have to cope with looking after the demanding sick child, but also have to attend to their own daily chores and work. Therefore, if possible, you or your spouse should take leave from work to look after your child. Try to take a nap when your child is sleeping during the daytime and leave the housework to the last.

After dinner, the parent on 'night shift' should also take a nap while the other attends to the sick child's needs. The message is to rest as much as you can and when you can, so that you will not be over-tired. Remember that when one is too tired, one's patience decreases and temper often flares up easily. It is very important that both you and your spouse understand this point and be more tolerant towards one another.

At the hospital

Sometimes, when you take your child to see the doctor, he may consider your child sick enough to warrant admission to hospital for investigations, treatment and/ or observation. Hospitalization can be a very stressful and traumatic experience for a sick child. To minimize the stress and trauma, it is important that at least one parent or someone whom your child is familiar and comfortable with accompanies him at the hospital throughout the stay even if this means taking time off from work. Rather than leaving it to the nurses to do all the caring for your child, try to get involved with the daily routine like feeding, changing nappy, bathing, or even giving medication under supervision. Your involvement with these activities will help your child feel more secure in the unfamiliar environment and help in his recovery. If possible, stay beside him when procedures like blood taking, injection, or dressing are done.

Bring along objects which your child is particularly attached to — things like his favourite teddy bear, pillow, towel, or toys. These items will make him feel more comfortable and secure. Bring along his favourite story books and read to him. If his medical condition permits, try to get your child involved in the playroom activities (if these are provided at the hospital) as this will make his stay in the hospital more pleasant and less traumatic.

Family physician versus paediatrician

Sometimes, you cannot decide whether to bring your sick child to see the family physician or a specialist. Generally speaking, if you are comfortable with the family physician, you should turn to him for consultation. The doctor may refer your child to a specialist if he thinks it is necessary. If your child has some pre-existing illness under the care of a specialist and his current symptoms are associated with the illness, you should consult the specialist first. He may direct you to see your family physician if he thinks the physician can handle the illness. If your child is less than 6 weeks old, it is better that he sees a paediatrician as many family physicians are not familiar with illnesses of the very young. If the newborn baby has fever, he will need admission to hospital for investigations and treatment under a paediatrician.

Medical emergency

There are occasions when a child's illness becomes a medical emergency when immediate medical attention, treatment, and hospitalization is necessary. When your child becomes drowsy, lethargic, listless, confused, unconscious, throws a fit or is having breathing difficulty, it is obvious that you should treat these as medical emergencies and take him to see a doctor straightaway. There are times when medical emergency may not be so obvious to you. For example, when your child has been having recurrent vomiting/diarrhoea for a few days and later develops sunken eyes together with decreasing urine output, he is actually quite sick. You should treat this as an emergency and send him to see a doctor, especially if he develops rapid and heavy breathing at the same time. This breathing pattern suggests that he is getting acidotic (too much acid in the body) and will require urgent fluids and electrolytes replacement in the hospital.

At times, you may want to treat a child with minor cough and cold at home. But if his fever and/or cough gets worse and he is having some difficulty in breathing, he may be developing pneumonia (infection of the lungs) and needs to see a doctor straightaway. Generally speaking, if a sick child is inactive and disinterested with the surroundings, with poor intake of fluids and little urine output, you should treat his condition as a medical emergency. In general, the younger the child, the more concerned you should be. However, there are times when you need to attend to the child's emergency first before you take him to the doctor.

Choking

Children, especially young babies, like to put things into their mouths. This is part of the developmental milestone they go through. It is called 'mouthing'. Unfortunately, a child may accidentally shallow or inhale the foreign body, causing obstruction of the airway or windpipe. He then starts to choke and may becomes breathless or wheezy. If he can cough, cry or talk, the airway is not dangerously obstructed and it is better that you do not attempt to remove the foreign body yourself. Take him to see a doctor straightaway. However, if he has breathing difficulty and is turning blue or is becoming unconscious, turn him face down on your lap and give his back four or five hard blows between the shoulder blades immediately.

If this procedure fails to relieve the child's problem, flip him over and place him on the floor. With the palms of your hands on either side of the lower part of the child's chest, give a sudden and forceful downwards and inwards compression. If this fails in the first attempt, you may alternate the two procedures for a few times. This will often help to dislodge the foreign body.

Another method that can be tried on an older child is to stand behind him and wrap your arms around his waist. Rest a fisted hand on the upper part of the abdomen and grasping the fist with the other hand, make a quick and sudden upward thrust. You may repeat the procedure if you fail to dislodge the foreign body the first time. This latter manoeuvre should not be tried on a baby or small child as there is a risk of injuring the internal organs in these children. Should all these fail, call for urgent medical assistance.

Never try to fish out a foreign body with your finger unless you are sure that you can get around it as there is a great risk that you will push it further back, causing more severe obstruction.

Peanuts is one of the commonest causes of foreign body in the lungs of children. Therefore, children less than 5 years old should not be given peanuts to eat unless it is in the form of peanut butter.

Accidental ingestion

Accidental ingestion of any chemical or medicine should always be treated as a medical emergency.

Children are always curious and are exploring all the time. When they get their hands on anything, they will put it into their mouth to taste it. Therefore, it is very important that you keep all harmful chemicals and medicine out of their reach. Always read the label and instruction on the bottle before giving any medicine to your child.

Should your child ingest any chemical or wrong amount of medicine, always contact your doctor or the nearest hospital by phone for advice. Make sure you have the following information ready — name of the substance or medicine and their ingredients, the amount taken, the time taken, and the age of your child. Report any symptom that your child may have like vomiting, breathing difficulty, or drowsiness. These information will help the person you speak with make a quick assessment of the situation and give advice accordingly. Never try to induce vomiting without first seeking medical advice and never do it under any circumstance when the child is drowsy or unconscious. When the child is conscious, you may get him to drink a lot of water or milk to dilute the poison. When you take your child to a doctor or a hospital, make sure that you bring along the container of the chemical or medicine, so that the active ingredients can be identified and proper treatment be given.

Specific antidotes are not available for most instances of accidental drug ingestion. What the doctor can do is to remove the ingested substance as quickly as possible before it is absorbed into the body. If your child is conscious and the chemical ingested is not corrosive, the doctor may induce your child to vomit be giving him 'peca'. If there is any impairment of the level of consciousness, your doctor may decide to do a stomach washout. This involve passing a tube from the mouth into the stomach to suck out all the stomach contents. Water is then introduced into the stomach and its contents are sucked out again. This is repeated until the aspirate from the stomach becomes clear. Following this, activated charcoal is often given unless there is some specific oral antidote. Generally speaking, your child will be admitted for further medical treatment and observation.

Burns and scalds

Unfortunately, accidental burns and scalds still occur in children — many of which are preventable. Often, these things happen in the kitchen during the cooking hours. Therefore, children should not be allowed in the kitchen during these periods. All hot pots and pans should be kept out of the reach of children. They should not be placed on top of the table covered with cloth which is within the reach of children.

Another common cause of burn is hot iron. Children should not be in the same room where ironing is being done and a hot iron must be placed out of reach of them.

When burn or scalding occurs, the first thing to do is to run cold tap water onto the burned site for about 10 minutes to cool down the burned area so as to prevent further damage to the skin. It will also help to alleviate the pain. Later, cover the burned area with a clean cloth. Do not apply anything on it. Do not prick the blister if any develops. You may give him some paracetamol to further relieve the pain. Take your child to see a doctor at once for assessment of the extent of the burn and treatment. He may advise hospitalization.

Head injury

Head injury resulting from a fall or due to being hit by an object is a frequent event in childhood. Often, a child will cry for a little while and then continues with whatever he was doing earlier. While crying, he may vomit one or twice. This is quite normal. Sometimes, you may find a bruise or swelling on the scalp. The latter is due to some bleeding underneath the skin. It is best managed by applying a cold compress over the lump. Do not massage it as this may cause more bleeding.

Most head injuries are not associated with concussion or damage to the brain and can be observed at home. However, should any of the following symptoms occur, you must bring your child to see a doctor straightaway — loss of consciousness (even if it is only momentarily), drowsiness, confusion, irritability, severe headache, persistent vomiting, fit, weakness of any limb, or unsteady gait. It becomes urgent if the pupils (the circular opening in the centre of the eyes) are unequal as this is an ominous sign.

If his level of consciousness fluctuates or when his breathing pattern is abnormal during sleep, you should also be concerned. Many parents are worried when their child falls asleep following a head injury. Getting sleepy after crying from a head injury is very common and you need not be too concerned provided that your child breathes normally and his colour is good. When he is awake, he should be alert and should behave normally.

Parents often ask for an X-ray of the skull to be done when their child has a head injury. Generally speaking, if your child has none of the symptoms mentioned earlier, he does not need an X-ray. Furthermore, a fracture skull does not necessarily mean brain injury. On the other hand, many head injuries with brain damage do not have skull fracture. However, they will have some of the symptoms mentioned above. Therefore, it is important to look out for them and consult the doctor when they occur. Brain injury can be confirmed by computed tomography (CT) scan (which is rather costly) and it is usually done only if the child has symptoms suggestive of brain injury.

Convulsion

A convulsion or fit is due to sudden outburst of abnormal electrical activity of the brain, causing spasmodic or jerky muscular contractions and transient loss of consciousness. During the attack, the child can stop breathing and turn dusty in colour due to lack of oxygen. Fortunately, this cessation of breathing is only transient and the child will soon start to breathe again. Mouth-to-mouth resuscitation may be given during the dusty episode, but is often unnecessary. Most fits will last only for a few minutes. Often, parents are understandingly panicky when their child throws a fit and will rush to take the child to a clinic or a hospital. This is not necessary. Manage the fit as mentioned above and take the child to the doctor only after the fit has subsided. However, if the fit lasts more than 20 minutes, you should consult your doctor and take him to the nearest clinic or hospital.

A convulsion can be due to many causes, but by far, the commonest one in children is febrile fit mentioned earlier. It can also be due to meningitis or encephalitis (infection of the brain). These are serious medical conditions which need urgent medical attention. A child with these conditions is often lethargic and listless with altered level of consciousness, unlike one with febrile convulsion who is usually alert and active before and soon after the fit.

There are times when medical emergencies may be less obvious to the parents. For example, a child may be observed at home for vomiting and diarrhoea or fever. When he starts to breathe fast and/or heavily and becomes lethargic, it is likely that he is getting dehydrated and acidotic (excessive accumulation of acid in the body) and is in need of urgent medical treatment. Any delay in medical consultation in situations like this may have serious consequences. Occasional vomiting or regurgitation is a very common thing amongst children and are usually no cause for concern. But if they are associated with stomachache or symptoms of dehydration and weight loss, medical attention should be obtained. Any vomiting which shows a yellowish or greenish liquid is also a medical emergency.

Generally speaking, it is wise to treat any deterioration of the child's medical condition at home as an emergency, especially if the child is a baby and the deterioration is sudden. Never put off the consultation in such circumstances just because you are too busy or it is not convenient at that moment. It can be a matter of life and death. Over the years, many lives could have been saved if only the sick children were brought to see the doctors earlier.

15
Medications

K VELLAYAPPAN & YIP Chin Ling William

All parents would like to have some medicines ready on standby to be given immediately to their child when he becomes sick. It may be all right to do so on most occasions but sometimes, it may mask the signs of a serious illness. The symptoms a child develops are warning signs of an illness. It is important to be aware of what these illnesses are. For example, the parents with a child who has asthma may know exactly what to do and what medicines to give when he gets an attack. The treatment plan will have been formulated by his doctor. On the other hand, a 1-month-old child with high fever may have meningitis (inflammation of the covering membranes of the brain). If his parents give him fever medicine, they are treating the fever and not the disease, which may be fatal if not treated promptly.

It is important for parents to realize that their baby is growing every day, and there is a tremendous increase in size in the 1st year and dosages of drugs will vary according to body weight and surface area. In a family, there may be two or three children of different ages and sizes. The appropriate dosage will definitely be different for each particular child. It is essential for parents to know that certain diseases may alter drug metabolism and excretion. Most drugs are excreted through the kidneys or livers. In general, in very young children especially those of less than 6 months old, this has to be taken into account when medicines are given.

Common over-the-counter medications and indications

There are minor complaints like fever, cough and runny nose which parents feel able to deal with or without consulting the doctor. Over-the-counter medications (those not requiring prescriptions) can be quite easily obtained for self-medication. Parents, however, should exercise caution in the use of these common medications as all drugs can give rise to side-effects.

Fever medicines (Antipyretics)

Antipyretics is the most commonly prescribed medicine which every parent should have at home. There are so many different types of fever medicines and they come in different colours and different strengths. They are available as syrups, suspensions, droplets, and suppositories. The basic chemical ingredients is paracetamol (acethaminophen). It is not abnormal for a child between 6 months and 2 years of age to get an average of 6–9 infections per year. These infections are usually due to viruses and fever is the commonest symptom. It may last 3–5 days.

During viral infections, the body temperature is being raised beyond the normal of 37–37.5°C. In order to make a child's environment unsuitable for the invader, mildly raised body temperature is good for him. However, when the fever becomes higher, for example, 38.5–39°C, the child becomes listless and irritable. In some children, a sudden high rise in temperature may precipitate a fit (convulsion). In viral infections, the child usually appears well. In other serious bacterial infections, for example, urinary tract infection, pneumonia and meningitis, the child appears unwell and very sick. You may give fever medicines to your child if he is more than 6 months old and appears well otherwise, apart from fever. In viral infections, the fever may rise every 4–6 hours and at times, may be high especially at night.

As a parent, you must be familiar with the fever medicines you are giving to your child. There are so many different types of fever medicines produced by different manufacturers. What is important for you to know is the strength of the medicine, that is, 50 mg/ml, 100 mg/ml or 120 mg/ml. In general, you should give 10–15 mg/kg/per dose every 4–6 hours. For a 10-kg child, you should give between 100 mg and 150 mg per dose (Table 15.1).

Table 15.1 Dosages of paracetamol according to preparations and body weight

Preparation	Strength	(5 kg)	(10 kg)	(15 kg)	(20 kg)
A	250 mg/5 ml	1 ml	2.5 ml	3–3.5 ml	5 ml
B	500 mg/5 ml	0.5 ml	1.5 ml	2 ml	2.5 ml
C	120 mg/5 ml	2 ml	5 ml	7.5 ml	10 ml
D	80 mg/0.8 ml	0.4 ml	1.2 ml	1.6 ml	2.4 ml
		$^1/_2$ dropper	$1^1/_2$ droppers	2 droppers	3 droppers

Most children can tolerate paracetamol well when prescribed in the appropriate dosage. Some children may vomit because of the unpleasant taste. For these children, paracetamol is available in the form of suppositories. Few may develop allergic reactions, especially in the form of a generalized rash which is usually itchy. The allergy may sometimes be due to the carrier medium of the syrup, rather than the paracetamol itself. For these children, paracetamol tablets may be given. Some are truly allergic to paracetamol and other forms of fever medicines may have to be given, for example, Ibuprofen and Mefenamic acid.

Some anxious parents may unwittingly give excessive quantity of paracetamol because their child's fever fails to settle with the usual dosage. As a result of the administration of paracetamol at higher strength or at shorter intervals, overdosage ensues toxic level of paracetamol in the blood and will cause inflammation in the liver, resulting in jaundice and sometimes, fatal liver failure.

One question often asked by most parents is: 'If my child vomits after taking paracetamol, is it safe for me to repeat the dose?' It depends on how soon and how much the child has vomited. If he has vomited immediately, the dose can be repeated. If he has vomited 1 hour after having taken paracetamol, half the dose of paracetamol can be given if he still has a fever. Always consult your doctor if you are uncertain of what to do.

Fever medicines are generally safe when used in the prescribed manner. If a child is truly allergic to paracetamol, alternative fever medicines are usually prescribed by the doctor.

Cough and cough medicines

When a child suffers from an upper respiratory tract infection, he develops not only fever, but also runny nose and cough. Mild runny nose and cough need not be treated. However, if he suffers from marked congestion of the nose and airways, medical relief is helpful. These mixtures belong to the class of medicines called antihistamines. As for fever medicines, there are many available preparations. It is important for parents to be familiar with one or two medications.

The different antihistamines include Promethazine (Phenergan, Xepagan) Dexchlorpheniramine (Polaramine), and Chlorpheniramine (Piriton). Common 'cough preparations' usually include an antihistamine and ephedrine and sometimes codeine. Some 'cough mixtures' include a mucolytic (medicine for 'dissolving' phlegm). In general, it is not advisable to give young children preparations of cough mixtures containing codeine. As codeine may suppress respiration, a child may literally be drown in his own secretions. Cough mixtures with codeine should only be given after consulting a doctor.

Common cough mixtures are Benadryl cough syrup which contains Diphenhydramine, Ammonium Chloride, and Menthol. Sudafed expectorant contains Pseudoephedrine with Guaifenesin. Pure mucolytics are available as Bisolvon, Fluimucil, Mucosolvan, and Rhinathiol.

Diarrhoea medicines

In general, a child with diarrhoea usually do not require medications. He needs to be given some clear liquids, for example, a mixture of glucose and salt solution (Paedialyte, Gesus, Repalyte, Servidrat) or rice water. He needs to avoid cow's milk for a few days or has cow's milk substituted with soya bean milk or milk low in fat and lactose. Diarrhoea in children is usually due to viruses causing infection in the intestines (gastroenteritis).

Smecta, which comes in the form of sachets, can be given to a child (by mixing with water or milk). It possesses a powerful coating property on the gastrointestinal mucosa. It increases the resistance of the mucosal gel in response to infective agents. Another commonly used drug is Lacteol forte which is actually the metabolic product of killed lactobacillus acidophilus. It aids in restoring the normal flora of the intestines. Some doctors advise on the use of Kaolin. It is usually of little value in the treatment of gastroenteritis in children.

Wind medicines

Babies, especially those below 3 months of age, may develop bouts of incessant crying during the night. This is thought to be due to trapped air in the intestines. The commonly used medicine is Simethicone (Infacol). It can be added to milk or given separately few minutes before a feed.

Laxatives

Laxatives should not be used routinely. The dietary method of treating 'constipation' is best with a lot of fluids, vegetables and fruit. Inspite of these measures, some children are really constipated. They may benefit from preparations like Fybogel and Lactulose. In older children, you may use preparations like Liquid Paraffin occasionally. Suppositories (Dulcolax, Glycerine) to evacuate the hard stools may be used at times.

Vitamins and minerals

If a child takes a balanced diet, additional vitamins and minerals are not necessary. Most milks are fortified with vitamins, minerals, and iron. For premature babies, children not feeding well and failing to gain weight and those not on a balanced diet, vitamin preparations may be useful. Most vitamin preparations are safe and it is best to stick to one. Some parents, hoping that their child will put on weight quickly, give two or three types of vitamin preparations a day. This is an unhealthy practice as some fat soluble vitamins (A, D, E, K) may get deposited in the body and cause untoward side-effects.

Common prescriptions and indications

Of the common medications that can be obtained with a doctor's prescription are those used for the treatment of bacterial infections and asthma. Medicines like these should only be used with professional advice. They should only be used for proper indications and with good knowledge of the side-effects and special precautions for those children with other co-existing medical problems.

It is wise to let your doctor know if your baby is already taking some medications. He may decide to change the medicines or alter the dosage. Do ask your doctor about the possible effects or side-effects of the medicine prescribed.

Other fever medicines

If a child is truly allergic to paracetamol, the doctor has to prescribe other types of fever medicines.

Ibuprofen (Brufen)

Ibuprofen is an alternative to paracetamol. It is to be prescribed with caution to babies below 6 months old. It comes in the strength of 100mg/5ml (i.e. 1 ml = 20 mg). The dosage prescribed is 5mg/kg/dose every 6–8 hourly (Table 15.2).

Table 15.2 Dosages of Ibuprofen according to body weight

Weight	Dosage	Dosage
5 kg	25 mg	1.25 ml
10 kg	50 mg	2.5 ml
15 kg	75 mg	3.5 ml
20 kg	100 mg	5 ml
25 kg	125 mg	6 ml

Most children tolerate Brufen well. Some, however, may be allergic to it and develop a generalized itchy rash. Other side-effects include nausea, vomiting, abdominal cramps, headache, and tiffitus (pain and noise in the ears). If a child is given an overdosage of Brufen, depression of the central nervous system function may occur, resulting in drowsiness. Depression of the respiratory system may also occur, resulting in the child breathing slowly.

Mefenamic acid (Ponstan)

Mefenamic acid is another medicine which can be used for children with fever but who are allergic to paracetamol. Ponstan is also effective for headache, abdominal pain, and muscle ache. It should be used with caution in babies below 6 months old. It comes in the strength of 50 mg/5 ml (i.e. 1 ml = 10 mg). The dosage prescribed is 6.5 mg/kg/dose every 6–8 hourly (Table 15.3).

Table 15.3 Dosages of Mefenamic acid according to body weight

Weight	Dosage	Dosage
5 kg	32.5 mg	3 ml
10 kg	65 mg	7 ml
15 kg	97.5 mg	10 ml
20 kg	130 mg	13 ml
25 kg	162.5 mg	16 ml

Side-effects of Ponstan include diarrhoea, rashes, and drowsiness.

Diclofenac sodium (Voltaren)

Some children mount up a very high fever with certain infections while a proportion of these children may develop a fit (febrile fit or febrile convulsion). For these children, it is advisable to use an effective medical preparation to bring down the fever quickly. Over the past few years, one such available medicine is Voltaren suppository. This medicine is usually used in adults with rheumatism. It has an anti-inflammation action and has the capacity to bring down the fever quickly. It is to be used with caution in children below 1 year of age. The suppository comes in two strengths — 12.5 mg/suppository and 25 mg/suppository. The dosage is 0.5–1 mg/kg/dose, given usually 8 hours apart. Side-effects include profuse sweating, headache, giddiness, bleeding from stomach. It has to be used with extreme caution in children with asthma and gastroenteritis (Table 15.4).

Table 15.4 Dosages of Diclofenac Sodium according to body weight

Weight	Dosage	12.5 mg suppository	25 mg suppository
10 kg	5–10 mg	$^1/_2$–$^3/_4$ suppository	–
12 kg	6–12 mg	$^1/_2$–1 suppository	$^1/_2$ suppository
15 kg	7.5–15 mg	$^3/_4$–1 suppository	$^2/_3$ suppository
18 kg	9–18 mg	1–1$^1/_2$ suppositories	$^3/_4$ suppository
20 kg	10–20 mg	1–1$^1/_2$ suppositories	$^3/_4$ suppository
25 kg	12.5–25 mg	1–2 suppositories	$^1/_2$–1 suppository

Antibiotics

Most infections in children are due to viruses. Children usually get better with medicines to relieve the symptoms. Though some doctors use antiviral preparations, these are usually not necessary. Ensure adequate nutrition so that a child's own immune responses can get rid of the viruses. In about 20–30 per cent of children, the infection may be due to bacteria in which a doctor usually prescribes an antibiotic. Sometimes, doctors cannot be absolutely sure that the infective agent is viral or bacterial. Thus, an antibiotic is prescribed. Some parents request the doctor to prescribe an antibiotic each time their child has a fever. In most cases, antibiotics are unnecessary. They are used for proven and suspected bacterial infection.

Macrolides

Erythromycin is the commonest example in this group. There are many preparations and they come in different strengths and colours. The usual dosage is 30–50 mg/kg/day and it is best taken before meals, three or four times a day. It is concentrated in the liver and excreted in the bile. It is usually used in infections of the respiratory tract like a throat infection, bronchitis, or infections caused by the germ called **mycoplasma**.

The Penicillins

The most commonly used synthetic penicillin is amoxicillin and it normally comes in two strengths — 125 mg/5ml and 250 mg/5ml. It is a broad spectrum penicillin and is active against infections caused by streptococcus, staphylococcus, E. coli, proteus, and salmonella. Depending on the severity of the infection, it is used at a dosage of 35–100 mg/kg/day given three times a day. It is given for infection of the respiratory tract, middle ear infection, urinary tract infection, and infection of the gastrointestinal tract.

The Cephalosporins

This group of antibiotics are used in the treatment of the respiratory tract infection, urinary tract infection, middle ear infection, and skin infection. One of the commonly used cephalosporin is cefaclor, given at a dosage of 30–40 mg/kg a day in three divided doses.

Antibiotic combination

The commonly used antibiotic combination is Bactrim or Septrin. It is a combination of trimethoprim and sulphamethoxazole. It is available as a suspension (40 mg of trimehtoprim and 200 mg of sulphamethoxazole per 5 ml) and as a tablet which is twice the dosage of 5 suspension. It is used in children with urinary tract infection, respiration infection, and gastrointestional infection. Children with G6PD deficiency should not be given Septrin and Bactrim which can cause severe and anaemia due to breakdown of the red blood cells. It is given at a dosage of 6 mg of trimcthoprim plus 30 mg sulphamethoxazole/kg/day in two divided doses.

In general, antibiotics are safe. They should only be prescribed in children with proven or suspected bacterial infection. A certain percentage of children may develop allergic reactions to some antibiotics. These include generalized itchy rash, diarrhoea, and vomiting. If a child develops any of these side-effects, antibiotics should be stopped immediately. If there is no adverse reaction, the antibiotic course should be completed in about 5 days. In some serious infections like sinusitis, pneumonia, otitis media and urinary tract infection, antibiotics may have to be given for a longer period of 7 days to 2 weeks.

Asthma medicines

The mechanisms that cause the symptoms during an asthmatic attack are multiple. They include bronchoconstriction, mucosal swelling, and increased bronchial secretions. The management of asthma includes treatment of the acute symptoms caused by bronchoconstruction by a group of asthmatic drugs called **relievers** and prevention of recurrence of attacks by a second group of drugs called **preventers**.

Relievers: Bronchodilators

The acute symptoms in bronchial asthma result from the obstruction of the airways from bonchoconstriction. Relievers are medicines that can bring relief to the acute symptoms through relaxation of the smooth muscles of the airways.

Sympathomimetic

Sympathomimetic are medicines which dilate the airways. They come in the form of syrups, tablets, inhalers, and nebulizing solutions. Commonly used medicines in this group are Salbutamol (Ventolin) and Terbutaline (Bricanyl). These medicines are adrenergic agents given as inhalers or nebulizing solutions, and can be used every 4 hourly. As a syrup, it can be used three or four times a day. The general trend now is to use them as inhalers or as nebulizing solutions, as the dosage delivered to a child is small and the onset of action is quickened. Hence, the relief to the child is faster. With the help of a spacer, inhalers can be used in children as young as 1 year of age. The side-effects of sympathomimetics are minimal. These include sweaty palms, tremors, palpitations, and muscle crams.

Aminophyllines

This group of medicines is not that commonly used as the sympathomimetics. However, they do have a place in the treatment of asthma in some children. They augment the action of sympathomimetics to dilate the airways. They can be used alone or in combination with Salbutamol or Terbutaline. They come in the form of syrups and tablets (Nuelin) and as slow release capsules (Nuelin SR, Austyn and Theovent). The slow release preparations can give relief to nocturnal symptoms of asthma. Common side-effects include abdominal pain, nausea, and vomiting. Overdosage can cause toxic level of drug in the blood. Heart irregularities, and convulsions may occur. One important drawback of this drug is the individual variability in dose response. To have maximum benefit from the drug, blood level of the drug has to be in the optimal range of 10–20 mg/L.

Preventers

About 20–30 per cent of children with asthma are those with frequent episode attacks or chronic asthma. They will require medicines to prevent such an attack. There are different preventers available, the choice of which depends on the age and severity of the condition.

Ketotifen

For younger children, some doctors use Ketotifen, an oral form of preventive medicine, but the drawback is that it may be effective in only 20–30 per cent of the children. This medicine has Antianaphylactic properties and antihistaminic effect. It has to be used for a period of 6 months to a year. It is given at a dosage of 1 mg twice a day for children between 6 months and 3 years of age and 2 mg twice a day in children 3 years old and above. One common side-effect is an increase in appetite which is a bonus to some children. It may cause drowsiness in some children.

Inhaled steroids

These medicines are being used commonly recently for children with frequent episodic asthma/chronic asthma. Asthma is an inherited inflammatory disease, and steroids are potent anti-inflammatory agents. If used as inhaled steroids in the standard dosage, the common side-effects of the oral steroids are not seen at all. There are a few different preparations in different strengths available, for example, Becotide, Flixotide, Pulmicort. The usual dosage is 200–300 ug/day. Inhaled steroids are usually prescribed for a period of 6 months to 1 year. Once the child is symptom-free, the dosage is reduced and the inhaled steroid is finally taken off. After 6 months, if the symptoms are not controlled, the dosage is increased. In this conventional dosage, no systemic side-effects of steroids are observed. Local side-effects may, however, occur. This include hoarseness of the voice and fungal infection of the mouth which can be minimized by proper oral hygiene and mouthwash after steroid inhalation.

Administering medications: Oral/Suppositories

In general, medicines for children are given orally. In European countries, medications in the form of suppositories are used more commonly. Administering medicines to children can be very tiring. They refuse to open their mouth or refuse to swallow the medicines. They may even spit or vomit most of the medicines. This is because it is rather difficult to coax a child or the medicine is not palatable. Parents must learn to administer medicines properly. This will come with patience and practice. Medicines may be mixed with fruit juice or milk.

If a child is difficult, medicines may have to be given in small portions at a time. With the use of a syringe, medicines may also be dropped in small amounts to the side or back of the mouth to avoid the sensitive taste buds in the front part of the tongue. It is important for parents not to force in all the medicines at the same time. It might be better to allow an interval of $1/2$–1 hour in between different medicines in a difficult child. It is also important for parents to realize that most medicines can be discontinued if the child is symptom-free with the exception of antibiotics which are usually given for a period of about 5 days.

In really difficult children, some medicines are available in the form of suppositories. Paracetamol and Voltaren suppositories are prescribed for treatment of fever. Dulcolax suppositories are used for constipation. Antivomiting suppositories may be given to children with distressing vomiting due to viral infections of the stomach and intestines. For children with recurrent convulsions, Diazepam (stesolid) rectal tubes are available for insert into the rectum. The liquid content of the tube can be squeezed out. Rapid absorption of the medicine through the rectal mucosa will effectively stop most convulsions.

References

Drug index of Malaysia and Singapore Annual, (1997) Singapore Eight Edition, Singapore.

Drug index of Malaysia and Singapore, (1997) Vol. 26, No. 3, Singapore.

16

Neurodevelopmental Problems

LEE Wei Ling

The common concerns that parents have about their child's neurological or intellectual development are delayed or abnormal speech, abnormal behaviour, and learning difficulties. The more serious disorders such as intellectual disability and autism are usually apparent in the first 2 years of life, whilst less serious disorders such as dyslexia may not be suspected until the child is challenged by having to learn in school.

It should be noted that no two children develop at the same rate and some children are better at certain aspect of their intellectual functions and weaker at other aspects. Hence, when doctors talk about intellectual development, they are referring to a wide range of normality. You should not compare the development of your baby with another baby but compare him with the general population.

Speech and language disorders

The terms 'speech' and 'language' are used interchangeably by laymen but a more precise usage restricts the meaning of **speech** to the activity of articulating speech sounds, whereas **language** refers to the communication of thoughts by the use of meaningful symbols combined in a systematic way.

Problems with the physical production of speech include disorders affecting the tongue, lips and palate, voice disorders caused by disease or stress of the vocal cords, and disorders in the neurological control of articulation, for example, dyslalia and stuttering.

Lisping and dyslalia

Lisping and dyslalia are common among preschoolers where up to 15 per cent may be affected. In lisping, the sound 's' is replaced by 'th', for example, *thimple* for *simple*. In dyslalia, there are multiple substitutions or omissions of consonants. Milder degrees consist of difficulty in pronouncing one or two consonants. For example, 'r' may be incorrectly pronounced so that it sounds like 'w' or 'y' — *'running a race'* becomes *'wunning a wace'* or *'yunning a yace'*. In severe cases, speech may be almost unintelligible. In more than 90 per cent of cases, these articulatory abnormalities disappear by the age of 8, either spontaneously or in response to speech therapy. Speech therapy may be started if these conditions persist into the 5th year. Lisping and dyslalia are often present in otherwise normal children. However, they are more frequent among the intellectually disabled or those with delayed language development than in normal children.

Stuttering

Stuttering attracts attention becasue of an interruption in the normal rhythm of speech. During the development of speech, most children repeat syllables and words (echolalia) and some normal adults stammer under emotional stress in just the same way as habitual stammerers. Repetition of words and syllables occurs about 45 times in every 1000 running words in normal children between the ages of 2 and 5. When it occurs more than 100 times in every 1000 running words, a noticeable stutter is produced.

What causes stuttering?

A strong family history is found in many cases, suggesting a genetic origin, but the mode of inheritance is unknown.

How common is stuttering?

Stuttering occurs in 1–2 per cent of the school population. It often disappears in late childhood or adolescence; by adulthood, only about one in every 300 individuals suffers from a persistent stutter. Males are affected more often than females with a ratio of 4 : 1.

What problems do stutterers have?

Stuttering is due to a disorder of rhythm of speech — an involuntary, repetitive prolongation of speech due to spasm of the articulatory muscles. The spasm may be tonic (continuous) and may result in a complete blocking of speech (stammering) or clonic (inter-mittent), with a series of spasms interrupting the emission of consonants, usually the first letter or syllable of a word (stuttering). There is no valid reason to distinguish between these two forms of the disorder, since they are intermingled, and the terms 'stammer' and 'stutter' are now used synonymously. Certain sounds, particularly 'p' and 'b', offer greater difficulty than others; *paperboy* comes out as *p-p-paper b-b-boy*. The severity of the stuttering is increased by excitement and stress, as when making a speech, and is reduced when the stutterer is relaxed. The muscles involved in stuttering function normally in all actions other than speaking so that chewing, swallowing, and even singing are normal. Intelligence, comprehension of language and writing are also normal in stutterers.

The time of onset of stuttering takes place mainly at two periods in life — between 2 and 4 years of age when speech and language are evolving, and between 6 and 8 years of age when these functions extend to reciting, reading aloud, and writing in the classroom. However, there may be a later onset. If stuttering is mild, it tends to be present only during the periods of emotional stress, and in four out of five children, it disappears during adolescence or early adult years. If severe, it persists throughout life regardless of treatment but tends to improve as the patient grows older.

The disappearance of mild stuttering with maturation has been attributed incorrectly to all manner of treatment (hypnosis, progressive relaxation, speaking in rhythm, etc.). Since stuttering may reappear at times of emotional stress, it has been hypothesized to be caused by psychological problems. In fact, if there are any psychological problems in the stutterer, they are secondary rather than primary. Many stutterers do become increasingly fearful of talking and develop feelings of inferiority because of their stuttering. By the time adolescence and adulthood are reached, emotional factors are so prominent that many doctors have mistaken stuttering for neurosis. Usually, there is little or no evidence of any personality abnormalities before the onset of stuttering, and psychotherapy, though helpful in relieving emotional tension and assisting the patient's adjustment to the condition, has not had a consistent effect on the stuttering.

What assessments should be done for children who stutter?

A consultation with a paediatrician is usually all that is required. Psychological, psychiatric and speech therapist evaluations often do not add further information nor are they helpful in planning treatment.

How is stuttering treated?

On the whole, the therapy of stuttering has been frustrating. Schemes such as the encouragement of associated muscular movements and the adoption of a 'theatrical' approach to speaking have been advocated. Common to all, such efforts have difficulty of achieving carryover into the natural speaking environment. Progressive relaxation, hypnosis, delayed auditory feedback, loud noise that mask speech sounds, and tranquillizers help temporarily.

What causes articulation problems?

Abnormalities of speech are rarely caused by anatomical abnormalities of the oro-pharyngeal structures. The cleft palate is the most frequent anatomic basis for articulatory disorders. This diagnosis is usually obvious to both parents and the doctor, and treatment is surgical repair of the cleft palate and speech therapy.

Tongue-tie is NOT a cause of delayed speech. There are still surgeons who are more than willing to operate on children with delayed speech to release the 'tongue-tie', and some children are seen by their doctors again after the operation because their speech have not improved.

Delayed or abnormal language development

Delay in speaking is a very common complaint which brings young children to the doctor. The main causes are 'late maturation' in a normal child, mental retardation, developmental language disorder, hearing impairment, and autism.

When should I worry about my child's language development?

No or inconsistent response to sounds is abnormal at any age and a hearing test should always be obtained without undue delay.

Most babies say their first words with meaning by 13 months, and if they have not done so by 24 months, it is definitely abnormal.

By 24 months, most babies are able to join two different words to form a phrase or sentence. Inability to do so by 3 years old indicates the need for medical evaluation. Combining two words which are the same (e.g. no, no), saying a word with more than one syllable (e.g. aeroplane) or a Chinese word made up of more than one character (e.g. *feiji* for aeroplane in Mandarin), do not qualify.

By 36 months, most children can speak in sentences and engage in conversation. If a child's speech is totally unintelligible, if he repeats what is said to him rather than answers appropriately (echolalia), if he says the same thing over and over again, he has a language disorder. Echolalia is normal at 18 months — it helps the child learn to speak by repeating what someone else says. It is abnormal only when it persists up to 36 months.

Most babies are able to point to indicate objects they want by 13 months. If they have not started doing so by 18 months, this suggests a disorder in non-verbal communication. Pointing is a symbol, equivalent to the word 'that' or 'I want that'. The absence of pointing or the inability to use gestures to communicate is often seen in children with autism.

Some children may achieve most or all the speech and language milestones at the expected age, but they may speak without communicative intent, for example, they may recite television advertisements instead of saying 'hello' when they meet someone, that is, they speak to speak, not to communicate with another person. This abnormality is seen especially in autism.

What assessments should be done for disordered language development?

The child should be investigated for hearing impairment, intellectual disability, developmental language disorder, and autism. A general medical evaluation by a paediatrician and a formal hearing test (not just ringing a bell and observing whether the child responds) are all that is required in most cases.

The most important condition to diagnose early is hearing impairment. If this is detected late, normal speech may never develop.

'Late maturation' of language ability in a normal child can only be diagnosed with confidence when the child eventually develops normal language at a later age. This means that the paediatrician cannot confidently reassure the parents when their child is first seen for delayed speech. However, there are several clues that suggest a good prognosis. If the child is delayed in speaking but has normal comprehension and general intelligence, he is more likely to acquire normal language later. If comprehension is impaired, if there is delay in many areas of development including social and visuo-spatial abilities and if expressive vocabulary is severely delayed, the prognosis is poor.

Parents with children with intellectual disability usually seek medical attention for delayed speech. Those with moderate or severe disability will be slow in learning to walk, run, feed, and dress themselves as well. However, many preschoolers with mild disability may appear to be delayed only in the area of language if no formal IQ testing is done.

Children with developmental language disorder have unexplained difficulties in acquiring language. This condition is also called 'specific language impairment'. As the name implies, these children do not have hearing loss, neurological disease, severe environmental deprivation, or autism. They differ from children with intellectual disability by having normal non-verbal IQ which can be shown by formal IQ testing, by their ability in non-language areas, for example, assembling jigsaw puzzles, figuring out how to operate television sets, and the use of gestures to communicate.

Except for hearing impairment which requires a formal hearing test, assessment for the other four common conditions causing disordered language development can be done by a paediatrician, usually without the need for blood tests, study of brain waves (electro-encephalography), or imaging studies of the brain such as CT (computer tomography) scan or MRI (magnetic resonance imaging). An assessment by a psychologist is helpful but not crucial. Many children will not cooperate for formal IQ testing at this age, especially children with developmental language disorder, intellectual disability, or autism.

How is disordered language development treated?

If a child has a significant hearing impairment, hearing aids and speech and language therapy should be instituted as soon as possible. Even then, many children with severe hearing impairment, if they ever learn to speak, have speech that is harsh, poorly modulated, unpleasant and accompanied by many peculiar squeals and noises of a snorting or grunting kind.

The role of serous otitis media (fluid in the middle ear) on language development is controversial. The current consensus is that it is unlikely to be an important cause of speech and language disorders. If there is no or only mild (less than 40 dB) hearing loss associated with the serous otitis media, operations to drain the fluid will not improve speech or language development.

For children with intellectual disability as well as those with developmental language disorder, 'speech therapy' is the only treatment available. There is no medication or operation that will help these children comprehend or speak. Whilst the common terminology is 'speech therapy', the aim of these programmes is to teach language, not just how to pronounce words as is implied by the term 'speech'. The term 'speech therapy' is used here to indicate both speech and language therapy.

In the past, most forms of speech therapy involved teaching language skills directly by imitation and modelling. The therapist identifies which aspects of the child's language system are impaired and focuses on these in drills that provide opportunities to work selectively on areas of difficulty. The area where this approach is still commonly used is in treating problems in articulation as in dyslalia. The aim is to identify the pattern of errors that the child makes, and then to give extensive practice in producing contrasting sounds. Few children below 5 years old are likely to cooperate during these programmes.

In recent years, there has been a move away from structured programmes, especially when teaching grammatical competence and appropriate language use. One reason was that therapists became dis-illusioned when they found that children who could produce acceptable language in therapy sessions persisted in using impaired language in more natural situations. Perhaps, formal language therapy sessions encouraged children to give correct responses to speech therapists, but do not teach them to use language to communicate needs.

The swing of the pendulum away from structured approaches to language training led to an advocation of a policy of general language stimulation, especially where the home background is thought to be disadvantaged. In practice, language stimulation is often interpreted to mean attendance at a nursery, where there is plenty of opportunities to mix with other children. However, a study in Britain has shown that working-class mothers used much more complex language with their children than did nursery teachers, and children used language for complex purposes more often at home than at school. Thus, although a great deal of language is produced in the nursery setting, individual children experience relatively few language interactions with adults. Nurseries can provide plentiful and stimulating opportunities for play and social interaction with peers, but they are noisy places, where the language-impaired child has to compete for adult attention with other children with more sophisticated language skills. In other words, sending children with language disorder (including mental retardation, autism or developmental language disorder) to a mainstream nursery will not help their language development.

Kindergartens in Singapore follow much more structured curricula than those in western countries. Often, the basic academic skills of learning to read, write, and count start by the 1st year in kindergarten. This may be suitable for normal children who, by the age of 4, have acquired all the basic language skills necessary for social communication. Children with language disorder will not benefit from this curriculum because they have not even learnt to comprehend and speak adequately, and will not learn anything meaningful in the mainstream kindergartens.

What is the advice for parents of Singapore children with disordered language development?

Many parents worry that it is the home environment that is causing their child's language problems. They blame themselves for leaving the child to the care of a maid, for exposing the child to multiple languages simultaneously, and for not spending enough time teaching the child to speak. There is no evidence that any of these factors can cause major language difficulties in normal children. It is possible (though not proven) that these risk factors may slow language development in a child who is destined to have language disorder, but the effect is unlikely to be major.

Practical things that parents can do to promote language development are as follows:

- Talk to your child, using a language level that is just a little more sophisticated than his. Do so in a naturalistic setting during everyday activities, for example, whilst sweeping the floor, say to your child, "Mummy is sweeping the floor".
- Encourage all your child's attempts to communicate whether verbal or non-verbal including gestures. Any means of communications is better than no communication.
- Do not use coercion to 'teach' language. Strategies such as withholding a sweet until your child repeats a word are likely to be counter-productive.
- Remind everyone to slow down the pace of conversation to give the language-impaired child time to formulate utterances if members of your family usually speak very fast. If your child has a comprehension problem, use simple, straightforward language when speaking with him.

Autism

The terminology in autism are very confusing. Terms parents are likely to hear include 'pervasive developmental disorders' (PDD), 'Asperger's syndrome' and 'autistic spectrum behaviour'.

PDD are a group of disorders characterized by qualitative abnormalities in reciprocal social interactions and in patterns of communication, and a restricted, stereotyped, repetitive repertoire of interests and activities. These abnormalities are a pervasive feature of the individual's functioning in all situations.

Autism, Asperger's syndrome and a number of other disorders are all included under the term 'PDD'. Autism is a type of PDD that is defined by abnormal development which is apparent before the age of 3 and abnormality in reciprocal social interaction, communication, restricted interests, and stereotyped, repetitive behaviour. Asperger's syndrome is similar to autism except that there is no retardation in language or intellectual development.

Autistic spectrum disorder is now frequently used to describe all degrees of the autistic condition. All those with autistic spectrum disorder have the triad of impairment that include difficulty with social interaction, communication and a restricted, stereo-typed, repetitive repertoire of interest and activities, but the degree of disability may range from never learning how to talk and sitting in a corner all day lining up blocks to a highly verbal individual who is able to complete university education but still experience considerable difficulties in social interactions.

What causes autism?

Autism can be caused by a variety of conditions affecting brain development occurring before, during, or after birth. Examples include fragile X syndrome, tuberous sclerosis, and maternal rubella. In many instances, genetic traits appear to be important though the actual genes which are abnormal are often unknown.

Autism is not due to emotional problems or emotional deprivation. It has nothing to do with the way parents bring up their child.

How common is autism?

The autistic spectrum disorder occurs in one or two per 1000 population in all countries and all races. Males are affected more frequently than females with a ratio of 3 : 1.

What problems do autistic children have?

Of the many disabilities seen in autism, it is the aberrations in **social** development that are the most handicapping and persistent. Individuals with autism have difficulties in reciprocal social interaction and the ability to form relationships. As babies, some autistic youngsters do not like to be held and do not hold their arms up to be lifted or adjust their bodies when being held, while others are very clingy or indiscriminately cuddly. What these behaviours have in common is a difficulty with the give-and-take of social behaviour.

In the preschool years, autistic children can be differentiated from mentally retarded children or children with language impairment by a lack of interest in other children, a limited range of facial expression, and unusual eye contact. By the time they are 4 or 5 years old, many autistic children are distressed by separation from their parents. However, they often do not greet their parents upon reunion or follow them about or want to be part of the family. They do not attempt to share their own enjoyment, such as getting their parents to come to school when they have something interesting to show or when a favourite television character appears. However, it is important to note that most autistic children do not show deficits in all of these areas; many children have one or more behaviours for brief periods of time or in particular situations that seem surprisingly social.

Although autistic children have delayed language development, the most striking feature is the deviant quality of the communication. Some children understand little or no language and never learn to speak. Even communication using gestures is impaired and many autistic children do not point to indicate what they want.

When speech develops, it is not used for social communication, and the child does not carry on with to-and-fro conversation. Some autistic children are talkative but their speech are repetitious or a monologue where they go on talking about a subject which they are obsessed with. Although they are able to speak, some autistic children do so only to ask for things.

Other special characteristics of the language of autistic children include reversing pronouns (e.g. referring to themselves as 'you' or 'he'), delayed echolalia or stereotypical speech borrowed from other people or the media (e.g. repeating commercials or phrases from their teacher out of context), abnormalities of pitch, stress, rhythm and intonation (e.g. talking in a monotone or with sing-song intonation).

Autistic children have restricted and repetitive interests and behaviours. This becomes noticeable in older autistic preschoolers when they become preoccupied with a specific part of a toy, such as spinning the wheels on a toy car. Some autistic individuals may carry out stereotyped, repetitive movements, particularly of the hands and fingers. Some autistic children injure themselves deliberately, for instance, by biting their wrists, banging their heads, or slapping themselves. Autistic children may become upset if their daily routines are not followed to minute detail (e.g. sandwiches not cut on the diagonal) or if trivial aspects of the environment are changed, such as repositioning the furniture in the room. Unusual reactions to sounds or sights, such as extreme agitation when someone sings a particular song, occur in some autistic individuals.

Approximately three-quarters of individuals with autism are also mentally retarded. Even those with normal intelligence quotient (IQ) often have learning disabilities. A significant minority of autistic individuals have unusual cognitive skills (special talent) as well as deficits earning them the title of *idiot savant*.

How is autism treated?

There is no cure for autism. The most important intervention in autism is early and intensive special education that addresses both behavioural and communication disorders. The effective approaches use a highly structured environment with intensive individual instruction and a high teacher-to-student ratio.

Education

Because of the wide spectrum of disabilities seen in autistic individuals, a range of educational provision is required. One question concerns integration or mainstreaming and the extent to which autistic children should be placed in self-contained classrooms specifically designed for autistic children, self-contained classrooms for more broadly defined groups (e.g. learning disabilities, mental retardation) or attend normal schools with additional specialist support. Few autistic children are able to cope behaviourally in the mainstream with no extra support, and of those who do, it is not clear that they are benefiting academically from the exposure.

On the other hand, there are social benefits to being surrounded by non-handicapped children. Much seems to depend on whether the programme is well structured, positive in attitude and prepared to cope with the individual needs of the children. For many children with autism, mainstream education is both appropriate and desirable. For others, however, such an environment can be terrifying and confusing, where things happen at random and in unexpected ways. This leads to distress for the child and disruption for the school. Higher-functioning children with autism, whose social difficulties make them vulnerable to bullying or abuse, need support and guidance to prevent them from becoming increasingly isolated in the mainstream environment.

Medication

There are no drugs that can cure autism, and many patients do not require medication. However, certain drugs that target specific symptoms such as repetitive behaviour, self-injurious behaviour, and aggression may help substantially. Parents should consult either a child psychiatrist or a paediatric neurologist as general paediatricians are not usually familiar with these problems and the relevant drugs.

Behavioural therapy

Behavioural therapy is often effective in dealing with tantrums and destructive behaviour as well as teaching self-help skills.

Unconventional therapy

Many desperate parents turn to unconventional and often expensive, dietary, medical and other therapies that, despite no proven efficacy, are widely used. Any therapy which claims to dramatically improve or cure autism must be viewed with skepticism.

What is the long-term outcome in autism?

The best predictors of long-term outcome are IQ and degree of language impairment. However, even autistic individuals who are of normal intelligence with minimal language impairment and have a good level of social adjustment in adult life never achieve complete normality. They may be gainfully employed, earning enough to support themselves, but most will require a certain degree of shelter in their work and support in their living arrangements. The majority of autistic individuals who are retarded or have moderate or severe language impairment will remain severely handicapped and dependent on others for help in meeting their day-to-day needs throughout life.

Where can parents of autistic children get help in Singapore?

The Rainbow Centre runs the Margaret Drive Special School and the Balestier Special School. Both schools offer the STEP programme (Structured Teaching for Exceptional Pupils), a highly structured individualized teaching programme to serve children with autism, autistic tendencies, or associated severe behavioural problems between the ages of 2 and 12. It caters to patients with moderate and severe autism associated with mental retardation. The programme is implemented by special education teachers. Much of the work is undertaken on a 1 : 1 teaching ratio in purpose-built cubicles which provide a distraction-free environment for the child. Activities include cognitive skills training, receptive and expressive communication, pragmatic and social skills, motor development, and academic development. Computer-assisted instruction is also part of the programme. The Margaret Drive Special School is located at 501 Margaret Drive, Singapore 149306. The telephone number is 4727077 and the fax number is 4739739. The Balestier Special School is located at 18 McNair Road, Singapore 328517. The telephone number is 2956591 and the fax number is 2956594.

The Reach-Me Project is a new project which started in April 1998. It provides an assessment and diagnostic service. The child will be given a detailed assessment and diagnosis which will provide a complete picture of his skills and disabilities. His family will be given advice on the type of support and services needed. An outreach service will have teachers trained in the education of autistic pupils. They will provide a specialist service to support and maximize the learning and development of pupils with autistic spectrum disorder in mainstream schools. An information and advice service will provide information and advice on all aspects of autism. It will manage an enquiry service and an information centre library. Finally, the Reach-Me project will provide training for parents, families and professionals involved in the care, management and education of autistic individuals. Reach-Me Project is located at Blk 437, Clementi Avenue 3, #01-98, Singapore 120437. The telephone number is 7781031, the fax number is 7787630 and the e-mail address is reachme@pacific.net.sg.

Learning difficulties

Most children with normal intelligence, normal vision and hearing, no emotional or psychiatric problems and adequate teaching should be able to learn in a regular school in Singapore, be streamed to EM1 or EM2 in Primary Four, and pass the Primary School Leaving Examination (better known as the PSLE) in Primary Six. Obviously, intellectual disability, severe visual or hearing impairment, emotional or psychiatric problems and poor teaching can all impair learning. However, there is a small but significant group of children, who, in spite of the absence of any of the above causes, seem unable to learn. These apparently bright students who cannot learn — no matter how hard they try, are termed 'learning disabled' or LD. In the last few years, researchers have made great strides in identifying and treating learning problems. But the explosion of knowledge has also led to an epidemic of diagnosis in the United States. In 1996, 2.6 million children (4.4 per cent of all students in the United States) were in publicly funded learning-disability programmes. In 1977, only about 800 000 (1.8 per cent of the student body) had been diagnosed. Providing special education for this large number of students is obviously a huge financial strain to the educational system. In addition, it is possible that some students are using the diagnosis of 'LD' as an excuse for their poor academic performance.

There are probably as many learning disabilities as there are academic skills that students have to acquire. As reading, writing and mathematics are the basic skills that all students are expected to acquire, the major learning disabilities are dyslexia (disability in reading), dysgraphia (disability in writing), and dyscalculia (disability in mathematics). Attention deficit disorder with hyperactivity (ADHD) is a behavioural disorder which is often associated with poor academic achievement and other school problems. Of the many different types of LD, only dyslexia and ADHD have been adequately studied with scientific methods.

Dyslexia

Dyslexia is a learning disability which results in difficulty with reading, spelling, and written prose. It is not due to poor teaching, low socio-cultural background or low intelligence. It is more easily detected in those with average and above average intelligence because of the obvious difference between their literacy skills and intelligence and abilities in other spheres. It can occur in those with below average intelligence as well, but is more often not suspected because the difficulties with reading and spelling are ascribed to the low intelligence.

What causes dyslexia?

Dyslexics have impairment of phonemic awareness. Phonemes are the smallest meaningful sounds in a language. English has 44 phonemes that its speakers combine to make all its words. 'Cat', for example, has three, 'kuh'–'aa'–'tuh'. In order to learn to read, one must understand that sounds in words can be broken up in this way, that is, phonemic awareness. In addition, one must also know what sounds each letter or combinations of letters represent.

Visual perceptual difficulties rarely cause the reading disability seen in most children with dyslexia. It is a common misconception that errors of letter reversal (b/d), inversion (m/w), transposition (was/saw) are typical of dyslexics. In fact, normal children learning to read and write also make these errors. However, dyslexics continue to make these errors at a time when normal children have learnt not to. They do so not because they cannot recognize the difference between the correct letter or word and its opposite image, but because they cannot remember which is the correct choice.

Many dyslexics have a family history of difficulty with written language and/or spoken language, and heredity plays an important role in dyslexia.

How common is dyslexia?

Depending on the criteria used for the diagnosis of dyslexia, estimates range from 3–15 per cent of the population from various studies in the western countries. In almost all studies, dyslexia was more common in males than females. In a study on Chinese primary school children in Singapore, dyslexia in reading Chinese and/or English was 4.8 per cent; dyslexia in Chinese only was 3.8 per cent; dyslexia in English only was 1.4 per cent; and dyslexia in both languages was 0.4 per cent. Similar to findings in western countries, males outnumbered females in all groups of dyslexics with an overall ratio of 4.3 : 1.

What problems do children with dyslexia have?

Since dyslexia is a disability in reading and spelling, problems may not appear until the children have to learn to read and spell. However, some children with dyslexia will also have difficulties in speech and language; for example, they may start talking later than normal children, may not pronounce clearly, may have difficulty finding the right words, and may have trouble learning numbers, letters of the alphabet and days of the week.

What assessments should be done for children with dyslexia?

Poor vision, hearing impairment, emotional problems, poor teaching may all cause difficulties in learning to read and write. They should be considered and excluded in the initial assessment of a child with dyslexia. Psychological assessment including testing of intelligence, language ability, spatial ability, reading and spelling ability, will show low reading and spelling ability relative to the other abilities in dyslexics. Special psychological tests for phonemic awareness will show impairment in this ability.

How is dyslexia treated?

There is no treatment that cures dyslexia. Medication plays little or no role in the treatment plan (unless the child has other associated disabilities such as ADHD). Treatment is remedial education, in particular, teaching the dyslexic how to split a word up into its constituent sounds (e.g. 'kuh'–'aa'–'tuh' in 'cat') and the correspondence between letters and sounds. In other words, the dyslexic needs to be taught phonics. While normal children may be able to learn to read via the 'look and say' or whole language approach favoured by most teachers, they do so because they have intuitively acquired phonemic awareness. Dyslexics have difficulty acquiring phonemic awareness even when they have been taught explicitly, and if taught solely by the 'look and say' approach, they may never learn to read.

What is the long-term outcome for dyslexia?

Dyslexics never outgrow their disability even after they have learnt to read and spell adequately to pass examinations. Speed reading and spelling are the biggest stumbling blocks which few dyslexics can overcome. This does not mean that dyslexics cannot succeed in life. With hard work, appropriate remedial education, and now with word-processing programmes, many dyslexics can cope with and even excel in professional careers.

Dyslexia in Singapore

Dyslexia also occurs in Singaporeans. However, the diagnosis of dyslexia is more difficult because of our multilingual environment. For someone whose first language is not English, difficulty in reading and spelling English may be due to dyslexia or may (more likely) be due to a poor command of the English language.

Another question is whether dyslexia can occur in reading Chinese. Chinese characters and words are not made up of letters which correspond to phonemes. Some students who are dyslexic in Chinese, are not dyslexic in English. The underlying defect leading to their difficulty with reading Chinese is still unknown, nor do we know what kind of remedial education will help them.

If you suspect that your child has dyslexia in English, you should speak to his English teacher or the principal. They will arrange for your child to be assessed by a special teacher (learning support co-ordinator) who may refer the child to the Dyslexia Association of Singapore (DAS) after testing. To assess your child's dyslexity, you can also directly contact the Dyslexia Association of Singapore, People's Association, located at Block C, Unit C2, Kallang, Singapore 397750. The telephone number is 3483540 and the fax number is 3483544.

At present, there is no provision in our education system for children who may have dyslexia in Chinese. However, most children from English speaking homes who have difficulties learning to read and write Chinese do not have dyslexia in Chinese. Instead, they have a poor command of spoken Chinese and/or poor motivation to learn Chinese. A very similar situation occurs in children from Chinese speaking homes who have problems learning English.

Attention deficit hyperactivity disorder (ADHD)

In 'attention deficit hyperactivity disorder' (ADHD), the individual (usually a child) is inattentive, impulsive and hyperactive, and manifests these behaviours in a variety of situations. The same characteristics are often seen in children with mental retardation, autism or other psychiatric disorders, but these patients show additional features which are typical of their disorder. Moreover, their long-term outcome are very different from that of children with ADHD alone, hence they are excluded from the definition of ADHD as well as the following discussion.

What causes ADHD?

Whilst many factors have been associated with ADHD, we do not know what causes it. A child with ADHD is four times more likely to have family members with the same difficulty, suggesting a genetic cause. However, parents with aggressive and/or antisocial behaviour, discordant family life and other non-genetic familial factors can also cause ADHD to occur in multiple members of the same family. There is no convincing evidence that brain damage causes ADHD.

How common is ADHD?

The prevalence of ADHD varies widely from one in 2 000 children in the United Kingdom to one in 100 children in the United States. This does not mean that North American children are much naughtier than British children. Just as fashions in dressing differ from country to country, so are fashions in medical practice. Doctors in the United Kingdom are less likely to label children brought to see them for behavioural problems as having ADHD and are less willing to put them on medication than doctors in the United States. The prevalence in Singapore is not known.

Studies from different countries all show that ADHD is more common in boys than in girls. The average ratio from many studies is 4 : 1.

What problems do children with ADHD have?

The behaviours which characterize children with ADHD are as follows:

- **Inattention**: These children are easily distracted, flit from task to task, forget instructions, and may appear dreamy or 'spaced out'. However, with adequate motivation, they can concentrate; a typical example being the ability to concentrate on video games for long periods of time.
- **Impulsiveness**: These children speak and act without thinking. They may break rules or get into dangerous situations.
- **Over-activity**: These children are restless, fidgety, and always 'on the go'.

In addition, many children with ADHD also have aggressive behaviour, learning disorders, and poor motor coordination. All these problems contribute to social rejection by their peers and teachers.

What assessments should be done for children with ADHD?

Children who may have ADHD should be referred to a paediatric neurologist or child psychiatrist. A complete medical history and physical examination, a detailed description from parents about the child's behaviour at home, as well as information from teachers about behaviour and academic achievement in school are needed. Emotional problems, autism, intellectual disability and developmental language disorders are all associated with hyperactivity. They should be considered and excluded in the initial assessment of a child with possible ADHD.

Psychological testing including testing of intelligence, language ability, spatial ability, reading, writing, and arithmatic should be done. Many children with ADHD will show low reading, spelling, and mathematical ability relative to their IQ scores indicating academic under-achievement.

Further medical investigations such as electro-encephalography, computer tomography (CT) scan, or magnetic resonance imaging (MRI) of the brain rarely add further information and are usually normal.

How is ADHD treated?

There is no single treatment for ADHD. Treatment is targeted at all the problems and these occur in different combinations in different patients.

Explanation

Explain what ADHD is to the child, family members, teachers and the child's peers. Tell the child in words he can understand. Be straightforward, honest and clear. Be sure to tell the child what ADHD is not. He is not stupid or bad. Also tell the teachers and other parents that the child has ADHD and that he is not being deliberately difficult but requires understanding and appropriate management strategies. Caution the child not to use ADHD as an excuse. It is an explanation, NOT an excuse, and he is still responsible for what he does.

Medication

The most powerful treatment is medication with stimulants such as dextroamphetamine and methylphenidate. These drugs are very effective in reducing hyperactivity and can improve academic performance at least for the short term. However, there is no scientific evidence for long-term benefits. This is partly because studies to evaluate the long-term effects of stimulants are difficult to conduct so that the absence of proof does not prove that stimulants are useless, but that we do not know the correct answer. Adverse effects of medication are seldom severe. They include loss of appetite, insomnia, and slowing of growth. The use of stimulant medications varies greatly between the United Kingdom and the United States. In the United Kingdom, the doctors are much more conservative and medication is used only when other treatment strategies have failed. In the United States, stimulants are prescribed very freely. In Singapore, most doctors are unfamiliar with ADHD, and are therefore reluctant to prescribe stimulants. It is obvious that the use of stimulants is a very controversial issue.

Behavioural modification

Behavioural modification is useful for many affected children. It may be less powerful than medication, or perhaps, it would be fairer to say that it is slower than medication in its effects, for the comparisons with medication have all been made upon the basis of short-term trials.

The best way to improve the child's behaviour is to encourage the desired behaviour. Children will repeat behaviours which are rewarded, so if wanted behaviour is rewarded, it is more likely to occur again. Parental attention is a powerful reward for most children. Unfortunately, when you are scolding, arguing with, shouting or even smacking, you are giving a great deal of attention, thus increasing the frequency of those very behaviour you want to stop. Whenever your child has been good, reward him. Praise your child and tell him WHY you are pleased with him. Ignore behaviours which may be irritating but not dangerous like whining, arguing, swearing and throwing tantrums by avoiding eye contact and discussion. Although these behaviours may get worse before they get better, they will decrease if you persevere.

Children need to be imposed with limits and parents need to set limits. Decide on the rules and ensure that ALL adults in the house agree with them. Give one instruction at a time, clearly and consistently. Do not make threats you are unable or unwilling to carry out or that could frighten your child. Do not give way just because he protests.

Promotion of learning

Children with ADHD learn better when they are taught one-to-one for short periods. A lot can be achieved by a person who is tactful and patient in maintaining a child's attention on a task and highlighting the relevant aspects of the task in hand. Such a person need not be a teacher but will need training in the job.

School teachers who have to cope with children with ADHD should have experience and training in the techniques of behaviour modification. At present, there is a shortage of these teachers in Singapore.

Diet

The fad for dietary therapy for ADHD was started by Feingold in 1975 who suggested that food dyes and preservatives cause behaviour and learning problems in children. Since then, cow's milk, wheat flour, citrus fruit and sugar have been added to the list of offending foods. The vast majority of children whose parents believe them to be intolerant of certain foods are not. When they eat the offending food items unknowingly, there is no change in behaviour. A very few individual children may be helped by elimination of specific items from their diets. In these cases, the parents have usually seen a change in their child's behaviour due to particular foods. If the parents have not noticed the association of behaviour with ingestion of particular food items even when it is suggested to them, food is unlikely to be a contributing factor to the child's ADHD.

What is the developmental course of ADHD?

In the toddler, over-activity is a very common complaint made by parents. This is often hard to evaluate because activity is very high in normal children at that age. After the age of 3, the normal course of development involves a reduction of the level of activity in some settings but not others. Starting school makes prolonged attention more necessary. The persistence of inattentive and hyperactive behaviour becomes more and more of a problem, and may be associated with academic failure and social isolation. The more worrisome problem is the development of aggressive and antisocial behaviour and delinquency.

Adolescence is the worst time. Adolescents with ADHD are more likely to be expelled from school, to require psychiatric treatment, and to suffer multiple accidents.

Many children grow out of their hyperactivity, and the stormy course during school age and adolescence can sometimes be followed by a relatively happy adult adjustment. Outcome in adult life is determined more by the individual's intelligence, aggressiveness and family relationships rather than by just how hyperactive they have been as children.

Conclusion

Although there is controversy regarding many aspects of ADHD, the last 10 years have seen advances in our understanding of the problem. It is clear that management of the problem does not depend on medication alone, but requires cooperation between professionals from different disciplines and the family members, especially the parents.

Index